29.95

Russia and
Its New Diasporas

Russia and
•••• Its New Diasporas ••••
Igor Zevelev

UNITED STATES INSTITUTE OF PEACE PRESS
Washington, D.C.

UNITED STATES INSTITUTE OF PEACE
1200 17th Street NW
Washington, DC 20036

First published 2001

Printed in the United States of America

The paper used in this publication meets the minimum requirements of American National Standard for Information Sciences—Permanence of Paper for Printed Library Materials, ANSI Z39.48-1984.

Library of Congress Cataloging-in-Publication Data
Zevelëv, I. A. (Igor' Aleksandrovich)
    Russia and its new diasporas / Igor Zevelev.
      p. cm.
    Includes index.
    ISBN 1-929223-08-0 (alk. paper)
    1. Russians—Foreign countries. 2. Russians—Former Soviet republics. 3. Nationalism—Russia (Federation). 4. Russians—Ethnic identity. 5. Russia (Federation)—Politics and government—1991– I. Title.

DK510.36 .Z48 2000
320.54'089'9171—dc21   00-063360

Contents

MAP   vi

FOREWORD *by Richard H. Solomon*   vii

ACKNOWLEDGMENTS   xi

INTRODUCTION: "The Russian Question" into the
Twenty-First Century   1

CHAPTER 1. Russian Nation-State Building and Diasporas
in the Security Context   11

CHAPTER 2. Transformations of Russian Identity   29

CHAPTER 3. The Politics of Nation Building in Modern Russia   63

CHAPTER 4. Russians outside Russia before and after
the Breakup of the Soviet Union   91

CHAPTER 5. Policy of the Russian Federation toward the
Russian Diasporas   131

CONCLUSIONS AND IMPLICATIONS   159

NOTES   177

INDEX   207

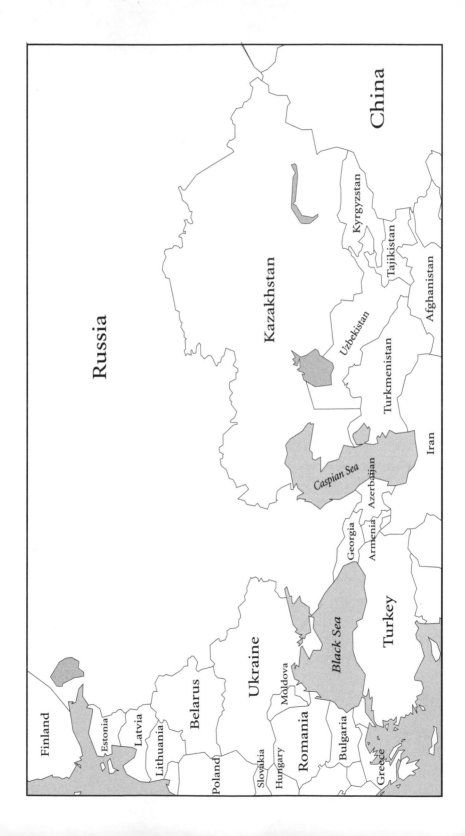

• • • • • • • Foreword • • • • • • • •

I MAGINE YOU WOKE UP ONE MORNING and discovered you were in a different country—not physically transported there; in fact, you have awakened in the same place, along with the same neighbors. But the name of your country has changed, you're supposed to salute a different flag, your loyalty is supposed to be for a different president.

This is the situation millions of ethnic Russians—more than twenty-five million by some estimates—found themselves in on December 26, 1991, when the Soviet Union was dissolved, heralding the independence of its fifteen constituent republics. Among the fifteen, Russia seemed first among equals, assuming the role of leader of the former Soviet space.

Indeed, ethnic Russians over many, many decades spread—through migration and political offices—throughout the imperial and Soviet territory, locating mostly in the urban centers and enclaves in neighboring lands and, later, Soviet republics. Their presence was unquestioned: After all, people in the Soviet Union owed their allegiance to the capital of the "socialist federation" in Moscow. Russians and the non-Russian republics' indigenous nationalities were "Soviets" rather than members of specific ethnic groups. With the USSR's sudden demise, have these sources of identity really changed?

One thing that hasn't changed are the ethnic Russian communities in these newly independent states. These "diasporas," as Igor Zevelev explains in the following pages, are not "refugees"; nor are they displaced people. In fact, they continue in their role as valued members of the work force in most of these newly independent states. There have not been any serious ethnic clashes with titular ethnic groups. There has been no mass exodus of ethnic Russians back into the Russian Federation, although there has been a steady stream of such migration.

What is of greater concern, though, is on the other side of these borders—that is, in the Russian Federation. The ethnic situation in these Soviet successor states remains generally stable, but the situation offers considerable political capital for Russian politicians who seek to tap into a spirit of nationalism, of Russian "greatness" that once held sway over these neighboring lands. The neo-imperialist bombast of Vladimir Zhirinovsky is rivaled by that of a considerable number of other, subtler Russian politicians who realize the potential to run on political platforms that could tap an otherwise inchoate nationalist sentiment.

Most Russian officials realize the potential of the diasporas issue slightly differently, considering these ethnic Russian communities as a distinct component in constructing the post-Soviet Russian nation-state. The *problematique* of contemporary international relations is that the political construct of the state and the historical and cultural construct of the nation have rarely converged on the same territory—certainly not the way they did in nineteenth-century Europe—and Zevelev provides here an excellent historical and intellectual survey of Russia's ongoing quest to define both concepts as part of a congruent whole, despite the country's cultural affinity for universal values and the manipulation of national identities during the Soviet period.

Up to now, moderation has served as the leitmotif of Russian policy toward ethnic Russians in the "near abroad," the term most of the Russian Federation's citizens use to describe the neighboring Soviet successor states. Since the beginning of the post-Soviet era, Zevelev tells us, successive Russian governments have been ambiguous in their attitudes toward the Russian diasporas. The resulting policy has reflected, on the one hand, the fear of mass migration of Russians back into the federation and an inability to provide jobs and welfare to this sizable contingent of potential citizens and, on the other hand, the appeal of an issue that could be used to exert considerable influence over the former Soviet republics. Russian president Vladimir Putin may be dramatically changing this policy, as suggested in his mid-November 2000 comments about bringing Russians home from the near abroad and strengthening the country's borders.

Such influence may be welcome in economically tenuous Kazakhstan, where ethnic Russians constitute a sizable presence in the country's northern provinces, but the Baltic states view their ethnic Russian communities with suspicion at best; at worst, they have decided to settle a historical score with what could be called discriminatory language and citizenship policies against the generations of ethnic Russians who moved to these states after the Soviet Union annexed them during World War II. As prospective candidates for membership in the North Atlantic Treaty Organization (NATO), the former Soviet republics of Estonia and Latvia compound the Russian Federation's aggravation over the prospect of NATO's expansion so close to its borders with domestic policies that appear decidedly anti-Russian.

If there is a constructive way to view the Russian government's policies toward the ethnic Russian diasporas, it lies in the concept of integration. Yet there are as many motives behind integrative schemes as there are programs—ranging from disguised proposals to re-create the centrally controlled Soviet political space to Kazakhstani president Nursultan Nazarbaev's economically driven Eurasian Union concept. Each proposal for such integrative schema, of course, puts a premium on a different dimension of integration. The Russia-Belarus union, a treaty initiative concluded during the Yeltsin administration and given a renewed mandate under Putin, seems to be the Russian government's ideal for such an integrative approach. Yet, despite the union's apparent exclusivity, Putin seems to envision the extension of the union to other Soviet successor states with large ethnic Russian and "Russian-speaking" populations.

If integration is the key to Russia's future as a positive member of the international community and as a way to construct a coherent nation-state, we should look for an emphasis on economic integration and open borders, not for a menacing and quite familiar pattern of bringing members of a scattered ethnic group "under one political roof." To dispel the air of suspicion surrounding any such attempt at integration that is lead by Russian officialdom, Zevelev appeals to the West to view such positive attempts as not bolstering the Russian state or nation, but as reiterating the historical fact of an extensive Russian-speaking civilization across Eurasia.

Igor Zevelev's work is the Institute's first in-depth examination of ethnodemographic security challenges on the Eurasian continent, and it joins quite a few closely related Institute initiatives and studies published by the Institute's Press. Among the former is the Working Group on the Future of Europe, bringing together veteran analysts on Soviet and Russian politics and how they affect European and transatlantic security institutions. The latter constitute a long line of publications on Russia's post-Soviet transition and its impact on global and Eurasian security, including Kenneth M. Jensen and Leon Aron's edited volume *The Emergence of Russian Foreign Policy,* Martha Brill Olcott's *Central Asia's New States,* Anatol Lieven's *Ukraine and Russia: A Fraternal Rivalry,* James Goodby's *Europe Undivided,* and Peter Reddaway and Dmitri Glinski's *The Tragedy of Russia's Reforms: Market Bolshevism against Democracy.* Undoubtedly, the issue of Russia's evolving role in the international community is one we will continue to address.

RICHARD H. SOLOMON
PRESIDENT
UNITED STATES INSTITUTE OF PEACE

• • • • Acknowledgments • • • •

For generous institutional support, I would like to thank the Woodrow Wilson International Center for Scholars, the Kennan Institute for Advanced Russian Studies, and the United States Institute of Peace. I would also like to acknowledge the continuing assistance of my home institution, the Institute of World Economy and International Relations of the Russian Academy of Sciences. Macalester College and George C. Marshall European Center for Security Studies provided a stimulating intellectual climate during the final stages of my work on this book. Some of my arguments were discussed in seminars at the Berkeley Program in Soviet and Post-Soviet Studies and the Center for Slavic and East European Studies, University of California at Berkeley, and I am grateful to all of the participants.

I would like to take this opportunity to acknowledge my debt to many colleagues and friends in Russia and the United States who provided invaluable insights during the research and writing of the book. I would especially like to thank Pierre van den Berghe, Sally Blair, George Breslauer, Karen Dawisha, Herbert Ellison, Joel Migdal, Blair Ruble, Peter Rutland, and Nodari Simonia. Joseph Klaits provided constant support and encouragement. Thanks also to Peter Pavilionis for insightful comments and help with the final preparation of the manuscript. I owe a debt of gratitude to Daniil Rosental and Erika Croxton for their research assistance.

I greatly benefited from discussions with many Russian officials who have been involved in policymaking in the areas relevant to my research. My special thanks to Vladimir Chernous, consultant to the Russian Federation government's Department for CIS Affairs; Vyacheslav Igrunov, deputy chairman of the State Duma Committee on CIS Affairs and Relations with Compatriots; Abdulakh Mikitaev, former chief of the

Citizenship Directorate of the Presidential Administration; Sergei Nasinovsky, senior adviser at the Foreign Ministry; and Konstantin Zatulin, former chairman of the State Duma Committee on CIS Affairs and Relations with Compatriots.

The views expressed in the book are, of course, my own and do not necessarily reflect the position of the above-mentioned institutions, officials, or scholars.

As always, my greatest debt is to my family, which has been patient and supportive.

Earlier versions of some sections have been previously published. A short version of chapter 5 appeared in *Post-Soviet Affairs* 12, no. 3 (July–September 1996): 265–84. Some sections of Chapters 1 and 2 were published in *Global Security Beyond the Millennium: American and Russian Perspectives,* ed. Sharyl Cross, Igor Zevelev, Victor Kremenyuk, and Vagan Gevorgyan (London: Macmillan, 1999).

. . . .

Introduction:
"The Russian Question"
into the Twenty-First Century

FROM FYODOR DOSTOEVSKY and Vladimir Solovyov to Nikolai Berdyaev and beyond, Russian philosophers, writers, poets, and historians have been recurrently haunted by "the Russian idea," the people's spiritual mission in the world.[1] Now, at the dawn of the twenty-first century, thinkers seem to be more concerned with "the Russian question." This change of terminology in theoretical discourse on the fate of Russians reflects an abrupt devolution of perceptions of the country among its leading sages. The image of the Russian people as the bearer of a messianic, universal idea has been transformed into only a semblance of a fading community—a community whose continued existence in the new millennium suddenly has been thrown into question. In short, "the Russian question" is one of survival and a search for a new identity.[2]

This book is an attempt to come to grips with one particular and often overlooked aspect of the Russian question after the collapse of the Soviet Union: the impact of new diasporas on the current quest for a new Russian identity.[3] Post-Soviet geopolitical rearrangements in Eurasia have been accompanied by what is perceived by many Russians as separation of their twenty-five million coethnics from a new Russian state. I will argue that Russia, while trying to establish special ties with its "compatriots abroad" is not only seeking domination in Eurasia but also looking to resolve the haunting legacy of its empire, an empire in which, ironically, Russians denied themselves for centuries an articulated ethnicity.

Instead of the expected triumphalism over the fall of communism, there is a growing pessimism and despair among many Russian intellectuals and the public in general. Why is this the case? Are the economic difficulties, social dislocations, and fragility of democratic institutions sufficient explanations for such a mood? Aleksandr Solzhenitsyn, Russia's most dedicated foe of communism and the only contemporary Russian writer who can be called great without a second thought, has tormented himself with issues that to him became much more fundamental than economic reform and democratization. He has argued that Russia has been "flattened," "smashed, run over, stunned, corrupted," that Russians are in a "national faint," "national pulverization," and that there is a danger of its total disappearance from the earth.[4] According to Solzhenitsyn, Russians became a divided nation when the Soviet Union collapsed along the Bolshevik-drawn administrative borders.[5] Even worse, he believes, "We have lost the feeling of one people."[6] For Solzhenitsyn, the issue of the Russian diaspora in the "near abroad," as many Russians call other Soviet successor states, became a litmus test for the state of the Russian question. Public indifference to Russians who flee to Russia from the near abroad prompted him to argue that "the fate of miserable refugees is a menacing prophecy of our own all-Russian fate." Without understanding of the refugees plight, "there is no understanding of today's Russia, or of the modern Russian people."[7] Solzhenitsyn studied the Russian question without leaving his strong nationalist convictions behind.

Is it possible to address the Russian question in the framework of an Anglo-American tradition of political thought? To be sure, such an attempt faces serious theoretical difficulties. Modern Russian thinkers talk about the fate of the Russian people as a collective entity that makes its own journey through history. But for Anglophone theorists since John Locke, any notion of the "people" as something more than a collection of independent individuals has been almost taboo.[8] This intellectual prohibition stands in sharp contrast to German and Russian traditions, which suggest more collectivist versions of nationhood, with an emphasis on the *spirit* of the people.[9] Karl Marx and John Mill strongly disagreed on whether humans were a social derivative or whether society was no more than a product of independent individuals' activity.

Perhaps if we replace the notion of a collective "people" (with its dangerous allusion to the German *Volksgeist,* though such an allusion is absent in the Russian language) with "nation," a term more common to modern political science, it would be easier to find an appropriate theoretical framework for discussing the Russian question. However, there are many theoretical challenges to the idea of nation as well. Anthony Smith contends that "there is an inherent instability in the very concept of the nation, which appears to be driven, as it were, back and forth between the two poles of *ethnie* and state which it seeks to subsume and transcend."[10] Indeed, very few countries have experienced as strong a tension between ethnicity and the state as has Russia, and the result is extreme ambiguity concerning the definition of the Russian nation. Most Soviet successor states construct their nations on the basis of myths of common blood and soil. Yeltsin's regime did not take this route, and there is little evidence thus far that President Vladimir Putin will radically change policy in this area. However, the issue of state boundaries and membership in a political community, taken for granted in Western political theory, remains contested by Russia's main political actors.

David Laitin argues thus: "The boundaries of states are territorially defined, and despite border wars, remain fixed over time. Classic theories of international relations assume fixed boundaries. But the boundaries of nations are defined by the cultural stocks of people, and these boundaries are forever ambiguous."[11] In such a way, Laitin expertly sums up why any attempt to implement the old European idea that the boundaries of the state must approximate those of a nation may face fierce resistance from those who interpret the boundaries between nations differently. The question of nations' limits is a field where individual and collective identities, their differing interpretations by intellectuals and political entrepreneurs, geopolitics, and the interests of the states meet and often clash—and sometimes clash violently. That is why the problem of the Russian quest for a new post-Soviet identity is more than a purely academic issue.

The term "diaspora" has become especially popular in Russia since 1995.[12] Often, the term has been used together with or instead of such terms as "Russians and Russian-speakers," "compatriots," or the oxymoron "ethnic citizens of Russia," which appeared in political and

theoretical discourse from 1991 to 1994.[13] The reconceptualization of
large groups of the population in the near abroad as "the Russian diaspora" reflected the attempt to emphasize the connection of these people
to Russia proper, a collective memory and myth about a common homeland, a traumatic experience, and a troubled relationship with host societies. This term is in many respects opposite to a term favored in the
diplomatic lexicon since World War I—namely, "national minority,"
which explicitly places the subjects under the jurisdiction of the former
Soviet Union's newly independent states.

The impact of the diasporas on a new Russian collective identity is
different from what is known about the experience of classic diaspora
peoples—for example, Jews, Greeks, Armenians, and Chinese. The
intellectual and political influence of the Russians from the near abroad
on their "historic homeland" has been minimal thus far, unlike the effect
of Jewish, Greek, or Armenian diasporas on their respective homelands. However, those "other Russians" play an important role as subjects
of Russian theoretical, political, and foreign policy deliberations and
actions. The reference group for those who debate, conceptualize, and
shape a new Russian identity by political means has been extended beyond the state borders of the Russian Federation—a new phenomenon
for Russia. Throughout the past several centuries, the state reached well
beyond the territory where Russian culture, language, religion, and traditions held sway. After the collapse of the Soviet Union, however, the
official Russian body politic no longer covered the entirety of this
domain, while continuing to include entities that can hardly be said to
belong to Russia culturally; Chechnya is the most striking example.
Very few modern nations have succeeded in attaining congruence
between ethnicity and the state, and the issue of minorities exists in
many countries. While having this problem, Russia is also confronted
by the question of its diasporas. In this way, Russia faces a double challenge to nation building—internal and external: Russia must address
the issues of both the minorities inside and ethnic Russians outside its
state boundaries.

Tension between the concepts of the Russian state and the Russian
nation—if major political actors acknowledge ethnicity as its important
component—has the potential to undermine the evolving system of
international relations throughout Eurasia and to embroil this vast territory in conflict. This book argues that there are many factors that may

strengthen a relatively dormant Russian ethnonationalism in the years to come, and the plight of the Russians in the near abroad and an attempt in Russia to mobilize politically around this issue should be considered one of the most important of these factors.

It should be acknowledged that there are at least three major ways to contest this argument. First, one could suggest that the economic, political, and international cost of ethnonationalist mobilization in Russia is too high. Russian leaders and the public understand that they will lose too much and gain too little by embarking on such a path. The horrible predicament of Serbia, which tried to unite all ethnic Serbs under one political roof and extended its support to coethnics in the neighboring states, serves as a warning against this policy. Second, one can counter that Russia's self-definition has been traditionally supra-ethnic. Russian identity can be called imperial or universalistic, depending on political preferences, and in any case, Russian ethnic identity is too weak to be the basis for political mobilization. Third, Russia has been morally and physically exhausted by centuries of imperial overextension and communist rule, and it lacks the appropriate ideas, institutions, and leaders for any kind of mobilization. The paralyzing combination of a weak state and a weak, atomized society precludes the rise of a strong ethnonationalist Russia.

These are respectable perspectives, yet they are insufficient to make sound predictions. The first perspective is based on a rational model of policy. Ilya Prizel has shown convincingly that an irrational concept of nationalism and national identity has been a vital element of the foreign policies of many countries, although contemporary scholars shun this approach.[14] Prizel's argument can be easily extended into domestic politics as well.

The second perspective underestimates the situational and constructed aspects of national identities. When studying the post-Soviet states, David Laitin, Ronald Suny, and others have argued that nations as a rule are not "out there"; rather, they are a function of social, political, and economic processes.[15] Prizel has argued along similar lines: "While the redefinition of national identities is generally a gradual process, under situations of persistent stress even well-established identities can change at a remarkable rate, and a people's collective memory can be 'rearranged' quite quickly."[16] Modern Russia is under such a condition of persistent stress, and there is no reason to believe that it will necessarily and indefinitely cling to its old universalistic traditions. Ethnicity could become the major building block in the efforts of the Russian elite to construct a new nation.

The third argument, which emphasizes the extreme weakness of Russia, has been the major concern of Aleksandr Solzhenitsyn as well as a theme in the disturbing, epic account of the debacle in Chechnya by Anatol Lieven, one of the most thoughtful Western observers of Russia.[17] Certainly, this perspective adequately reflects the current state of the Russian nation. However, it lacks dynamic and comparative components. Russia in the early seventeenth century and after the collapse of statehood in 1917, China throughout the first half of the twentieth century, Germany and Japan after defeat in World War II—all were fragmented or devastated to such an extent that nobody awaited their rise as meaningful political entities. There is not enough evidence to prove that Russia's current dire situation means that the country cannot reappear on the global arena of the twenty-first century in some new and important role. What exactly this role will be is, of course, a debatable issue. While I contend that it is too early to write off Russia, I do not mean that its political future is necessarily that of a Western-style liberal democracy.

In today's Russia, many intellectuals believe that the country must readdress and reshape the very core of its existence, beginning with a redefinition of its identity. The redefinition of national identities always contains a significant destabilizing component and, therefore, can be considered a potential security threat. This threat presents a challenge to Russia, its Eurasian neighbors, and, because of Russia's size and nuclear arsenal, the world. With the collapse of the Soviet Union, Russia has lost its old identity but has not yet found a new one. Nearly a decade has passed since the collapse of the Soviet empire, but debates are still taking place concerning the boundaries of the new Russian state, as well as the very meaning of being Russian. This book argues that the fate of the new Russian diasporas, the twenty-five million Russians who suddenly found themselves "outside Russia" after the breakup of the Soviet Union, is an essential element in defining the new Russian identity.

The purpose of this book is to analyze the interrelationship between identity, diasporas, foreign policy, and conditions for international security in and around Russia. Most of the researchers working in the field of international relations are separated from those who address questions of identity transformation and modern diasporas.[18] Theoretical advances in the research of nationhood, ethnonationalism, and diasporas made by Margaret Canovan, Anthony Smith, Walker Connor, Rogers Brubaker, Liah Greenfeld, Robin Cohen, Roman Szporluk, and others are of particular importance and underlie the approach applied in this book.[19] Chauncy Harris, Vladimir Shlapentokh, Munir Sendich and Emil Payin, Paul Kolstoe, Neil Melvin, Jeff Chinn and Robert Kaiser, David Laitin, A. I. Ginzburg, S. S. Savoskul, Vladimir Kozlov, Valery Tishkov, Sergei Kuleshov, T. Poloskova, G. Vitkovskaya, and other scholars have begun analyzing Russian communities in the countries of the former Soviet Union.[20] Nikolai Rudensky, Elizabeth Teague, Neil Melvin, and Aurel Braun outlined some aspects of Russian policy toward the diasporas in the near abroad in the context of relations between the former Soviet republics.[21] However, these advances have not been applied to broader questions of Russian identity and to security studies. The question of how the problem of the diaspora is perceived inside Russia by politicians, intellectuals, and the public, and how Russia is addressing the issue in its foreign policy is still open. We know little about the history of the issue, the concrete manner in which the modern Russian elite redefines Russian identity, or the effect of all of this on international security in Eurasia. Are Russian communities in the near abroad perceived in Russia as parts of the Russian nation? What role have they played in Russia's foreign policy agenda from 1991 to the present? What are the consequences of Russian policy for international peace and security in the vast Eurasian region? These questions are related to a fundamental theoretical problem: After having been an empire for centuries, is contemporary Russia finally becoming a nation-state?

Chapter 1 begins with the assertion that the idea of becoming a nation-state within the current borders is entirely new and still problematic in Russia. It will show that the forceful building of a nation-state in Russia may put painful and explosive issues concerning the Russian people's frontiers on the country's political agenda. Emphasizing Russian ethnonationalism politicizes the question of the diasporas in the near abroad.

Chapter 2 argues that in both the Russian Empire and the Soviet Union the cultural and historical boundaries of the Russian people were blurred. This lack of clarity had several causes, including the combination of somewhat intertwined ethnic and imperial components in the national consciousness, the overlap of cultural and historical distinctions among Eastern Slavs, the suppression of Russian nationalism, the concept of "the Soviet people" (and the reality that supported this concept), and, finally, weak state institutions of the Russian Soviet Federated Socialist Republic (RSFSR). Chapter 2 also argues that intellectual history has not provided modern Russian thinkers and politicians with the foundation for an innocuous attitude toward the new geopolitical situation and a painless reconciliation with the new state boundaries. On the one hand, the supraethnic (imperial) tradition of defining "Russianness," dominant in the nineteenth and early twentieth centuries, points to the breakup of the Soviet Union as a historical defeat of the Russian state. On the other hand, the primordialst Soviet conception of *ethnos* is instrumental for the rise of modern Russian ethnonationalism and for an assertive policy toward the diasporas—which, within such a conception, can be easily stated to be parts of the Russian nation.

Chapter 3 analyzes the essential link between the Russian intellectual quest for a new identity and specific governmental policies, a link that consists of the domestic politics of nation building. Findings show that there are five major perspectives on building the state and nation in contemporary Russia: new state-building, ethnonationalism, restoration of the Soviet Union, integration of the post-Soviet states, and hegemony/domination. Chapter 3 also argues that ethnonationalism gradually strengthened its position in the political arena in the 1990s, not because of the rise of pure ethnonationalist groups, but as a result of incorporation of their ideas by major opposition parties, namely the Communist Party of the Russian Federation (KPRF) and the Liberal Democratic Party of Russia (LDPR). However, the forces that accept state building within current borders and advocate de-ethnicized nation building maintained stronger influence on concrete policies from 1991 to the present.

Chapter 4 addresses those features of the Russians of the near abroad that affect Russia's quest for a new identity and argues that the conditions of the Russian communities in the near abroad are as varied as the states and regions in which they live. Only nationalist ideology can reduce all of the complexities of these diaspora communities to a single problem with a single solution. As of yet, there are no noticeable horizontal ties among the Russian communities and few prospects that such ties will be constructed. Most Russian communities are very poorly organized, and political mobilization, solidarity, and cooperation along ethnic lines are in fact entirely new concepts for this once-dominant ethnic group. Nevertheless, there are important factors that might unite the Russian communities to a certain extent: a common culture and language, and the psychology of "victims" of the Soviet Union's dissolution. However, absent the Russian government's involvement, problems arising within the diasporas are likely to remain local issues. The only major factor that could make the problem significant for international security is the existence of a common "external homeland" for the diasporas—a regionally dominant Russia.

Chapter 5 argues that, contrary to the belief that Russian policy in the near abroad has been imperialistic and aggressive over issues concerning the Russian diasporas, Russian policy has instead been reasonably moderate in some aspects and tremendously ineffective in others. Indeed, in those undertakings that could destabilize the whole region, Russian policy has been particularly ineffective so far. As a result of both moderation and ineffectiveness, there is a great discrepancy between the boastful, assertive rhetoric of Russia's leaders and the actual policy of Russia in its relations with the Russian diasporas. In situations where Moscow has encountered determined resistance from other governments on an issue, it has simply backed off. In light of such responses, integration in Eurasia might further temper Russia's ethnonationalist and imperialist ambitions, however slight they may be at present.

If all these arguments hold, the most general conclusion must be that the Russian question was not resolved in the twentieth century and it will remain in the center of Eurasian political development in the new millennium. U.S. foreign policy officials must take this into account in their attempts to outline a long-term strategy in the region. Such attempts will require rethinking some theoretical assumptions about nation-state building, a realization that Russia may respond in several different ways to the evolving situation around its diasporas, and, finally, a search for new approaches to Eurasian regional development.

Russian Nation-State Building
and Diasporas
in the Security Context

T HAS BECOME almost commonplace to say that dramatic changes
have taken place in Russia since the beginning of the 1990s. From
an international perspective, the most significant transformations
have occurred in Russia's geopolitical situation, its role in global affairs,
and its military might. Russia's territory has reverted to that of the seventeenth century, and it has lost its most prized territorial possessions
in Europe. Russia was abandoned by all of its Soviet-era allies; its military is in dismal condition. As a result of these changes, Russia is now
geographically more detached from western and central Europe than
in any period since that of Peter the Great.

Nevertheless, many still view Russia with suspicion and perceive it as
a potential threat. According to many popular viewpoints, prerevolutionary Russian imperialism persisted throughout the communist
period, remaining at the heart of Russian foreign policy even after the
Soviet collapse. This is the view of Henry Kissinger, Zbigniew Brzezinski, and many other scholars and politicians in the United States, and
it is largely shared by the eminent Russian historian Yuri Afanasiev.[1]
Steven Sestanovich has called this school of thought "geotherapy."[2]
Why does this perspective remain so strong despite the dramatic changes
in Russia? The issue seems to be even more interesting if one compares
the views of "geotherapists" with the position of those who can be

called "geomourners," who are easily found among Russian communists or members of Vladimir Zhirinovsky's Liberal Democratic Party of Russia, as well as among many true liberals.

Geomourners believe that Russia is about to disappear from the global arena. Vladimir Lukin, the former chairman of the Committee on Foreign Relations of the State Duma (the Russian legislature's lower house) and current Duma Deputy Speaker, former ambassador to the United States, and one of the leaders of the liberal political party Yabloko, argued that "the main Russian strategic interest in the coming two decades will be extremely simple: to survive."[3] Lukin singles out "civilizational" factors as the major threat to Russia and fears that the country's disintegration as a distinct community will result from gradual disappearance of common ideas, laws, and values uniting the country's population. Under such circumstances, any external threat to security, even a small one, might become fatal.

Why is there such a discrepancy between the prevalent perceptions of Russia in the context of international security? On the one hand, there is an image of an aggressive, scheming, conspiring, imperialistic state. On the other hand, there are concerns for an endangered nation struggling to survive. However, there is an important affinity between the two schools of thought. Paradoxically, both geotherapists and geomourners rely on the assumption that Russia lost its old imperial identity and is still searching for a new one. Geotherapists fear that Russia will fail to find such a new identity and revert to its traditional role by attempting to create a new empire. While also fearing that Russia will fail to find a new role, geomourners are more concerned about the possibility of chaos, disintegration, and the gradual fading away of Russia. Viewed in this light, the two seemingly opposite perspectives seem to be not so different. Both adumbrate postimperial transformations of Russia and the loss of its previous identity. The major difference between these two schools is in the perception of potential threat. Geotherapists are concerned with the possibility of imperial restoration; geomourners perceive chaos and disintegration as the worst possible outcome. The positive alternative seems to be similar for both geotherapists and some of Russia's liberal geomourners who claim that Russia will cease to be a threat to the world and to itself when it becomes a "normal" European nation-state, abandoning its imperial ambitions.

Nation Building as a Potential Security Threat

One may argue that the construction of a new nation-state within current borders and treatment of ethnic Russians in the near abroad as foreign citizens would be an ideal solution to the Russian question. If the term "nation-state" is intended to define a situation in which the borders of a nation approximate those of the state, Russians spent several centuries building an empire, not a nation-state. British historian Geoffrey Hosking recently reinterpreted Russian history of the 1552–1917 period, attempting to demonstrate how and why the Russians failed to develop a strong sense of nation and arguing that the process of empire building obstructed nation building in Russia.[4] Relying on his earlier work and combining it with Hosking's ideas, Richard Pipes has proclaimed that building a nation-state in Russia was an immediate political task and even came up with a formula, assuming that history develops in a clear "progressive" direction toward some well-known and well-defined goal:[5] "The Russians of today would be well advised to give up fantasies of reconquering their lost empire—fantasies common to both conservatives and democrats—and concentrate on building a genuine nation-state. Nationalism, defined as 'a feeling of community and solidarity,' which the West has put behind itself and which it has turned into a reactionary doctrine, is distinctly progressive at the stage of history at which Russia happens to find itself."[6] Martin Malia may disagree at times with Pipes, but not on this issue. In Malia's words, "Russia surely needs remaking as a cohesive nation-state in order to wean her from a now anachronistic imperial heritage."[7]

Thus geotherapists' deliberations on foreign policy and security have been placed into a seemingly solid theoretical framework with a deep historical perspective. Drawing partly on this framework, U.S. policy in Eurasia has been based on the assumption that Russian neo-imperialism is the major obstacle to a positive and progressive process of nation building on the territory of the former Soviet empire. Brzezinski has argued that the prime task of U.S. policy in Eurasia would be the creation of an international environment that would stimulate Russia to become a "normal state," not an empire.[8]

Indeed, both common sense and political theory (and the two so rarely concur!) suggest that people need a bond of collective identity, especially after the collapse of despotic regimes that ruled over them. The process of democratization makes the search for a new bond even more urgent, because it is no longer provided by old authoritarian structures. Respect for basic human rights and the establishment of democratic institutions are possible only when there is some kind of integrated community, usually in the form of a nation-state, to which individuals are loyal. A "people" is created out of such a collection of individuals. Therefore, cultivating a devoted political community is essential for Russia's survival as a meaningful polity, which cannot be taken for granted at present. According to all these theories, a nation-state is the best possible framework for creating such a community.

Yet the idea of building an instant nation-state in today's Russia might be seriously flawed, not only theoretically and historically, but also from an international security perspective. It is a problematic and dangerous political goal for the Russian elite to undertake and for American political strategists to encourage. The issue of the Russian diasporas is one of the key elements that is overlooked by those who advocate building a nation-state in Russia. It is precisely the issue of diasporas that throws into doubt the theoretical foundations of the nation-state–building concept and makes it politically dangerous in the Russian context.

The history of the United States explains the instrumental, easy-going approach that some American scholars bring to the project of engineering the nation-state from scratch. As Khachig Tololyan has observed: "It is not accidental that USA, like IBM, is an acronym for an establishment (as in Est. 1776) that was founded fairly abruptly, not in the intimate coevolution of a people and nation over centuries, like France and the French, say."[9] To be sure, the nation-state is not a uniform condition. It is in fact a highly specific historical phenomenon that does not, and most probably never will, exist in most of the world. Is it likely (and desirable) that Russia (or any other modern state) will simply retrace, step by step, the path that the western European countries followed several centuries ago?

More to the point, does the process of accelerated globalization have any impact on today's nation building? Keep in mind that the stage of history at which Russia happens to find itself now is not the relative technological backwardness of the eighteenth century, but the nuclear and information age.

On the more concrete level of national security, the question is whether it is possible to risk the tumultuous perils of building a genuine nation-state in a country with nuclear weapons. Western European nation-states emerged out of centuries of wars and oppression. Michael Howard, an eminent scholar of the history of war, has argued: "From the very beginning the principle of nationalism was almost indissolubly linked, both in theory and practice, with the idea of war. . . . In nation-building as in revolution, force was the midwife of the historical process."[10] Too often, the "feeling of community and solidarity" has been founded on hostility toward others. The advocates of nation-state building in the former Soviet Union often overlook these historical realities.

From among these concerns, two crucial questions emerge in the process of building a nation: namely, who should belong to the nation, and what should its boundaries be?[11] The most destructive feature of any nation-building process has been the amalgamation of smaller political entities (ethnic and religious minorities) or the breaking up of bigger ones (typically multiethnic states). The boundaries of any western European state and corresponding nations were usually defined by numerous wars and internal violence, or a combination of the two.[12] In today's Russia, such a definition is more complex—and seems to mean so much more. The issue of the Russian people's boundaries determines their attitudes toward the diasporas, the non-Russians within Russia, Russia's relations with neighboring newly independent states, and the international security of Eurasia.[13] For Russia, constructing a nation-state on the rubble of the empire may challenge its federative structure, which contains a number of ethnoterritorial units, and jeopardize the issue of external borders that are still based on artificial administrative boundaries drawn by the Bolsheviks, effectively excluding twenty-five million ethnic Russians from their presumed homeland. Indeed, such a nation-state–building effort could easily undermine the entire system of regional and global security.

Hosking wrote that "Britain *had* an empire, but Russia *was* an empire—and perhaps still is."[14] The collapse of the Soviet Union meant much more for Russia than simply the loss of colonies. It was a loss of identity. Political, historical, cultural, and ethnic boundaries, as well as subjective mental maps that are held by most Russians, no longer share any congruence. There have been no clear and historically consistent criteria for distinguishing "we" from "they" in the Russian consciousness. Confusion over the boundaries of the Russian people has been the major factor in Eurasia's historical development for at least three hundred years. This phenomenon has enormous and contradictory implications for current issues of stability, security, and peace in the region. Unfortunately, this issue has not been adequately incorporated into the study of international relations and foreign and security policy. Such a lacuna can be explained, to a great extent, by the fact that during the Soviet period there was practically no connection between issues of Russian (different from Soviet) identity and foreign and security policy. The existence of artificial barriers between these two disciplines hindered the examination of the newly emerging link between them after the end of the Cold War. In the years following the breakup of the Soviet Union, there has been a comfortable blanket of silence over the issues of Russian identity, its boundaries, and the fate of Russian nationhood. Boris Yeltsin, the driving force of the empire's dissolution, went out of his way to downplay "national" themes, emphasizing instead the conflict of socialism versus capitalism, communists versus democrats, and slow versus rapid reform.

Without addressing the issues bound up with Russian identity, it is impossible to understand, for example, why Yeltsin and Vladimir Putin unleashed full-scale wars to keep culturally and politically alien Chechens within Russia, while at the same time ignoring the strong desire of six million Russians compactly living in adjacent northern Kazakhstan to be a part of Russia.[15] Does this mean that the major challenges for peace and security in Eurasia will come from Russia's internal disintegration, or is it possible that this threat will come from conflicts between Russia and the newly independent states? The wars in Chechnya demonstrated that Yeltsin and Putin were ready to resort to extreme measures to achieve their goal of building the Russian state within current borders. Notably, the United States showed an unusual tolerance in this situation. However, one can only speculate on what America's reaction would be if Yeltsin or Putin had decided to encourage and support irredentism among ethnic Russians in neighboring states. Because firm and unconditional support of the Soviet successor states' sovereignty is a pillar of U.S. policy in the region, aimed at curbing Russian neo-imperial ambitions, the U.S. response would probably be incomparably stronger, especially if Ukraine, the Baltic states, or the countries adjoining the oil-rich and strategically significant Caspian Sea were involved.[16]

A national redefinition of identities always contains a significant destabilizing component and, as such, could be considered a security threat. The war in Chechnya proved that almost any solution to the Russian question, understood as the unfinished quest for identity, might have serious consequences. Even the seemingly peaceful and democratic idea of preserving sovereignty and territorial integrity of the post-Soviet states within their current borders might end up giving their rulers a free hand within those borders, with sometimes horrible consequences for minorities. Such a strategy might also freeze in place frontiers that are not viable in the long run and stimulate the growth of tensions between the governments trying to build sovereign nation-states and the millions of people attaching their loyalties to another country.

Of course, a proper understanding of the crucial difference between territorial and ethnic nations would probably benefit from an objective, scholarly analysis of the distinction. "The first type, as the name suggests," writes Anthony Smith, "takes its basis from a sense of territory, and from the effects of interaction within *clear-cut geographical boundaries.*"[17] It is formed as a community of laws and legal institutions, with a strong sense of citizenship and common culture. The second type was formed "on the basis of pre-existing ethnie and ethnic ties, so that it became a question of 'transforming' ethnic into national ties and sentiments through the process of mobilization, territorialization, and politicization. In general, this produced a rather different conception of the nation, one that emphasized elements like genealogy, populism, customs and dialects, and nativism."[18] It is evident that these two concepts of nation are no more than ideal types. Most nations exhibit territorial and ethnic components in varying proportions at particular moments of their history. As dynamic entities, they are constantly reconstructed and redefined. The analysis of nation-building processes led Smith to the conclusion that to become a political community on the territorial and civic model, the nation often paradoxically seeks to emphasize or invent myths of common descent, historical memories, and homelands that are not just some terrain, but historic, sacred territories where their ancestors lived.[19] This is the way the nation strengthens itself by forging intimate ties between the state and the people.

If Smith's concept is applied to Russia, one may argue that territorial nation building does not preclude, and possibly even warrants, the use of ethnic components. Moreover, in comparative studies of nationalism, it is common to emphasize that Central and Eastern European, Russian, and Middle Eastern nationalism tends to regard the nation-state as the natural expression of pre-existing ethnic unity.[20] The idea of constructing a nation-state in Russia ignores profound differences between Western and Eastern nationalisms.

To sum up, nation-state building may be a serious security threat for Russia and Eurasia as a whole, because it might lead to ethnicization of Russian politics and eventual attempts to redraw state borders by absorbing Russian diasporas in the neighboring states. The blurred political map of Eurasia might be more in line with the accelerating process of globalization than the two-centuries-old system of nation-states that emerged from bloody wars. Boundaries between nation-states are becoming increasingly less significant as a result of globalization, and there is no reason for Russians and other Eurasian peoples to repeat all the steps and mistakes made by western Europe. "The German question" was finally resolved within the framework of European integration when the borders that the Germans had fought over for a century became subsumed within a broader economic community. Forcing construction of the nation-state in Russia may place painful and explosive issues concerning the frontiers of the Russian people onto the country's political agenda. It is probably better to keep these issues behind the lines of Russian internal politics and foreign relations, because it might lead to ethnicization of nation building in Russia.

Globalization and Diasporas as Potential Security Threats

For at least a decade, social science literature has been challenging the preponderance of the nation-state system.[21] Criticism of excessive focus on the nation-state in international studies gained momentum with the spread of the "globalization" paradigm emphasizing economic, political, and cultural processes that transcend national boundaries.

Ronald Robertson thoughtfully defined globalization as "the crystal-lization of the entire world as a single place."[22] The features of this phe-nomenon most often pointed to are the erosion of national sovereignty formally enjoyed by independent nation-states, the rise of multinational and transnational institutions, and cultural homogenization.[23] Global-ization is often viewed as conflicting with the divisive impact of ethnic-ity.[24] Yet the connection is not as straightforward as it might appear at first glance. In some situations, globalization may go hand in hand with the strengthening of subnational ethnic ties. This is particularly true of ethnic diasporas that may flourish and bring about new divisive lines under conditions of globalization.

The traditional nation-state is a bordered territory occupied by a settled population under a sovereign government. Globalization leads to the waning importance of territoriality. James Rosenau contended that "globalization is rendering boundaries and identity with the land less salient."[25] Politicization of subnational ethnic groups, and espe-cially the spread and sustaining of ethnic diasporas, can undermine the sovereignty and preponderance of nation-states in a manner similar to globalization by transferring important social functions to levels other than the nation-state. Globalization actually facilitates the erosion of nation-states by diasporas, because it provides easy links between ter-ritorially dispersed communities by the means of global mass media, affordable transportation for frequent travel, cyberspace connections, and so forth. It is no longer true that transnational bonds necessarily entail permanent resettlement or territorial claims.[26] Benedict Ander-son has argued that "the telephone, electronic banking, videotapes, radio, and television, to say nothing of e-mail, are making a sort of 'vir-tual,' portable nationality more and more possible, and, exactly because of people's nomadic experience, more and more attractive. The implica-tion is a widening split between citizenship and affective nationality."[27] These phenomena further multiply identities, creating various loyalties and challenging unconditional devotion to one country.

Even in well-established states, the immigration and rebirth of diasporas challenge identities, which were recently taken for granted. For example, it has been argued that the "melting pot" paradigm does not reflect all the realities of ethnic relations in the contemporary United States; indeed, assimilation is not the only ethnic trend in the country. The "diasporas" contribute to the erosion of "one nation, indivisible."

Chinatowns, for example, often demonstrate detachment from and indifference to the host state.[28] The debates over bilingual education, the spreading of hyphenated identities, even the support of Mexican soccer teams by Mexican-Americans in San Diego—all reflect the new multicultural face of America. The state continues to insist on its exclusive right not only for political obedience from its citizens but also for their devotion and even love of country. But solemn ceremonies pledging oaths of allegiance cannot hide the fact that residence and citizenship are used more and more frequently as mere economic conveniences.

To be sure, we live in a world "in which identities are less closely married to residence in specific 'national' territories."[29] Diasporas are important components of the new global order of liberal internationalism. But by weakening nation-states, the process of globalization may paradoxically stimulate a resurgence of ancient ethnic identities and provoke new localism and nativism. Diasporas represent a new global phenomenon of "a generalized condition of homelessness."[30] This may stimulate attempts to mentally create, in Salman Rushdie's words, "imaginary homelands."[31]

However, it would be premature to say, as Robin Cohen has, that diasporas "may, in significant respects, transcend and succeed the nation-state."[32] Khachig Tololyan, editor of *Diaspora: A Journal of Transnational Studies*, wrote the following in his opening editorial statement: "To affirm that diasporas are the exemplary communities of the transnational moment is not to write the premature obituary of the nation-state, which remains a privileged form of polity."[33] Diasporas represent one of the factors of the global system's reconfiguration, characterized by the relative erosion of the nation-state. Proliferation of multiple identities creates new tensions and conflicts, including those between state and nonstate actors. It separates "nation" and national constructs from functions of the nation-state.

Many authors have pointed to the connection between "globalism and tribalism,"[34] both being challenges to the system of nation-states. Benjamin Barber has highlighted the destructive features of both phenomena, such as anarchy, unaccountability, and indifference to civil liberty and democracy.[35] Similarly, Benedict Anderson has emphasized some worrisome implications of strengthening ethnic ties across state boundaries:

The politics that tend to emerge are not linked to democratic institutions or traditional accountability. They thrive on secretive narcissism of e-mail nets and lend themselves to violence and paranoid fantasies. It is not at all surprising that people active in these networks are often "disappointed" by those in their series who actually live in, say, Armenia, the Punjab, Ireland, or Croatia, whom they find too soft, too impure, too contaminated by "foreign" cultures. There is plenty to worry about when ethnicity escapes the nation. . . .[36]

Russian diasporas are too weak, disorganized, and disoriented to influence Russian politics in this way. It is actually the Russian state that, in concert with host states, ethnicizes Russians in the near abroad. Russia does it by establishing special ties with its "compatriots" in these regions, while the newly independent states do the same by introducing distinctions between "titulars" and "nontitulars." This situation is in sharp contrast with many other diasporas, which played a crucial role in state creation and nation building. The Jewish diaspora of Eastern Europe was actually a precursor of the state of Israel, and the Greek diaspora of Odessa and Vienna gave birth to Greek anti-Ottoman nationalism. These diasporas played crucial roles in the creation of corresponding states. A different example of diaspora activism is the Irish in the United States, who have been an important ally and lobby for nationalists in Northern Ireland. The Russian case is also very different from the role of Lithuanian, Latvian, and Estonian diasporas in building their respective nations. Baltic-Americans have taken a leading role in the politics of their "overseas homelands." American citizens have become the president of Lithuania, defense and foreign ministers of Estonia, and members of parliament in their respective countries (about 10 percent in Latvia). This particular diaspora activism has stood in sharp contrast with the fact that most ethnic Russians born in Latvia and Estonia could not obtain citizenship in these countries. As a rule, active participation of diasporas in nation building of their external homelands ethnicized the process.

Students of nationalism have long been intrigued by the formative influences of exiles and diasporas in the generation of nationalist movements.[37] However, Russian diasporas of the near abroad are not a source of serious ideological, financial, or political support for their homeland. On the contrary, they look to Russia as a source of such support. The pattern of interaction between diasporas and the homeland has been marked by the expectation of Russia's active involvement in and protection of the Russian diaspora in the near abroad. This position of Russian diasporas is very different from the attitude of "classic" diasporas, which are assertive, ethnonationalistic, and, in many cases, financially better-off than the majority of the population in their homeland. Yet the common feature of the Russian case and the "classic" links between diasporas and their homelands is the potential for ethnicization of the nation-building process. One cannot preclude the possibility of a Russian Sun Yat Sen, who would build his nationalist movement based on the Russian communities outside Russia and start a political struggle against the "IMF-backed comprador occupational regime" (the favorite term of the radical nationalist opposition) in Moscow.[38]

In summary, the processes of globalization, accompanied by the rise of new tribalism and the politicization of diasporas are inherently destabilizing factors for the international system as we have known it since the Treaty of Westphalia. Like attempts to accelerate nation-building in modern Eurasia, these factors might lead to the ethnicization of Russian politics and the redrawing of borders.

The Unfinished Quest for Identity and Its Security Implications: Three Scenarios

The problems of the interrelationship between Russian nation building, Russian diasporas, and Eurasian security might also be analyzed through a different approach: by studying Russian identity transformation and its impact on the system of international relations in Eurasia. A new Russia has begun to define its identity from the ground up, and very little from its past can be applied to the present. Intellectual history has not provided contemporary thinkers and politicians with adequate tools for assessing how Russia's age-old quandary concerning national identity fits in the new geopolitical situation. Nevertheless, three major options for the future development of a new Russian identity may be isolated: neo-imperial, ethnic, and civic.[39]

Throughout the past three centuries, Russian culture was formed within an imperial framework. "Universalism" *(vselenskost')* became the key feature of Russian "high culture." On the one hand, it helped it to gain worldwide recognition. Far from being provincial or narrow-minded, Russian culture easily absorbed the achievements of other, particularly European, cultures and made outstanding contributions to humankind. On the other hand, the attempts to include everyone, culturally and otherwise, into a limitless, universal Russia were in constant conflict with the particular aspirations of neighboring peoples, who largely did not want to become "universal." They saw Russification behind such universalism and perceived it as a threat to their very existence. These historical and cultural messianic traditions stand in sharp contrast to the new geopolitical situation in which Russia finds itself today.

Most of the current literature on foreign policy and security issues in Eurasia is devoted to the threats emanating from Russian attempts to restore the Soviet Union or dominate the post-Soviet space. This concentration on the neo-imperialist option has overshadowed serious perils to international security associated with the likely rise of Russian ethnonationalism, as well as the difficulties of building a new civic identity in Russia. No longer hidden under an imperial veil, ethnic identity has become more salient to Russians after the collapse of the Soviet Union. Although ethnonationalism in Russia is not politically well-organized, it might emerge ascendant, especially if the goal of nation-state building is introduced into contemporary political discourse—the term "nation" has had a strong ethnic, not civic, connotation in Soviet and post-Soviet academia, public opinion, and politics (see chapter 2). As has happened many times in the history of Europe, a well-articulated common culture may come to be defined as the ideal political boundary, serving as a historical precedent for ardent claims that all Russians must be reunited under "one political roof." As Anthony Smith notes, "Aggrandizing their homelands through the mobilization of ethnic sentiment among kinsmen outside the 'homeland' was the mark of many a European irredentism in the last century and later . . . and it has often led to sharp conflicts and even full-scale wars which threaten the stability of regional interstate systems and attract great power involvement."[40]

The redefinition of Russia in more concrete ethnic terms, in line with those of all Soviet successor states, may become one of the most dangerous undertakings in its history, primarily because of the inevitable redrawing of Eurasia's borders that would accompany the implementation of an ethnonationalist project. As will be shown in chapter 3, the essence of the ethnonationalist program is to restore geographical congruence between the state and the nation by, in this case, building the Russian state within the area of settlement of the ethnic Russian people and other Eastern Slavs. Politically, such a program means the reunification of Russia, Belarus, Ukraine, and northern Kazakhstan.

If the experience of other countries is any guide, nation building on the rubble of an empire is usually the endeavor of ethnonationalists. Kemalist Turkey started its experiment with a nation-state by subjecting its Armenian, Greek, and Kurdish minorities to genocide and expulsion.[41] Austrians welcomed the *Anschluss* following twenty years of living in a small postimperial state. Serbia and Croatia became aggressively nationalistic and began to redraw the post-Yugoslavian political map through the use of brutal force. All former Soviet republics have resorted to ethnopolitical symbology and historical myths to craft an image of the state as a homeland of "indigenous" people. Intellectually, all these policies have relied on the Romantic historicist tradition, claiming that humanity can be divided neatly into nations, stipulating that culturally—or ethnically—defined nations possessed sacred rights, and, as a result, allowing these nations' leaders to downplay individual human rights and due respect for minorities.[42] The policy of ethnonationalism is especially dangerous when it is supported by powerful outside forces that prefer to see anti-imperial struggle cast in rosy hues, ignoring the darker, potentially violent side. The real trouble in Eurasia will begin if Russia adopts a similar doctrine of nation building—that is, put simply, if Russians "go ethnic." The rhetoric of "historic justice" adopted by many ethnonationalists in Eurasia could very well result in a backlash if Russia does the same: the notion of "historic justice" is always subjective and one-sided.

The development of a more benign civic identity also delegitimizes Russia's current boundaries by questioning the collapse of the Soviet Union and its aftermath. Why was it impossible to build a de-ethnicized, democratized state within the old borders? The politically correct answer is that this option would not have met ethnonational aspirations of the non-Russians: they did not want to live in the old empire and thus created their own states. Russians, on the other hand, have again found themselves in a multiethnic milieu within new borders, and twenty-five million of them were left outside. "The national question" for Russians was not resolved by the collapse of the Soviet Union. On the contrary, it was created. Within its current borders, Russia is "more a bleeding hulk of empire: what happened to be left over when the other republics broke away."[43]

The development of a civic identity hardly matches the other options in the sense of a rapid mobilization potential; in fact, it may result in a rather weak state for an extended period of time. To build a true civic identity, it is necessary to have or develop a common idea, history, heritage, traditions, legitimate boundaries accepted by all citizens, and strong and effective state institutions. Thus far, none of these elements exists in Russia. As a multiethnic political community within the boundaries of the modern Russian Federation, the Russian nation is new, unstable, and weak. Regular elections, vibrant and accountable political institutions, and common economic and social problems and policies could gradually serve as the integument for this new political nation, further distinguishing and separating it from the other Soviet successor states. However, internal divisions, first between the Russian Federation's ethnoterritorial administrative units and the federal center, remain strong. Separatist Chechnya is an extreme example of the difficulties in building a common civic identity in Russia. Russia's eventual disintegration is an evident security concern not only for Russia, but for the rest of the world, which would undoubtedly be affected by a security and power vacuum on the Eurasian continent.

Russia is not alone in confronting the immense difficulties in building a civic identity. States in many parts of the world have been unsuccessful nation builders, and many governments have failed to induce their subjects to shift their primary loyalties from informal subdivisions (ethnic, religious groups) to formal, legalistic state structures.[44] Commenting on the perils of nation building "from above," with little input from society, Karen Barkey and Mark von Hagen emphasized: "The consequences of this pattern of nation building are to be seen today in relatively fragile, mutable, and wavering definitions of nationhood, in the absence of a sense of unity in a common project, and in the vulnerability of the societies to find appeal in particularly militant variants of communist or nationalist ideologies."[45] Even the objective realm of scholarship is not immune to such oversights. As Walker Connor observed, "Scholars associated with theories of 'nation building' have tended either to ignore the question of ethnic diversity or to treat the matter of ethnic identity superficially as merely one of a number of minor impediments to effective state integration."[46]

Many in Eurasia and the West view the vague boundaries of the Russian people as an unnerving and threatening phenomenon that could very well lead to imperial restoration. A Russian nation-state, on the contrary, is seen as a familiar, conventional, and peaceful alternative. The crux of this chapter's message is that the approach of nation-state builders overlooks many of the grave threats to international security that may evolve from an attempt to mechanically configure Russia with its (mostly ethnonationalist) neighbors, none of which have diasporas comparable in size and potential political significance to Russia's. Inarticulate Russian nationhood is one of the key factors explaining why the Soviet Union's demise occurred so peacefully, especially when compared with the debacle of another communist federation—Yugoslavia —where most Serbs encountered no ambiguity over their nation or national identity. A Russia without clear-cut frontiers may be the only peaceful solution to the Russian question after the breakup of the Soviet empire. Inconsistent and messy relations between Moscow and ethnic republics within the Russian Federation and moderate, though hardly effective, policies toward Russians in the near abroad might be a better solution for security in Eurasia than attempts to shape a clear-cut approach toward nation-state building and the inevitable redrawing of borders. It should be noted, however, that the Russian government often pursues such an ambiguous policy not because of its wisdom, but because of its weakness.

The issue of ethnic Russian diasporas can play a crucial role in building a new Russian nation. George Breslauer's sophisticated analysis of Boris Yeltsin's "invention of a Russian nation-state" led him to the conclusion that "Yeltsin's efforts to sell a formula that entailed de-ethnicized nation building within the territorial boundaries of Russia, but ethnicized governmental responsibility for Russians in the near abroad, highlighted and sustained the ambiguity about whether Russia was to remain an empire or become a liberal state."[47] Political choices made by the Russian government seem to prove that

> the Russian government's responsibility to this diaspora was the issue that could not be wished away. Yet addressing it entailed highlighting the contradiction between Russia as a consolidating nation-state and Russia as the

heir to an empire. Yeltsin tried to have it both ways, which may have been the best that an advocate of liberal nationalism could have done, given the objective and subjective legacies of empire and the challenges of political competition.[48]

In other words, debates on Russian nationhood in modern Russia have gone beyond state boundaries. Establishing special relations with "compatriots" might be viewed as an attempt to extend Russia's political space, yet Russia has few resources and little political will to become truly assertive in this field. Struggling through a deep economic crisis, facing serious social problems, and having a weakened and disorganized army, Russia can hardly afford to implement any project that would stipulate actually redrawing current borders. A weak state that does not collapse entirely may be a good prerequisite for moderation in relations with its neighbors. There is, however, a deeper factor that can explain the trend toward restraint: the weakness of Russian identity. The next chapter addresses this issue in more detail.

· · · · · · · · · ·

Transformations
of Russian Identity

RUSSIA'S FORCEFUL CONSTRUCTION of a nation-state is a dangerous path because it might lead to the rise of ethnonationalism
and the redrawing of Eurasian political boundaries. Why has
Russia not taken this path up to now? What factors restrain Russian
ethnonationalism? Are there counterforces that might lead to a redefinition of Russia's identity in ethnic terms? What is the role of the Russian
diasporas in these processes? The history, intellectual traditions, current theoretical debates, public opinion, and politics of these questions
form a background for actual Russian policies toward Russians in the
near abroad.

The key issue for Russia's perception of its diasporas is how its citizens define the boundaries of their nation. The hypothesis that Russia
will build a nation-state within the current borders of the Russian Federation and treat ethnic Russians in the near abroad as foreign citizens
derives more from wishful thinking than from an actual analysis of the
current trends. In Russia, nationalism and liberalism have been intellectually and politically separated for a century and a half, making Russia
strikingly different from many of its European neighbors. It is unclear
whether the fusion of these two concepts has become possible after the
breakup of the Soviet empire or whether Russian nationalism is still
hostile to an open society, democratic participation, and a limited representative government. To determine the answer, one must define the
new forms of nationalism in Russia and examine their effect on a civic
identity that is currently being constructed from the top down.

This chapter is organized as follows: Evidence for weak ethnic identity among Russians, characterizing historic factors that provided for their inarticulated nationhood and ambiguity over the borders of the Russian people, is considered first. Examination of nation-building issues in Russian intellectual history, again from the perspective of defining Russia's boundaries, follows. Then it will be argued that there are important trends in the Soviet and post-Soviet theoretical discourse on Russian identity that might lead to a redefinition of "Russianness" in more ethnic-oriented terms. This hypothesis will be tested by looking at recent shifts in public opinion.

The Boundaries of the Russian People: Theoretical Perspectives

This chapter's analysis is based on three major interconnected assumptions. First, there has been an extraordinarily wide range of social and political phenomena that are customarily identified as "national."[1] As mentioned before, nation and nationalism are not uniform conditions; they are highly specific historical phenomena that have varied greatly in time and space, and they might not exist at all in many countries and time periods.[2] Second, nationhood is fluid and dynamic. It may remain dormant for a long period of time and then suddenly emerge, altering political processes, interstate boundaries, and the identities of millions of people. It can change shapes and shift from ethnic-oriented to civic, or from exclusive and aggressive to inclusive, moderate, and liberal. Very little is predetermined in what kind of nationalism this or that people will embrace in the future. Third, nationhood is an extremely complex and somewhat elusive phenomenon. Russian philosopher Nikolai Berdyaev perceived it as something "mysterious, mystical, irrational."[3] Most theoretical approaches to nationalism contain some truth, but when applied universally, they ultimately lead to a dead end. Each of the concepts of a nation, such as a politically conscious ethnie, a cultural community, an act of willful consent and subjective identity, a product of modernization and nation-building by the state, does provide a valuable perspective.[4] However, each of these concepts in isolation is often one-sided and does not provide a comprehensive picture. In addition, most of these theories are not mutually exclusive, though their authors may believe them to be.

The issue of the Russian nation's boundaries is a key question in the analysis of diaspora issues and their impact on Russia's quest for a new identity. Whichever definition of a nation is adopted for academic or political purposes will be confronted by serious difficulties in defining the boundaries of the Russian nation.

As is the case with most other peoples, Russians have a national mythology of common descent. Long ago, however, they expanded beyond their primordial ethnic "core" (if it ever existed), and many other ethnic groups have been assimilated by or intermingled with Russians to a great extent. During the Soviet period, urbanization, industrialization, and standard education accelerated such assimilation and intermingling. These processes, in turn, led to a further blurring of ethnic "frontiers."

As a cultural community based on the Russian language, the Russian nation will, in the foreseeable future, remain a much broader entity than Russians living within Russia's borders; yet at the same time, this same nation will continue to exclude some groups within the Russian Federation. Chapter 4 will illustrate the fact that there are millions of people who identify themselves as non-Russians but admit, however, that they are "culturally Russian." Their identities are fluid. Cultural divides often run not between individuals, but within them.

As a subjective identity based on a collective sense of history, "Russianness" is a rather strong force. It has been experienced primarily in terms of belonging to a larger collective entity—the Russian people. Different traditions create different theoretical frameworks for discussing such issues as collective identity and national consciousness. While most contemporary literature on nationalism seems to agree that the crucial factor for turning people into a nation is consciousness, and not "objective" features, the literature divides on other issues. The Anglo-American tradition stresses the will of individuals to be parts of a nation, while collectivist schools of thought emphasize the destiny of an organic entity, its mission, and the duty of its individuals to serve the whole.[5] In Russia, many theorists believe that a nation is formed by relationships between individuals, and that for each individual it is "objective" in the sense that it cannot be altered by an individual, because he or she is born into it. Individuals perceive national identity as ascriptive in most cases. However, the identification of individuals as Russians, not only by themselves but also by others, has often been confusing. For example, practically everybody who came abroad from the former Soviet Union was called "Russian," irrespective of actual ethnicity.[6] In a similar vein, Soviet Jewish immigrants to the United States or Israel now call themselves "Russians," though it would sound strange for those Jews who remain in Russia. These are all indicators of the fact that the term "Russian" *(russkii)* may have not only an ethnic but also a civic connotation.

From this book's perspective, the most important issues are the subjective identity of those twenty-five million Russians who suddenly found themselves outside the borders of Russia after the collapse of the Soviet Union and the way in which they are perceived by Russians who reside in a new, post-Soviet Russia. Most of them, while being citizens of newly independent states, feel that they belong to the "Russian people," whatever that may mean. They are also perceived as such in Russia, thus making frontiers between the Soviet successor states seem artificial to many people.

There is probably only one definition of a nation that can provide a clear-cut answer to the question of the boundaries of the Russian state: a political one—a political nation is effectively a nation-state. According to British theorist of nationhood Margaret Canovan, however, "The first move serious analysts of nationhood tend to make is to distinguish between nations and states, pointing out that the two cannot be the same thing."[7] Congruence between the state and the nation is rather an exception to the rule. Moreover, the two were often at odds in the twentieth century. Many governments throughout the world have failed to induce their subjects to shift their primary loyalties from informal subdivisions of humankind to formal, legalistic state structures.[8] States in many parts of the world have been unsuccessful nation builders.

Confusion over boundaries of a seemingly limitless, shapeless Russian national identity suggests multiple, overlapping identities. For the purposes of better understanding these identities, one can isolate and define several concentric circles of Russian identities. The "core" inner circle is formed by ethnic Russians of the Russian Federation, who have little ambiguity over their identity. Broader circles surrounding this core include the nonethnic Russians of Russia (together with the core

Russians, they constitute a new civic identity of *rossiyane*); Russians of the near abroad, who might combine the core ethnic identity with another, civic one (for example, there are ethnic Russians in Ukraine who simultaneously identify themselves as Ukrainian citizens); and some Russian-speakers of the near abroad, who might have a Russian "cultural" identity along with several others (for example, a Russian-speaking ethnic Ukrainian who is a citizen of Kazakhstan). All this is further complicated by intermarriage that occurred for several generations. Such a multilayered hierarchy of identities in Eurasia has resulted in an inarticulate Russian nationhood. Obviously, any political project of building a new Russian nation is confronted by vexing problems of the boundaries of the Russian people.

Inarticulate Nationhood

Before the late 1980s, very few Western scholars called the Soviet Union an empire;[9] nor, for obvious reasons, were there any adherents to this framework of analysis within official Soviet historiography. With the beginning of the Soviet state's collapse, however, the concept of the Soviet Union as an empire gained ground in the West and was quickly adopted by some Russian historians as well.[10] This perspective usually emphasized the role of nationalism and national liberation movements in the state's collapse. The most insightful ideas were produced by those who put the postimperial transformation of the USSR into comparative context.[11]

Theories using the imperial framework were modified or challenged by those who emphasized the complexities of the notion of empire.[12] Yuri Slezkine suggested that some features of the Soviet Union did not fit a classic imperial model,[13] while Mark Beissinger argued that "empire and states are inherently subjective constructs rather than simply objective entities, and . . . a key difference between the two lies in the eye of the beholder."[14] Jeff Chinn and Robert Kaiser developed an alternative model of "relative deprivation theory."[15] One of the common denominators for all those who were not completely satisfied with the imperial model was their attention to two particular features of the former Soviet Union. First, the deliberate efforts of the Soviet state to build nations out of the numerous ethnic groups of the previous Russian Empire. And second, the unique status of the core group, the Russians, whose development as a full-fledged nation was effectively blocked. These approaches have resonated in the analyses of many Russian thinkers, who, while acknowledging that the Russian Empire and the Soviet Union were indeed empires, emphasized the paradoxical absence of an imperial nation. Aleksandr Solzhenitsyn has argued: "Russians in Russia became an embracing people, as if they were a woven basis of a multinational rug, which is a rare ethnic phenomenon. It was caused by many-centuries developments, their state-establishing role and inter-mittent geographic settlement. No, they were not an 'imperial nation.'"[16] Such perspectives have been vigorously challenged by political leaders and many scholars in the newly independent states, who see them as self-serving attempts to rewrite a history of oppression and domina-tion (see chapter 4).

Whatever perspective is adopted, it may be argued that because of various historical factors, Russians emerged from the USSR as an incom-plete nation with a surprisingly low level of national consciousness and lack of a mass-based national movement. This fact fundamentally differ-entiates Russia from the other former republics, particularly the Baltics, Georgia, and Armenia. It also explains why there has not yet been any influential mass-based movement advocating reunification with the diasporas. Russian scholar Sergei Savoskul noted that careless and indif-ferent attitudes of Russians toward their own as well as others' national values was a characteristic feature of their consciousness and was typical of a "big" people.[17] However, being big still does not necessarily lead to a people's being careless and indifferent toward issues of nationhood. There must be some deeper explanation for this phenomenon. Five major factors that contributed to the formation of a specific, inarticu-late Russian nationhood are outlined below.

First, the Russian Empire and its successor, the Soviet Union, were continuous land-based empires, like those of the Hapsburgs or the Ottomans, with no natural boundaries between the center and the periphery.[18] In the Russian and Soviet cases, the center was represented by the capital city—first Moscow, then St. Petersburg, then Moscow again—not by some well-defined core territory. Geography played an important role in the formation of Russian national consciousness, a fundamental characteristic of which was the partial combination of ethnic and imperial components. Richard Pipes, Roman Szporluk, and Richard Sakwa contend that the Russian Empire was formed before the modern national identity of Russians emerged.[19] Further, Geoffrey Hosking demonstrated that the Russian elite was more interested in expanding the boundaries of the empire than promoting the belief in nationhood. Unlike Pipes, Hosking attributes the nonemergence of the Russian nation not to the backwardness of the country, but to specific geographical, historical, and political circumstances.[20]

Various authors also point to different periods of history when trying to identify a boundary between the supranational and ethnonational orientations of the Russian Empire. Russian historian Nikolai Tsymbayev found that the shift to ethnonational policy occurred at the turn of the eighteenth century.[21] Richard Sakwa suggests the 1880s as a watershed.[22] In his assessment, Sakwa is more in line with the Russian liberal tradition: Pavel Milyukov pointed to the period of Alexander III as the beginning of suppression of non-Russian nationalities and the rise of Russian nationalism.[23] Yet both orientations have existed throughout Russian history, including the Soviet period. One or the other may have prevailed at different times, but the Soviet era encompassed periods of stronger internationalism in the 1920s and stronger Russian ethnonationalism from the 1930s through the early 1950s.

The absence of clear boundaries between the empire and its Russian core has led some analysts to conclude that there was no dominant ethnic group: all groups, including Russians, were subjects of an imperial center.[24] This thesis, though seemingly serving the self-justification of Russians, plays an extremely important role in their post-Soviet psyche. There is practically no significant theory or political force in present-day Russia that views the empire as a vehicle for Russian interests at the expense of other peoples. This thesis obviously stands in sharp contrast to emerging ideology and official historiography in the newly independent states. More important, it reflects a deep-rooted belief in the Russian consciousness that the empire did not serve Russians' interests and was instead a burden (Solzhenitsyn); or a benefit for all peoples and not only Russians (Gennadi Zyuganov); or, during the Soviet period, detrimental to everyone because of its communist nature (Russian liberals). The latter were totally unprepared for the alleged anti-Russian stance of national movements in the Baltic states and Ukraine after the collapse of the Soviet Union. It turned out that many non-Russian nationalists fought not against a faceless empire, but against Russian domination. This split in what were all initially called "democratic movements" reflected the differences between more nationally-minded non-Russians and more "internationalist" Russian democrats.

The second factor inhibiting the development of mass-based Russian nationalism is the overlap of cultural, linguistic, and historical distinctions between Russia, Belarus, and Ukraine, leading to a confused boundary between Russians and other Eastern Slavs.[25] For centuries, it made the Russian elite soft-pedal its nationalism, much like the existence of the "home empire" of Scotland, Wales, and Northern Ireland in the United Kingdom allegedly suppressed English nationalism.

The third factor contributing to the weakening of Russian national consciousness was the concept of the "Soviet people" and the reality that supported it. People from mixed marriages, those living outside their "homelands," and Russians from large urban (and more cosmopolitan) centers were the most responsive to this concept. Russians accepted it more readily than other ethnic groups, because to be "Soviet" implicitly meant being a Russian speaker and acknowledging the "civilizing" mission of the Russian culture and its extraterritorial nature throughout the entire Soviet Union. In theory, there was much in common between the "melting pot" paradigm in the United States and the "Soviet people" concept in the USSR. (The notions of multiculturalism and diversity in the American experience also had an ideological cousin in the USSR: the "free union of flourishing nations.") The first attempts to develop a theory of the "Soviet people" can be traced back to Nikolai Bukharin.[26] Nikita Khrushchev revisited this theory, emphasizing the fusion of nations under communism and promising its attainment in the near future. In the 1970s, this idea was revived when it was solemnly pronounced that the "Soviet people" were a "new historical entity," not just a concept.

Some Russian nationalists claimed that the imperial role deprived Russians of their ethnic identity. Slavophile writers grouped around the magazine *Nash sovremennik* worried that "Soviet patriotism" was

UNITED STATES INSTITUTE OF PEACE

. . . .

An independent institution established by Congress to strengthen the nation's capacity
to promote peaceful resolution of international conflicts

June 2001

Dear Reviewer:

The United States Institute of Peace is pleased to enclose a
review copy of a new publication

Russia and Its New Diasporas
by Igor Zevelev

July 2001 • 240 pp. • 6 x 9
(paper) 1-929223-08-0
$19.95 • £14.50

Ten years after the fall of the Soviet Union, Russia continues to
dominate headlines of international news. The current president,
Vladimir Putin, struggles in his efforts to develop a new, stable,

This volume addresses the interrelationship between identity, diasporas, foreign policy, and conditions for international security in and around Russia. It focuses on the question of Russian identity and Russia's territorial reach and, in particular, explores the implications for Eurasian Security.

Should you review this volume in your publication, please send two copies to my attention at the Institute's corporate address. Please see the enclosed catalog for pricing and order information. If you need additional information about this or any other USIP Press book, do not hesitate to contact me.

Thank you for your consideration.

Sincerely,

Kay Hechler
Sales & Marketing Manager

Tel: 202-429-3816   Fax: 202-429-6063
email: kay_hechler@usip.org

1200 17ᵀᴴ STREET, NW   WASHINGTON, DC   20036-3011
TEL 202-457-1700 ● FAX 202-429-6063 ● TDD 202-457-1719 ● WEB www.usip.org

undermining Russian national consciousness and were concerned because Russian city dwellers frequently referred to themselves as the "Soviet people." It is fashionable but unwise to easily discard any reality that stood behind the concept of the "Soviet people"; it adequately reflected some trends (intermingling of peoples into a new entity) while ignoring others (national awakening).

There are two major perspectives on the construction of the "Soviet people" in Western literature. One emphasizes the efforts of the Communist Party of the Soviet Union (CPSU) to build a new supraethnic entity and points to the failures in this undertaking.[27] The other perceives "ethnocultural indigenization" and the formation of nations at the republican level as a result of little effort on the part of the Soviet authorities to create a "Soviet nation."[28] Robert Kaiser's argument about a contradictory process of interaction between state policy and nationalization from below seems the most accurate in describing the complex relationship between stated goals, policy implementation, and actual social developments in the Soviet republics; yet his dismissal of any reality that stood behind the concept of the "Soviet people" does not seem convincing.[29]

Fourth, throughout Soviet history—from Vladimir Lenin to Mikhail Gorbachev—one common policy denominator greatly weakened the formation of the Russian national consciousness, further blurring its imperial distinction and simultaneously contributing to a possible nationalistic revival in the future. This was the struggle, though not a consistent one, of successive Soviet regimes against Russian nationalism. Lenin developed the concept of two nationalisms—one of an oppressive nation and one of the oppressed; the former was dubbed as reactionary, triggering his theoretical and political crusade against "Great Russian chauvinism." The struggle against Russian nationalism was continued by Nikolai Bukharin and, later, by Joseph Stalin, the most inconsistent warrior against Russian nationalism.[30] Stalin initially upheld Lenin's perspective on Great Russian chauvinism as the major threat and local nationalism as a justified response to it in his "Report on National Factors in Party and State Development," published in 1923.

However, from the Sixteenth Party Congress (1934) until his death in 1953, Stalin's rhetoric and deeds amounted to a complete departure from Lenin's ideas and his own earlier views. Stalin's actions during that period were characterized by a vigorous policy aimed at promoting Russian achievements rather than Soviet internationalism. This shift was reflected, among other policies, in the promotion of the Russian language in the USSR's non-Russian republics (Russian Communist leader Gennadi Zyuganov currently glorifies this stage of Soviet nationality policy). However, even in the 1950s, when Russian nationalism was used for state purposes, it was still not fully embraced by the regime. Valery Solovey was probably right when he argued that there was not enough evidence to believe that Stalin's Soviet Union was "Russified." The policy was *velikoderzhavnoy* ("great power"), not pro-Russian;[31] yet it was perceived as pro-Russian by many minorities.

Decades later, in 1972, Aleksandr Yakovlev, then the acting head of the CPSU Central Committee's Department for Propaganda, made a name for himself by denouncing Russian nationalism.[32] Yuri Andropov, then the head of the Committee for State Security (KGB), reportedly considered Russian nationalism, rather than liberal dissidents, a major threat to the security of the Soviet state.[33] According to very revealing memoirs of Gorbachev aide Anatoly Chernyaev, the specter of Russian nationalism was present in some discussions at the highest levels of the CPSU Central Committee. For example, Yakovlev told Chernyaev in 1987: "Inspiring Russian nationalism now means provoking such a wave from the borderlands . . . that it will make our whole empire crack."[34] "The systematic constraint of Russian nationalism"[35] was the price the Soviet leadership was ready to pay for the preservation of the multinational state.

With his instruments of terror, Stalin was probably the only Soviet leader confident enough in his strength to allow Russian nationalism to develop, because he was not afraid of the expected reaction from the non-Russian nationalities. Russian nationalism, if kept under control, could serve as a convenient instrument of mobilization in times of crisis, as during World War II. Yet in this regard, Hugh Seton-Watson may be correct when he concludes that "in the Soviet period there has been more Russification than Russian nationalism. The Russification has been less a conscious policy than an unintended consequence of the political and economic centralization of the Soviet empire. The Soviet leadership, from 1917 to the present day, has not been inspired by Russian nationalism."[36]

Fifth, state institutions facilitate nation building. In the twentieth century, states have more often created nations than the other way around. The entire Soviet Union was a homeland for Russians, which stood in sharp contrast with other ethnic groups whose members were inclined to identify only with the titular republic as their homeland. The Russian Soviet Federated Socialist Republic, which was supposed to be a republic for Russians (and not only for ethnic Russians, but also for many nationalities of its autonomous republics, okrugs, and oblasts[37]) within the framework of the USSR, lacked many of the attributes of other Soviet republics. The imperial center had merged with the ethnic Russian center; the RSFSR had neither a separate capital city, nor (until 1990) its own Communist Party, nor (unlike Ukraine and Belarus) its own seat in the United Nations. In short, the institutional weakness of the RSFSR contributed a great deal to the underdevelopment of Russian national consciousness and confusion over the boundaries of the Russian people.[38]

Rogers Brubaker suggests a provocative parallel between Russians in the USSR and whites in the United States.[39] Both groups serve as an "invisible core," a zero-value for their countries. While other communities could afford to emphasize their distinct cultural heritage, Russians in the USSR and whites in the United States, while actually shaping their respective countries' dominant cultures, downplayed their ethnic distinctiveness vis-à-vis smaller ethnic groups. Not surprisingly, this particular status gave rise to grievances among politically marginal and potentially violent groups of Russian nationalists and militant white separatists in the United States. Vladimir Bondarenko, a leading publicist of the Russian nationalist newspaper *Zavtra*, has frequently published apologetic commentaries on what he calls the "right-wing patriotic movement" waging a "holy war" of "white resistance" in the United States and predicts the failure of the "American multicultural experiment," the disintegration of the United States, and mass suffering of American whites. The common denominators among Russian nationalists and right-wing American patriots are extreme suspicion toward globalization, often associated with "Zionist capital," and deep-seated mistrust toward multinational institutions.[40] It should come as no surprise then that extreme nationalists have so far been the most vocal advocates of building a Russian nation-state.

Problems of Identity
in Russian Intellectual History

Mass-based nationalism often follows the "nationalization" of a country's elite. As discussed previously, many factors have blocked the emergence of Russians as a strong ethnopolitical community with well-defined boundaries. But what about Russia's intellectuals? Have they tried to "awaken" the Russians nationally? Have they developed any concept of Russians as a distinct nation with established frontiers?

For a century and a half, the debate over Russian identity, nation formation, and Russia's future has focused primarily on Russia's relation to and interaction with the West.[41] However, the Russians' interaction with the neighboring peoples of Eurasia and definition of the boundaries of the Russian people are of equal importance, and at the end of the twentieth century this aspect is becoming even more important in the search for a new Russian identity. Nevertheless, this "Eurasian question," while having its own history of intellectual reflection in Russia, has often played a secondary role—or has been totally neglected—in the debate.

It is possible to identify two traditions in Russian intellectual history in the nineteenth century: universalist and statist. "Universalists" emphasized the expansiveness of Russia as an ethical and moral entity, while "statists"—whether they be pan-Slavist or imperial—drew concrete boundaries for Russia. Universalists were represented by Slavophiles, Fyodor Dostoevsky, and Vladimir Solovyov. The second tradition included such different, and often politically opposite, thinkers as Nikolai Danilevsky, Pyotr Struve, and Pavel Milyukov.[42]

The roots of this Western-oriented discourse on Russian identity can be traced back to the nineteenth-century debates between Slavophiles and Westernizers. Slavophiles emphasized the unique character of Russian civilization, based on Slavic Orthodox communitarian traditions, and they were opposed to alien Western civilization, with its alleged rationalism and faceless codified law. In contrast, Westernizers argued that Russia should emulate and learn from the rationalism of the West. The problems brought on by the multiethnicity of the Russian Empire, the interactions between Russians and other peoples, and the frontiers of the Russian people played no significant role in these debates, establishing a tradition for many Russian intellectuals.

Characteristically, the specific problems of Russia's national minorities were first raised in a relatively consistent theoretical manner, not in the intellectual salons of St. Petersburg or Moscow, but in Kiev, by the Brotherhood of Saints Cyril and Methodius. Led in 1846 by a Ukrainian poet and public figure, Taras Shevchenko, and a Russian student of Ukrainian history, Nicholas Kostomarov, these debates could hardly countenance the separation of Slavic kin. In fact, Shevchenko and Kostomarov elaborated the idea of a pan-Slavic federation of liberal states, including Russia, Ukraine, Poland, Bohemia, Serbia, and Bulgaria. (At that time, present-day Belarus was not defined as something distinct.) It can be argued that the first problem theoretically addressed by Russian thought regarding the issues of multiethnicity of the empire and Russian identity was the diversification and unity of Eastern Slavs, with an emphasis on unity.

In 1869, Danilevsky, in his *Russia and Europe,* tried to fuse Slavophilism, pan-Slavism, and a policy of imperialism.[43] Danilevsky essentially recast the liberal pan-Slavic idea into a conservative imperialist concept. Slavic culture, in his view, could serve as a basis for Russian leadership of a newly created federation of Slavic peoples with Constantinople as its capital.

There was one more significant intellectual development in the nineteenth century that left an important imprint on later discussions: the idea of the "universal" character of the Russian identity. Started by Slavophiles, this idea was developed by Dostoevsky, who wrote in his famous 1880 speech on Pushkin: "For what else is the strength of the Russian national spirit than the aspiration, in its ultimate goal, for universality and all-embracing humanitarianism?"[44] In his deliberations, Dostoevsky, like both Slavophiles and Westerners, referred only to Europe: "Yes, the Russian's destiny is incontestably all-European and universal. To become a genuine and all-around Russian means, perhaps (and this you should remember), to become brother of all men, *a universal man,* if you please."[45] Universality for Dostoevsky was limited to the Christian world:[46]

> Oh, the peoples of Europe have no idea how dear they are to us! And later ... we ... will comprehend that to become a genuine Russian means to seek finally to reconcile all European controversies, to show the solution of

> European anguish in our brethren, and finally, perhaps, to utter the ulti-
> mate word of great, universal harmony, of the brotherly accord of all
> nations abiding by the law of Christ's Gospel!

It could be argued that Dostoevsky expressed with remarkable passion some very important features of Russian national consciousness: its openness, inclusiveness, and messianism. While Danilevsky drew boundaries, though very broad ones, Dostoevsky went beyond them; Dostoevsky admired Pushkin for his ability to understand and include the entirety of European culture into the Russian soul.[47]

The universalism of Dostoevsky was further developed by Vladimir Solovyov. While harshly criticizing Danilevsky for his particularism,[48] Solovyov himself paradoxically endorsed Russian imperial policy. Writing about the addition of formerly Polish lands to Russia by Catherine the Great, he argued that "Russia acted here not as a nation, which conquered and suppressed the others, but as a superior force of peace and truth, which gave every nation what it was entitled to."[49] For Solovyov, the justification of imperial policy was its Christian, or universalistic, character. He argued that the behest of Peter the Great and Catherine the Great to Russia was: "Be faithful to yourself and your national peculiarity, so be universal."[50] Nikolai Berdyaev wrote that Solovyov believed that Russians were the people of the future because they would resolve all the problems that the West was incapable of addressing.[51] Solovyov strongly believed that Russia's mission was universal and unifying, not particularistic and exclusive. The boundaries of the people in this context are practically limitless.

Russian policy in the nineteenth century, however, was driven not so much by these ideas, but by the doctrine of "official nationalism," formulated by Count Sergei Uvarov. Orthodoxy, autocracy, and national spirit were proclaimed the pillars of the empire;[52] the third principle, national spirit *(narodnost')*, was the most ambiguous, especially after the Polish revolt of 1830 and the nationalization of ethnic groups in the second half of the nineteenth century. In mid-nineteenth century Russia, *narodnost'* in most cases meant belonging to a people or a community,[53] but this was a subject for very different theoretical and political interpretations. Yet the central question remained unresolved: Was the Russian Empire a state of and for ethnic Russians, or was it a multiethnic entity that somehow required loyalty to the monarchy? In combination with the principle of Slavic Orthodoxy, it seemed that the former proposition was true. In this case, did it imply Russification or religious and cultural tolerance? The answer was pragmatic: Throughout the centuries, the Russian Empire co-opted those who accepted its rule into a system of government that was rather diverse in the non-Russian regions and granted a lot of freedom on local cultural issues. At the same time, however, tolerance could end abruptly if there were demonstrations of political defiance.

The key factor that informed theoretical discourse in Russia was the fact that nationalization processes among Russians and many non-Russians were evolving simultaneously, but at different speeds. While responsive to the nationalization process, the Russian intellectual elite usually lagged behind the developments among some non-Russians, who had already constructed collective mental boundaries between themselves and Russians by the second half of the nineteenth century. Slavophiles and Westerners, as well as Danilevsky, Dostoevsky, Uvarov, and others, were concerned with the issues of Slavic unity, the Russians' connection with Europe, or their place and mission in the universe, and not with relations between Russians and other peoples within the empire. In their minds, the "Little Russians" (Ukrainians), the "White Russians" (Byelorussians), and the "Great Russians" (the "core" ethnic Russians) comprised one Russian people, while many others (Asiatics and Jews, usually referred to as *inorodtsy*) were practically excluded from theoretical discourse. This bifurcation occurred because both an ethnic and a broader national consciousness (among both the elite and the masses) were still relatively weak in this premodern empire. Evidently, it was a mistake to ignore the developments in the empire's western part, especially Poland, where national consciousness was becoming stronger.

The interest of the Russian elite in its cultural roots was not backed by the process of "national awakening" among Russian peasants, who remained very local in their outlook. The abolition of serfdom in 1861 initiated the process of nationalization of the masses, but there was a long way to go before the peasants started to identify themselves primarily as Russians. This was also true for many peoples in the east and the south of the empire. Although nations as mass-based communities had hardly evolved in most regions of the empire, the more developed western parts of Russia were paving the way by World War I.[54]

When the nationalization process gained momentum in the second half of the nineteenth century, the policy of Russification started to take shape in the Russian Empire, especially under Alexander III. There was an evident shift from the de-ethnicized mindset of the imperial court, which was mostly concerned with loyalty of the subjects to the czar, to more ethnically articulated attempts to either turn the non-Russians into Russians or secure Russian dominance over the "awakening" peoples. This shift established a background for defining Russians as a separate nation.

However, by 1917, when loyalty to the czar among the Russians had thoroughly eroded, they did not yet constitute a modern, cohesive nation. There is no consistent evidence in Russian intellectual thought or social history to support the assumption of Chinn and Kaiser that "nation and homeland—rather than czar and religion—became the focus of Russians' loyalty."[55] In fact, most Russian thinkers stressed the opposite. Pyotr Struve wrote: "The collapse of the monarchy, after a brief period of general shock, showed the extreme weakness of national consciousness in the very core of the Russian state, among masses of the Russian people."[56] Struve argued that in prerevolutionary Russia, the nation was opposed to and in disagreement with the state; hence he favored a reunion between the state and nation. Amazingly, like the Slavophiles of seventy years earlier, he addressed neither the problem of multiethnicity in the Russian "nation" nor the place of ethnic Russians in the state as something of crucial significance. In that regard, he was very much in line with other liberal thinkers and politicians of the time. For example, Pavel Milyukov, the leader of the Constitutional Democratic Party, wrote about the formation of Russia's "new supraethnic nation," which had begun to develop well before 1917. He argued that there was a moment in history (in the late nineteenth and early twentieth centuries) when "nationalities took the path of establishing a common Russia's *(rossiiskaya)* state 'nation.'" He attributed the failure of this attempt to the defeat of Russian democracy and freedom. [57]

An important contribution to the debate on Russian identity was made by "the Eurasians," a group of young intellectual émigrés (Pyotr Savitsky, Nikolai Trubetskoy, Georgi Frolovsky, Pyotr Suvchinsky, and others) in the 1920s. Unlike the Slavophiles, they went beyond their Slavic roots in search of the basis for the Russian nation. Arguing that Turkic and Finn-Ugric elements also played a key role in the formation of the "Russian superethnos," they were the first to incorporate the non-Slavic peoples into the discourse on Russians' identity. According to them, Eurasia was cemented by a common geographic space and self-consciousness; it was neither European nor Asian—it was Eurasian. Though the Eurasians differed significantly from other thinkers in many respects, they continued the tradition of a nonethnic definition of Russianness.

The Bolsheviks seemed to be the party that devoted the greatest attention to "the nationality question."[58] The most important features of their view were the denunciation of the Russian Empire as a "prison of the peoples," the accusation of "Great Russian chauvinism," and the proclamation of the right for self-determination for all the peoples of the country. Contrary to these principles, the Bolsheviks gradually re-created a highly centralized state within borders similar to those of the empire. The price they paid was the suppression of Russian ethnic nationalism and the creation of ethnoterritorial units with different levels of autonomy for the non-Russians.

Soviet leaders' theories of "the nationality question," as well as policies pursued in this realm, were far from consistent for more than seven decades. Up to the early 1920s, the internationalist perspective was dominant. Relying on Karl Marx, Russian revolutionaries Pyotr Lavrov, Pyotr Tkachev, Georgi Plekhanov, and Vladimir Lenin believed that the nationalities question was subordinate to broader social issues and that nations would disappear, or "merge," in a future communist paradise. The Russian nation envisioned by Milyukov was transformed into the global communist one by Lenin. While neither liberals nor Marxists saw a future for the nationalities question, there was an important difference between them. To gain allies in the struggle against the tsarist empire, Bolsheviks were ready to make significant concessions to the non-Russians by giving them ethnoterritorial homelands and the right to self-determination. The regime was sure that Russians, as a more "advanced" nation, did not require such enticements as a homeland because they would be satisfied with the Bolshevik social ideal. For Lenin, the national interests of Russians did not exist separately from the interests of world proletariat. In this respect, Dostoevsky's "universality" of Russians took a new, Marxist form, while remaining practically the same in its essence: Russians were supposed to dilute their ethnic identity in broader humanitarian and social missions.[59] This "universality" stood in sharp contrast to the implicit notion that Russians represented the vanguard of a brave new world. The difference between the interests of Russia and the interests of humanity were often blurred.

When the goal of a world socialist revolution was indefinitely postponed, temporary concessions to nationalities within the Soviet Union became long term. Centralized party rule was a critical counterbalance to this ethnonational federal system. When the party dissolved and then collapsed under Gorbachev, the state itself fell apart.

Soviet and Post-Soviet Theoretical Discourse on Russian Nationhood

So far, it has been argued that there have been many significant factors weakening the ethnic component of Russian identity. Historical and intellectual traditions shaped Russianness primarily as an inclusive cultural phenomenon, while the state was primarily supraethnic. Russian high culture was strongly influenced by the ideas of universalism and was mostly separated from its ethnic roots. However, some new, forceful intellectual and political trends emerged after the collapse of the Soviet Union that may lead to a redefinition of the Russian people in more primordialist, nativist terms. Such a redefinition would be a rather unusual trend for a people that constitutes an overwhelming majority of the population (Russians make up more than 80 percent). Unlike minorities, established dominant groups are more inclined to associate themselves with the state, not with a particular ethnicity (English in Great Britain, Castilians in Spain, white Protestants in the United States).

The reinterpretation of Russian identity in ethnic terms by influential intellectuals and a positive public response to it might force political actors to reconsider attitudes toward Russian diasporas and seek political unification with them. An important factor that creates a favorable climate for such a chain of events is the universal phenomenon of backlash against globalization. In Russia, it gained momentum as a reaction of the general public and many intellectuals against what is seen by many as Western-imposed, market-oriented economic reform that resulted in mass dislocations. The spread of Americanized mass culture that accompanies the new market economy has led some people to seek refuge in traditional Russian values,[60] a trend that has been documented by opinion polls.

A second important factor that has facilitated the strengthening of ethnonationalism in Russia is the political path chosen by many post-Soviet nations whose identities are being redefined in ethnic terms (see chapter 4). Yet another factor is the internal administrative structure of the Russian Federation, which contains ethnoterritorial units—republics—for the non-Russians, but no similar arrangements for the Russians. Combined with the plight of Russian diasporas in the near abroad, this situation has led to ethnic Russians' dissatisfaction with the state, which, in the view of many, does not seem to represent their interests. These new trends find solid theoretical background in both mainstream and dissident Soviet ethnology.

Elitist perceptions have also played an unusually important role in post-Soviet ethnopolitics. Many experts on ethnic problems became high-ranking state officials in post-Soviet Russia.[61] Intellectuals holding doctoral degrees in the social sciences or humanities became the leaders of several newly independent states.[62] Throughout the former Soviet Union, communist bosses turned to rhetoric loaded with ethnic studies terminology. The balance of this section addresses the role of theory in shaping Russian attitudes toward the emergence of new Russian diasporas.

• • • • • • • • • ***Soviet-Era Primordialists*** • • • • • • • • • •

It might seem surprising that a Marxist sociological theory of the nation in its Soviet form had a strong primordialist component. That component manifested itself in the theory of "ethnos" developed by the leading Soviet theorist Yulian Bromley, director of the USSR Academy of Sciences' Institute of Ethnography. This theory sought to find a common "essence" in the historic triad of "tribe-nationality-nation,"[63] which dominated the official Soviet thinking on nationality questions since Joseph Stalin. Although the term "ethnos" was absent in the writings of Lenin and Stalin and did not appear in official party documents, it surprisingly became the key concept among Soviet scholars. According to Bromley, ethnos is a stable group of people who have specific features of culture and psychology, awareness of their unity, and distinction from other such groups, which is expressed in their self-identification (ethnonym).[64] Ethnos is a territory-bound entity.[65] In other words, ethnos was perceived as an exclusive ancient group making its own "journey through history."[66] A "mature" ethnos could exist in the form of a nation when developed economic ties linked its members together.

Dissident scholar Lev Gumilev, whose books were banned in the Soviet Union until the late 1980s, effectively based his theories on similarly controversial and untested assumptions that ethnoses lived their own lives for 1,200–1,500 years and then died. Like his Soviet "official" alter ego, Bromley, Gumilev argued that ethnically mixed marriages were "anomalies" and "chimeras" even for large contemporary nations.[67] The views of Gumilev became extremely popular in the post-Soviet context, when political entrepreneurs in the newly independent states and republics within the Russian Federation based their political platforms and justified their ethno-exclusive policies on the existence of primordial, "natural" factors. Gumilev's mysticism, which became so popular in the "times of trouble" after the collapse of the Soviet Union, and his reputation as a dissident harassed by the communist authorities, made his intellectual legacy seem more attractive than Bromley's; the latter had been too closely associated with the Soviet establishment. However, some differences notwithstanding, both scholars had much in common, primordialist views first and foremost.

There is enough evidence to believe that the dominance of primordialism in Soviet thinking on nationalities contributed to the fact that the concept of a "new entity of people—the Soviet people"[68] never postulated that a new political nation, the Soviet one, had emerged or was in the process of formation. The term "nation" continued to have a strong ethnoterritorial connotation. Indeed, according to Bromley and the official Soviet policy, a "nation" was the part of an ethnic group that resided in its own ancient homeland. The "Soviet people" was not a nation in this theoretical framework because it did not have an ethnic core. Unlike the Soviet Union, Yugoslavia, a communist federation that copied many of the Soviet nationality policy features, permitted its citizens to report their national identity as "Yugoslav" if they wished to, though there was no such ethnicity.

How did the primordialist essence of the Soviet theoretical legacy influence theoretical discourse in post-Soviet Russia? Two mutually exclusive perspectives have evolved: the theory of a new Russian civic nation and the theory of primordial ethnic Russianness. In other words, in the theoretical arena, the major divide has been between liberals and ethnonationalists. Liberal and ethnonationalist theoretical frameworks have opposite implications for the issue of diasporas.

• • • • • • • • • • • • • *Liberals* • • • • • • • • • • • • • • •

The most influential, articulate, and politically important figures of what is considered to be a liberal school of thought are academics-politicians Ramazan Abdulatipov, deputy prime minister in 1997–98, and Valery Tishkov, minister of nationalities in 1992. Both have a reputation for being solid reformists, moderates, and theory-prone figures who shape or directly influence nationalities policy and often compete with each other. However, a closer look at the theoretical premises of Abdulatipov reveals a typically post-Soviet mix of self-styled democratic values with archaic primordialism. While acknowledging the importance of building a civic community, he has expressed his concerns about what he calls the imposition of the Western experience (in the form of individual human rights) on Russia. Collective ethnic rights have "probably more meaning" for him in what he calls a unique Russia.[69] Abdulatipov is a moderate, consensus-building politician equally concerned with interests of all ethnic groups in Russia, including the Russians. His stance on the issue of the Russian diasporas, which has not differed from the official mainstream (a mainstream formed partly by Abdulatipov himself), essentially was to defend the Russians' political and other rights in the near abroad, assist in meeting their cultural needs, and prevent mass migration to Russia. He has also expressed support for a more assertive policy in the form of granting dual citizenship to Russians in neighboring states.[70]

However, Abdulatipov's ethno-oriented framework of addressing state-building issues might be objectively in line with those who claim the need for reunification of all Russians under a single political roof. This is a conceptual catch for any advocacy of politicized ethnicity in the former Soviet Union. If it is applied to ethnic Russians, the whole of Eurasia is destined to start redrawing borders. In his theoretical deliberations and political activity, Abdulatipov has relied on the assumption that nations and ethnic groups are the same thing. This assumption is a widespread theoretical perspective in post-Soviet scholarship. Leokadia Drobizheva, one of Russia's experts on ethnicity who allegedly has been widely exposed to Western academia, nevertheless expressed her primordialist perspective in a disarmingly simplistic way: "I use *nation, nationality,* and *ethnic group* as virtually synonymous."[71] When these archaic paradigms are applied to complex social and political realities, and especially when they serve as a basis for policy recommendations, the results could be catastrophic.

Unlike Abdulatipov, Valery Tishkov represents a far more radical intellectual departure from the Soviet tradition in theoretical discourse on these issues. Sometimes mistakenly regarded in the West as a sort of moderate Russian nationalist, Tishkov is actually the most consistent liberal in today's Russia, relying on the "constructivist" school of thought and the modernization theory of Ernest Gellner, Eric Hobsbawm, and Ronald Suny. Tishkov broke the Soviet tradition of defining a nation in ethnocultural terms and outlined it as a purely civic, political entity.[72] In some respects, Tishkov has been close to the Russian liberal tradition of Pavel Milyukov and Pyotr Struve, who wrote about the formation of a supraethnic Russian nation before the Bolshevik Revolution. Tishkov deplored the adoption of Austro-Marxist ethnonational categories by the Bolsheviks, who started constructing many nations in the USSR "from above."[73] He suggested the complete removal of the categories of ethnicity, nation, and nation-state from scholarly discourse, as they were meaningless.[74] Anthony Smith's compromise notion of an "ethnic core" in a modern nation has never been addressed in Tishkov's combative writings.

When applying his theoretical views to Russian realities, Tishkov argued for de-ethnicized nation building within Russia's current borders.[75] His theories made their way into the political arena and President Yeltsin's official statements. The concept of "nation as co-citizenship" was included in the president's annual address to the Russian parliament in February 1994, and it triggered emotional and politically charged criticism from the whole spectrum of Russian politics.[76] It also theoretically undermined the Russian official policy of protecting Russian diasporas in the near abroad. Eduard Bagramov, formerly a leading Soviet expert on the national question and a high-ranking official in the Russian government, contended that this concept "may deprive Russian authorities of many arguments in defending the rights of ethnic Russians abroad."[77] Tishkov has argued for the preservation of ethnoterritorial units for the non-Russians within the Russian Federation (though disagreeing with this concept theoretically[78]) while not granting the similar privileges to the ethnic Russians.

In that regard—again, as in the Soviet Union—ethnic Russians were to remain an "incomplete nation," a notion that was unacceptable for too many in post-Soviet Russia. For example, historian Aleksandr Vdovin, whose prime concern was the absence of equal ethnoterritorial status for Russians and communist suppression of Russian identity, advocated the proclamation of Russia as a state for ethnic Russians, with ethnoterritorial units for others within it.[79] Vdovin's position reflects the sentiments of those Russians who claim that the superpower glory of the Soviet Union and a tacit acknowledgment of the leading role of ethnic Russians constituted a powerful compensation for the suppression of Russian ethnonationalism and that a new Russia could offer little in this respect. Tishkov's perspective, however, reflects post-Soviet political realities in the Russian Federation much more adequately.

An unrealistic point in Tishkov's concept and policy recommendations was his idea of integrating Russian diasporas into the host societies of the newly independent states. Theoretically flawless, this idea seemed like wishful thinking when applied to the ethnonationalist realities of most Soviet successor states. For example, Tishkov wrote of the ethnic Russians living in Estonia: "If these Russians become loyal citizens of the new state and participate in its economy and culture, why could they not be members of an Estonian civic nation . . . ?"[80] Tishkov's example seems to disprove his own theory. The Estonian government has built an ethnic nation-state, excluding most ethnic Russians by refusing to grant them citizenship. The ethnonationalism of the newly independent states makes diaspora Russians think of themselves in ethnic terms and compels Russia to protect them as co-ethnics. Tishkov's fine liberal theories are thus challenged by harsh, ethnonationalist, post-Soviet realities. Tishkov's implicit assumptions that ethnoterritorial autonomy for Russians in Kazakhstan, Estonia, Ukraine, and Moldova is a viable option also do not seem realistic, given the political conditions in these countries.[81]

• • • • • • • • ***Theoretical Ethnonationalism*** • • • • • • • • •

While neoimperialism is the major political adversary of liberalism in today's Russia, liberalism's major theoretical opponent is ethnonationalism. From 1993 to 1998, ethnonationalism was represented in the political arena mainly by small, often extremist, groups. However, because of ethnonationalism's alleged moral authority and written articulation, combined with the global factors mentioned previously, it is safe to predict that in the coming years, ethnonationalists will rise to higher levels of influence in Russia. Ethnonationalism addresses the most painful problems of the new Russian identity that is being formed after the collapse of the Soviet Union. However, this school of thought has thus far failed to transform its grievances into a consistent political agenda and program.

One of the most telling manifestations of ethnonationalism was the address to the Russian people adopted at the session of the Second World Russian Council, organized under the auspices of the Russian Orthodox Church in February 1995. The address claimed that the Russian people had been divided by the collapse of the Soviet Union and that Russia should conduct its policy under the assumption that this situation is only temporary.[82]

There are two major sources of modern Russian ethnonationalist doctrine: literary and theoretical. The spiritual predecessors of post-Soviet Russian ethnonationalism are the intellectuals, mainly writers, poets, and literary critics who have been grouped around the magazine *Nash sovremennik* since the 1970s (including Valentin Rasputin, Vasily Belov, and others). Their moral authority among intellectuals during the Soviet period stemmed from the fact that they were anticommunist, environmentally conscious, bold, and, in many cases, very talented writers. They deplored the collectivization of agriculture in the 1930s, advocated the return to traditional Russian spirituality still preserved in remote villages, and claimed that "Soviet patriotism" undermined Russian national consciousness. At the First Congress of People's Deputies in 1989, Valentin Rasputin was actually the first to publicly suggest that Russia should leave the Soviet Union, pointing out that the RSFSR subsidized other republics at the expense of the Russian people.[83]

Post-Soviet ethnic and nationalities studies based on the primordialist perspective have contributed to theories of modern ethnonationalism. After the breakup of the Soviet Union, leading ethnologist Viktor Kozlov claimed that following the collapse of communist ideology, Russia needed "a national idea, anxiety for the future welfare of its own ethnos."[84] He argued that the only way to insure the interests of Russians was the creation of a Russian *(russkaya)* republic. Working in a similar primordialist framework, V. M. Kabuzan studied historical demography and geography of the Russian ethnos and came to the conclusion that it was "totally inadmissible" to preserve the "Stalinist-Khrushchevist frontiers" after the collapse of the Soviet Union because many lands occupied mostly by Russians were now in possession of foreign states.[85]

The founding father of ethnonationalism as a consistent worldview in modern Russia is Aleksandr Solzhenitsyn. Modern Russian ethnonationalism is a radical departure from the mainstream Russian tradition shaped by both imperialist and liberal perspectives. Solzhenitsyn's overall outlook appears to be humanistic, inclusive, and moderate, with his major concern being the "Preservation of the People."[86] However, when applied to the concrete geopolitical situation in Eurasia, this perspective seems less benign. The essence of the ethnonationalist political program is to build a Russian state within the area of settlement of the Russian people and other Eastern Slavs. Politically, this means reunification with Russian diasporas and the territories of Ukraine, Belarus, and northern Kazakhstan (the last of which Solzhenitsyn calls "Southern Siberia").

Solzhenitsyn's contribution to the discourse on post-Soviet Russian identity and its effect on perceptions of the new Russian diasporas cannot be overestimated, though the Yeltsin regime tried to downplay the significance of the great writer's voice. Arguably, Solzhenitsyn is the first giant figure in Russian intellectual history to challenge the imperialist tradition. He has condemned the centuries of empire-building as detrimental to the Russian people, wasteful of Russia's resources, a misdirection of human energies. The magnitude of Solzhenitsyn's rebellion against tradition can be truly appreciated only if it is put in context. It comes at the end of several centuries of intellectual discourse that allowed Nikolai Berdyaev, a leading philosopher of the first half of the twentieth century, to call Russia "providentially imperialist."[87] In this context, Solzhenitsyn paradoxically looks like a radical Westernizer, although he speaks out against the Westernization of Russia. He effectively argues for building a Russian nation-state along the lines of nation building in nineteenth-century Europe. During World War I, Berdyaev contended that "our nationalism always makes an impression of something non-Russian, extraneous, sort of Germanic. . . . Russians are almost ashamed of their Russianness."[88] Solzhenitsyn is not ashamed of being a Russian. He has been more concerned with the preservation of his people, which, according to him, was almost ruined by the self-imposed burden of empire.

Solzhenitsyn has called Russia a "torn state," arguing that twenty-five million Russians found themselves "abroad" without moving anywhere from "the land of their fathers and grandfathers," thus creating "the largest diaspora in the world."[89] His ethnonationalism brings the issue of the diasporas and "false" post-Soviet borders to the fore. In *The Russian Question at the End of the Twentieth Century,* he writes:

> The trouble is not that the USSR broke up—that was inevitable. The real trouble, and a tangle for a long time to come, is that the breakup occurred mechanically along the false Leninist borders, usurping from us entire Russian provinces. In several days, we lost 25 million ethnic Russians—18 percent of our entire nation—and the government could not scrap up the courage even to take note of this dreadful event, a colossal defeat for Russia, and to declare its political disagreement with it—at least in order to preserve the right to some kind of negotiations in the future.[90]

In this book, Solzhenitsyn does not limit himself only to analysis, but also outlines policy recommendations. In comparison to his heart-rending assessment of the situation, however, the recommendations appear more moderate. He makes a clear distinction between different groups of Russians in the near abroad and prescribes different policies toward them—a distinction official Russian policy has often failed to make. He proposes the evacuation of those Russians from Central Asia and Transcaucasia who wish to leave those countries, while advocating dual citizenship to those who stay behind. He also urges Russian leaders to demand from the Baltic states compliance with international standards of national minority rights. Finally, and most important, Solzhenitsyn advocates that leaders work toward "possible degrees of unification in various areas with Belarus, Ukraine, and Kazakhstan, and strive, at the very least, for 'invisible' borders."[91] In a work published three years after *The Russian Question,* Solzhenitsyn becomes even more realistic and moderate on the Ukrainian issue, arguing that "stubborn estrangement (hardly veiled hostility) of the Ukrainian leaders ... blocks the perspective of tri-Slavic unification."[92] He concludes that the Russian government did not sincerely strive to protect Russians in the neighboring states and calls this apathy toward compatriots in dire straits a component of the "Great Russian Catastrophe of the 1990s."[93]

Those Russian ethnonationalists who have been more politically active than Solzhenitsyn usually prescribe more assertive solutions to the Russian question. Nikolai Pavlov, member of parliament from 1990 to 1995, and the leader of the National-Republican Party of Russia, has argued that "for Russian nationalists, a true tragedy is not the collapse of the Union, but the fact that a historical national Russia has not been restored yet and stays in its Leninist-Stalinist-Khrushchevist borders."[94] In such a way, Pavlov emphasizes the fundamental difference between ethnonationalist and imperialist perspectives: The possible restoration of the Soviet Union is viewed by ethnonationalists as a sacrifice of the Russian nation and the undermining of its vitality.[95]

Advocates of both ethnonationalism and neoimperialism argue for redrawing borders but along different lines. While neoimperialism implies restoration of the USSR, the ethnonationalist approach, according to Pavlov, "does not recognize the legitimacy of the current boundaries of the Russian Federation and suggests two options for solving the question: unification with Ukraine, Belarus, and Kazakhstan into one state or declaration of the current boundaries of the Russian Federation disputable and holding referendums on the territories of Ukraine, Kazakhstan, and other regions populated by Russians."[96]

Modern Russian ethnonationalism is implicitly suspicious of "the Russian idea" in its interpretations by Dostoevsky or Solovyov. According to the leading theorists of modern Russian ethnonationalism, universalism and messianism might only dilute a unique Russia and Russian Orthodoxy into a broader concept of supranationalism.[97] Like most ethnonationalists the world over, the theorists belonging to this school of thought in Russia adhere to the Romantic tradition, stipulating that "people" is a mystical collective entity with its own soul and fate.[98] According to Nataliya Narochnitskaya, a nation is a "successively living entity bound by spirit, worldview, common perceptions of good and evil, and historic emotions."[99]

Not surprisingly, ethnonationalist perspectives have led to an assertion that Russians are a forcefully divided people who have a legitimate and unconditional right to reunite all their historic lands into one state.[100] Narochnitskaya also suggests a concrete foreign policy based on the firm belief that reunification of the Russian people is natural and inevitable, and that until the Russian question is resolved, international stability is impossible. She writes:

> A responsible national government must avoid any formulation that might mean direct or indirect legitimization of the current state of the Russian people, and the seizure of its historic long-standing territories and sacred things, when concluding any international treaties and agreements, conventions and multilateral documents. West Germany's foreign policy did exactly the same. This is particularly true with regard to Sevastopol, a city of Russian honor, the Crimea, Pridnestrovye and many other problems, including a number of questions in the Baltic states.[101]

It is interesting to note that the German experience has been particularly popular among Russian ethnonationalists. Viktor Aksiuchits, chairman of the Russian Christian Democratic Movement, also praised West Germany's policy of not recognizing East Germany and has advocated peaceful reunification within one state of the "Russian people" in the territories of Russia, Belarus, Ukraine (excluding Galicia), and "Southern Siberia," as well as active support and resettlement of those Russians who found themselves outside these areas. Aksiuchits also asserted that the rest of the territory of the former Soviet Union must remain a zone of Russia's vital interests.[102]

The idea of Russians as a divided people made its way to the political agenda in the late 1990s. In April 1998, the Duma Committee on Commonwealth of Independent States (CIS) Affairs and Relations with Compatriots organized a conference on this issue. Sergei Baburin, then deputy speaker of the Duma, argued at this conference that Russians are a "divided nation" and that it was time to raise their international legal status as such. Vladimir Zhirinovsky contrasted the concept of a divided people with the notion of national minorities, suggesting that Russians in the near abroad should be perceived not as minorities but as parts of one people.[103] The conference, chaired by Georgi Tikhonov, chairman of the Duma Committee on CIS Affairs and Relations with Compatriots, recommended parliamentary hearings on the bill "On the Divided State of the Russian Nation." If this proposal results in a law, the ethnonationalist perspectives will be legitimized and institutionalized, and the issue of the Russian diasporas might dramatically change the political discourse in Russia. An important indicator of such an outcome's plausibility is the statement of Gennadi Zyuganov in November 1998: "Russians have become the largest divided people in the world."[104]

Public Opinion: An Overview

The vacuum left by theorists in Russia's discourse on the diasporas gives room for maneuvering by political entrepreneurs. They may capitalize on public opinion, which reflects all the historical and theoretical ambiguities over Russian identity. This section attempts to illustrate some points developed earlier by looking at the results of recent opinion polls and reinterpreting them from this book's perspective. The major focus will be on the ambiguities of Russian national identity, its underdevelopment, and the likely rise of ethnonationalism. This overview may lead to a better understanding of popular perceptions of the diasporas question in contemporary Russia. This section relies on data obtained mainly by Russian pollsters.

In today's Russia, opinion polls are numerous and not always reliable. Samples may not be representative, and questions often reflect the ideological preferences of pollsters and can miss important issues and perspectives. Unlike in the West, the same people often formulate questions, make samples, conduct polling, and interpret the results—in many cases, in politically charged ways. Opinion trends themselves are unreliable, as they may shift radically in unstable societies in a short period of time. A classic example is the behavior of Ukrainians in 1991, when 70 percent of those who participated (84 percent of eligible voters) cast a "yes" vote during a referendum on the preservation of the USSR in March, and more than 90 percent supported the declaration of independence just nine months later. Was this an indicator of rapid change of attitudes in a transitional period or just a misinterpretation of the referendums' questions by the public? Probably both.

The Ukrainian referendums also point to the relativity of any conclusions about public opinion in post-Soviet states. However, it seems plausible to argue that, if treated with caution, some general trends can be isolated, particularly through cross-examination of polls conducted by different teams of experts. The results of the polls conducted by the Public Opinion Fund and the Institute of Sociological Analysis, headed by Igor Klyamkin; the All-Russian Center for the Study of Public Opinion (VTsIOM); and the Center for Sociological Analysis of Interethnic Conflicts are the most valuable for purposes of this study.

The most general and striking impression one gets from studying the polling data is that Russians became a confused people in the aftershock of the Soviet Union's collapse: eclectic attitudes of many groups combine "contradictory" ideas and perceptions. At the same time, many analysts stress that the values of individualism, liberalism, human rights, rule of law, and private property have taken root in Russian society. Indeed, people have gotten tired of "grand ideas" and have concentrated on their private lives, higher living standards, and individual success. According to Klyamkin, 67–98 percent of the respondents shared liberal attitudes in 1996.[105] Liberal attitudes may be also seen in perceptions of the "nationality question": In 1995, 81 percent of the respondents in the poll conducted by the Center of Social Prognosis and Marketing thought that there were no "bad" or "good" nations.[106]

According to some polls, most Russians demonstrate tolerance and sensitivity to other ethnic groups' interests. Andrei Zdravomyslov's data indicate that 74 percent of respondents believe that "Russia is a common homeland for many peoples that influence one another. All peoples of Russia must have equal rights, and nobody must have any advantages."[107] Most pollsters and experts on public opinion in Russia seem to agree that radical ethnonationalism has not been popular. In 1995, Zdravomyslov claimed that only 7–17 percent of the population was sympathetic with the idea of Russian exclusiveness, a "special mission," and exclusive rights.[108] In 1996, Klyamkin, relying on other polling data, came to a similar figure: 16 percent.[109] It seems safe to argue that these figures reflect the size of the core constituency that would be very assertive on the issue of Russian diasporas, and it is not that large.

However, VTsIOM's data, based on Moscow polls, showed stronger ethnonationalist attitudes and less tolerance: 28 percent of the respondents "totally agreed," and 13 percent "generally agreed," with the statement that ethnic Russians must have more rights in Russia than other peoples.[110] As a rule, assertiveness vis-à-vis the non-Russians in the Russian Federation goes hand in hand with resolute support of unification with the diasporas. It is noteworthy to point out that Moscow, in many instances, takes the lead in changes of public opinion and is joined by the rest of the country with some time lag. Nationalism is getting more popular in Moscow. Should it be treated as a sign of change in the attitudes of all Russians?

It is particularly useful to keep in mind that in 1995, a solid plurality of Russians (46 percent) in the Public Opinion Fund's poll believed that their state should focus on exclusively traditional Russian values, while only 4 percent preferred purely Western ones (the rest chose "Soviet" or various "mixed" options).[111] Another polling center, VTsIOM, registered a dramatic rise in the numbers of those who advocated "a specific Russian way of development" in post-Soviet Russia: from 18 to 52 percent in 1992–1995. At the same time, the popularity of "a Western democratic path" declined dramatically: from 56 to 11 percent.[112] As such, these figures do not necessarily mean the rise of Russian ethnonationlism, but they may indicate the creation of a favorable climate for the activities of various political entrepreneurs, including those trying to mobilize the population with ethnonationalist slogans.

Of course, upbeat conclusions regarding the liberalism and tolerance of the public in post-Soviet Russia must be treated with caution—or, at least, with healthy skepticism; outbursts of nationalism do happen. The data contained in the results of the polls can be interpreted somewhat differently from the way they are explained by the authors who conducted them. It is particularly important to note that many respondents appear to hold views that could lead to attempts to redraw post-Soviet borders. These views reflect ambivalence about the collapse of the Soviet Union, confusion over the boundaries of the Russian people, and a transitional state of public opinion.

An international group of scholars led by Timothy Colton, Jerry Hough, Susan Leman, and Mikhail Guboglo found that an overwhelming majority (about 70 percent) of respondents in Russia in 1993 saw the breakup of the Soviet Union as "negative" or "more negative than positive."[113] According to a poll conducted by VTsIOM in 1994, 76 percent of Russians agreed that the collapse of the Soviet Union yielded more damage than good, while only 7 percent thought the opposite.[114] Four years later, in 1998, VTsIOM registered only 15 percent of Russians welcoming rather than opposing the Soviet Union's breakup.[115] However, the number of respondents under age 25 who regretted the breakup is half that of those over 55.[116] The polls conducted by the Public Opinion Fund have yielded similar results that indicated nostalgia for the Soviet Union. In 1998, 85 percent of Russians regretted the dissolution of the USSR, up from 69 percent in 1992.[117] The polls also registered a sharp fall, from 32 percent in 1992 to 13 percent in 1997, in the numbers of those who have no regrets about the breakup.[118] One should not interpret this data as an indication that a majority of all Russians are ready to fight for the restoration of the USSR or sacrifice some of their well-being for that goal. The populist army general Aleksandr Lebed formulated the widespread Russian attitude to the deceased Soviet Union better than anybody else: "Those who do not regret its collapse lack a heart, but those who think that it will be possible to re-create it in its old form lack a brain."[119] These attitudes reflect the fact that the Soviet Union, not the RSFSR, was the alleged homeland for most Russians.

Russian experts who conduct and interpret opinion polls sometimes underestimate the fact that there are actually two groups of people who might support policies leading to the redrawing of post-Soviet boundaries. As discussed previously, they are the ethnonationalists, who are concerned with Russians in the near abroad, and the imperialists, who would like to re-create the state within the former Soviet borders. In spite of many differences between these groups (addressed in chapter 3), there is one fundamental perception that unites them: the collapse of the Soviet Union along republican borders is not final. From this perspective, one can reconsider some interpretations of the results of the 1996 Institute of Sociological Analysis poll that downplayed nationalist attitudes in Russia. If the respondents who share positive views on redrawing Russia's borders are grouped together, the minimal estimate of their share in the Russian population is 42 percent.[120] The figure seems particularly high when viewed in the context of significant efforts of the government and the mainstream media to emphasize state building within the current borders of the Russian Federation.

The ethnonationalist inclinations of Russians can be assessed using the Public Opinion Fund's data for 1995: 43 percent of the respondents agreed that "it is necessary to seek the creation of the state where (ethnic) Russians are officially acknowledged as a chief nation," while only 38 percent disagreed with this statement.[121] This view has not made its way into state policy in a consistent and articulated way, but the poll suggests that caution is justified before declaring a victory of liberal values.

These data must be weighed against another important indicator: public perceptions of what constitutes a "Russian." It turns out that most

Russians are inclusive and even liberal in their perception of Russianness. The formal and legalistic dimensions of the issue are not overly important for most people. Bonds of blood seem to be the least important factor for the Russians: In 1994, less than a quarter of respondents agreed that in order to be a Russian, one had to look Russian or have Russian parents.[122] At the same time, love for Russia and perception of it as one's motherland was seen by 87 percent of respondents as an obligatory feature of a Russian. Attachment to Russian culture, customs, and traditions was supported by 84 percent, and knowledge of the Russian language was important for 80 percent of respondents. Formal features, such as citizenship or passport registration of ethnicity, were perceived as obligatory by 56 and 51 percent, respectively. Another important point connected to the diasporas question was that only 32 percent of Russians believed that it was necessary to live in Russia in order to be Russian.[123] All these polling data suggest that emotional attachment to Russian culture is perceived as much more important to most people in defining Russianness than bonds of blood or common citizenship; the data may also mean that a popular view of who is Russian is very inclusive. Most ethnic Russians and Russian speakers in the near abroad are perceived as *russkie*, a word that is usually translated as "ethnic Russian" but may actually include many others. Russian-speaking Ukrainians living in Kazakhstan, Belarusians from Uzbekistan, or Kazakhs from Russia would all be *russkie* in this framework. Many residents of the Russian Federation are inclined to think that foreign citizenship or "alien" lines of blood cannot separate those *russkie* from Mother Russia.

The data of the 1995 Public Opinion Fund poll are illuminating in connection with the issue of the Russians' attitude toward sister communities in the near abroad and the borders question in this context. Thirty-three percent of the respondents think that Russia must seek unification with adjacent territories of the former Soviet republics where most of the inhabitants are Russians, while 46 percent disagree. The idea of unification is more popular among less educated people (below high school degree), about half of whom approve. Pensioners and collective farmers are more sympathetic toward the idea of unification than other social groups.[124] Evidently, many Russians tend to perceive the problems of diasporas as an internal Russian matter, not as an issue of interstate relations. Nevertheless, most of those who share such a view do not want to resolve the problem forcefully. From 61 to 81 percent of respondents agree that Russia must promote respect for the human rights of Russians living in neighboring states, while only 5 percent of respondents think that it is not a concern for Russia.[125]

If opinion polls tell us anything about attitudes toward the new diasporas, it is that there is a liberal tendency in public opinion in the Russian Federation in general and toward Russians in the near abroad specifically. However, fluctuations in the various polling data may lead to the conclusion that such opinions are not well articulated and remain contradictory. Perceptions of boundaries and membership in the nation are vague. Such inchoate attitudes are a reflection of a broader problem —namely, the current extreme weakness of Russian nationhood. Margaret Canovan argued that "nationhood, once established, functions like a battery, a reservoir of power that can slumber for decades and still be available for rapid mobilization: the flag remains, and the people can be rallied to it."[126] Russian nationhood is a dead battery at present, but it can be charged by political entrepreneurs. They can charge it with many different things: big power restorationalism, ethnonationalism, or liberal patriotism. The next chapter will address the issues of the politics of nation building in modern Russia and different political projects of future Russian nationhood.

The Politics
of Nation Building
in Modern Russia

A S ALL STUDENTS of modern Russia agree, there is hardly a single issue in today's politics on which there is a consensus in Russian society. Reflecting this phenomenon, the political elite is fragmented into many factions. Thirty-five parties, movements, and associations were represented in the Federal Assembly from 1996 to 1999. Forty-three electoral associations (party coalitions created for election purposes) participated in the 1995 parliamentary elections. Twenty-six electoral associations and blocs participated in the 1999 elections; six party factions and three deputy groups were officially established in the third Russian State Duma in January 2000. Obviously, a unitary view among contemporary Russian political elites toward the Russian diasporas cannot be assumed. What, then, are the positions of the modern Russian political forces on the issues of nation building and diasporas? What is the real political weight of each perspective? What have been the major changes in Russia's politics of nation building throughout the period of independence?

This chapter will analyze political programs of parliamentary, as well as nonparliamentary, parties and groups and will suggest a typology of major perspectives on nation-building and diasporas issues. The chapter will also assess the respective political importance and evolution of each of these perspectives during the period 1992–2000.

There are significant limitations for this kind of research. In today's Russia, the multiparty system is far from mature. The number of groups claiming or having the status of a political party far exceeds what might be considered optimal for an informed voter decision. Coalitions and associations form, split, and dissolve on a regular basis. Parties and movements appear and then disappear from the political arena before a student of Russian politics is able to take notice. Prominent political figures migrate between parties and groups. Duma deputies are elected on one party list and then are registered as members of another faction. The key party leaders' views might be at odds with their parties' programs.

However, an analysis of the parties' positions could yield important insights useful for understanding the existing perspectives on nation-building and diaspora issues, as well as political options for the Russian government. The parties' programs adequately reflect the approaches that have crystallized within the Russian intellectual and political elite throughout the 1992–2000 period. Although the 1993 constitutional and political crisis and the subsequent adoption of the new constitution, as well as the 1993, 1995, 1996, 1999, and 2000 elections, changed the relative strength of each perspective, these events hardly led to the emergence of radically new ideas in the area of nation building. There is no evidence to support the claim that any future regroupings of political forces can reshape the framework for theoretical and political debate of state- and nation-building issues.

Nationalistic forces seem to be politically disorganized and fragmented into many small groups; in short, they lack influence in today's Russia. Yeltsin's rhetoric carried just a flavor of moderate nationalism. Nationalism plays a more important, but still not entirely dominant, role in the leftist ideology of CPRF leader Gennadi Zyuganov. It is too early to judge President Putin from this perspective. Will liberal views prevail within the Kremlin elite in the years to come, or will we witness the emergence of a more explicitly nationalistic regime in the near future, as some analysts predict? Will this nationalism be ethnic, exclusive, and aggressive, or will it be civic, inclusive, moderate, and liberal?

Historical Traditions and Parallels

The issue of nation building played an important role in Russia's party politics prior to the Bolshevik Revolution. Although the Russian diaspora did not exist in its modern form, the question of nationalities came to the forefront in the last decade of Imperial Russia. The analysis of the political parties' programs leads to the conclusion that there were three major perspectives: imperial, Russian ethnonationalist, and the approach that favored self-determination for minorities.

• • • • • • • • • • • • *Imperialism* • • • • • • • • • • • • • •

Imperialism was the dominant ideology among political elites, and mainstream liberal and conservative parties were imperialist as well. However, imperialist ideology had distinct differences on both ends of the Russian political spectrum at the time. Liberals of the early twentieth century, unlike their successors at the end of the century, advocated preservation of the empire. The leading liberal party—the Constitutional Democratic Party—downplayed "the national question" in its program adopted in 1905.[1] This approach was based on the views of party leader Pavel Milyukov, who claimed that a new supraethnic Russian nation was being formed (see chapter 2). The program emphasized individual human rights and cultural self-determination for nationalities. With respect to cultural autonomy for minorities, the leading leftist Jewish party, the Bund, which played an important role in Russian politics before the Bolshevik Revolution, held views similar to those of the Constitutional Democrats, though they borrowed their ideas from another source—the Austro-Marxists.[2]

The conservative version of the imperial tradition was represented, above all, by the "Union of October 17"—the Oktyabrists. Since 1906, they had emphasized the importance of Russia's unity, proclaiming the importance of this issue in the first section of their program. While objecting to any discrimination against the non-Russians, they were uncompromising unitarists. An important difference between this group and the liberals was the use of the term *russkie* by the former, not *rossiiskie*, citizens in reference to all subjects of the empire.[3] Traditionally, *russkie* stood for ethnic Russians, *rossiiskie* for citizens of Russia. The term "*russkie* citizens" reflected an attempt to emphasize the fact that there must not be ethnic differences between Russian citizens and a stronger inclination toward Russification of the non-Russians.

• • • • • • • • • • **Ethnonationalism** • • • • • • • • • •

Russian ethnonationalists at the beginning of the twentieth century, like their successors ninety years later, were militant, extremist, and underrepresented in the mainstream political arena. The major difference between the two generations of Russian ethnonationalists is that at the beginning of the century they stood for the preservation of the empire,[4] while modern Russian ethnonationalists argued that the empire was a burden for the Russian people. Unlike liberal or conservative imperialists, the four major groups of early Russian ethnonationalists— the Russian Assembly, the Russian Monarchist Party, the Union of Russian People, and Mikhail Archangel Russian People's Union—advocated unconditional primacy of ethnic Russians in the empire. The 1908 program of Mikhail Archangel Russian People's Union, for example, stated: "The Russian People . . . has the right to be a prime, ruling people in the state's life, even more so in the state's creative transformations. The Russian language is a dominant language in all domains of the indivisible Russian Empire."[5]

• • • • • • • **Self-determination for Minorities** • • • • • • •

Representing ethnic minorities, "national" parties favored one or more of the following principles: self-determination, federation, national-territorial autonomy, and full independence. As was the case in the Soviet Union many decades later, minorities did not want to support the creation of a new supraethnic nation, suspecting that behind this idea was the desire to secure domination of ethnic Russians. Most of the minority parties' leaders were ethnonationalists.

Bolsheviks and Socialist Revolutionaries supported the idea of self-determination, seeking an alliance with minorities in the struggle against the tsar. In reality, many Bolsheviks favored the preservation of the empire. In 1925, Pavel Milyukov challenged the sincerity of the Bolsheviks with regard to granting non-Russian nationalities a genuine right to self-determination to the point of separation. He showed that in the party documents of 1913, 1917, and 1918, the Bolsheviks actually claimed that this right was subordinate to the goals of building social- ism and could not be granted if it contradicted the general interests of the class struggle.[6] V. V. Zhuravlev, an eminent historian of Russian poli- tical parties, wrote that Stalin's imperial unitarism, disguised as "auton- omization," was a logical outcome of the prevalence of centralist ideas among Russian political elites in the first three decades of the twenti- eth century. Democratic federalism was not popular at all.[7] Actual Soviet policy, especially in the 1930s to 1950s, shared many important features with the imperial tradition.

The collapse of the Soviet Union in 1991 and the emergence of a huge Russian diaspora dramatically changed the political landscape of Eurasia. However, the centralist (imperial), ethnonationalist, and self- determination schools of thought, which were formed in the beginning of the century, have reappeared in the political arena of modern Russia. Naturally, they have changed to fit new realities. In addition, several new perspectives have emerged.

Five Projects of Nation Building

Examination of Russia's evolving multiparty system became a rapidly developing field of post-Soviet studies in the 1990s. The most popular framework of research is dividing all parties, movements, and associa- tions into democratic (liberal, reformist), communist, nationalist ("patriotic"), and centrist. A somewhat different grouping is necessary for the purpose of analyzing the politics of nation building.[8] The major criterion in separating various movements will be their attitude toward new Russian diasporas, which is inherently linked to a broader vision of postimperial nation- and state building.

In 1992–93, political parties and movements were polarized between the two extremes. Liberals—or "democrats," as they are usually called in Russia—advocated state building in a new, independent Russia and denounced the old Soviet empire. Their main political opponents, the Communists, favored the restoration of the Soviet Union.[9] Between late 1993 and 2000, a more complicated political configuration evolved, leading to the formation of several perspectives on nation-building and diasporas issues. Specifically, there were three major changes in comparison with the 1992–93 period. First, many individuals who were a driving force in dismantling the Soviet Union began to claim that they wanted to preserve the union, albeit in a new form. For example, on the eve of Russia's Independence Day in 1995, Boris Yeltsin alleged that "Russia never spoke against the Union."[10] Second, a theme of integration of the former Soviet republics became a common denominator for practically all political forces. Finally, there was a shift within the Russian political elite from ignoring or paying little attention to the issue of the Russians in the near abroad to emphasizing the importance of this topic.

The analysis of ideologies and programs of various political parties, groups, and prominent politicians leads to the conclusion that there are five major perspectives, or projects, on building the state and nation in contemporary Russia: new state building, ethnonationalism, restorationalism, hegemony/dominance, and integrationalism.

• • • • • • • • • • *New State Building* • • • • • • • • • • •

The concept of new state building dominated the official policy of the Russian government in 1991–92.[11] It was advocated by President Yeltsin and the Democratic Russia movement. Gennadi Burbulis, who was a professor of "scientific communism" at an institute in Sverdlovsk (Yekaterinburg) when Yeltsin was the party leader there, became the president's major political strategist in 1991–92. He was the author of the Russian (as opposed to Soviet) policies of his boss and an advocate of de-ethnicized state building. In late 1991 and 1992, after being appointed to the posts of deputy prime minister and state secretary, Burbulis became the most influential figure in the government, but he was dismissed from all official positions in December 1992. As was argued in chapter 2, the theoretical foundations of new state building have been laid out by Valery Tishkov, minister for nationalities in 1992 and director of the Institute of Ethnology and Anthropology. Unlike Burbulis, Tishkov did not push disintegration of the Soviet Union; rather, Tishkov tried to cope with the realities of post-Soviet Russia.

The essence of this project was state building through the creation and stabilization of new state institutions within the borders of RSFSR, inviolability of the borders between the former Soviet republics, and development of relations with neighboring states as fully independent entities. The problems of Russian ethnic identity and the new Russian diaspora were treated practically as politically insignificant. The project stressed civic patriotism and de-emphasized the allegedly artificial character of the Bolshevik-drawn borders of the RSFSR, which were much narrower than the domain of Russian culture, language, religion, and traditions. The strategy of the new state builders toward the diaspora included promotion of their integration into host societies, defense of their human rights, some assistance in cultural projects, and help for those who chose to migrate to Russia.

The political constituency for this project included the intelligentsia from Russia's major urban centers, who sought a quick and radical transformation from the communist state to a democratic system. It also included the Russian Federation's *nomenklatura* (high-ranking former CPSU and state officials) eager to get rid of the all-union state apparatus and establish its full control over Russia's resources.

* * * * * * * * * * **Ethnonationalism** * * * * * * * * * * * *

In 1991–93, the moderate versions of ethnonationalism were politically represented by the Christian Democratic Party, led by Viktor Aksiuchits, and the Constitutional Democratic Party, headed by Mikhail Astafiev. Later on, in 1995–98, Derzhava, headed by Aleksandr Rutskoi, and the extremist National Republican Party of Russia, headed by Nikolai Lysenko, became the more visible ethnonationalist movements on this side of the political arena. Ethnonationalist forces became largely marginalized on the political scene by 1999–2000, although they remained intellectually powerful.

Theoretically, this perspective relies on the ideas of Aleksandr Solzhenitsyn, prominent writers Valentin Rasputin and Vasily Belov, and mathematician and essayist Igor Shafarevich (see chapter 2). There have also been many small extremist groups, Pamyat' being the most notorious among them. These groups are known as "the Russian right" or the "Black Hundred" (named after notorious extreme Russian nationalists of the early twentieth century) and are similar to the moderate ethnonationalists in at least one respect: they emphasize the importance of Russian ethnicity for state and nation building.

The basic difference between extremists and moderate ethnonationalists is that the former completely reject the "Western values" of democracy, human rights, and the rule of law. The influence of the Black Hundred is thus far limited; however, in a time of social unrest they could become important and dangerous. Extremist and moderate ethnonationalist parties and groups were significantly weakened after 1993, when some of them were outlawed and their newspapers banned because of the support from many small, militant, ethnonationalist groups in organizing the defense of the Russian legislative headquarters during Yeltsin's assault on the country's parliament in September–October 1993. Yeltsin's repression targeted them as the most well-organized force of resistance.

The essence of the ethnonationalist political program is to unite Russia with the Russian communities in the near abroad and build the Russian state within the area of settlement of the Russian people and other Eastern Slavs (see chapter 2). Again, diasporic existence is viewed as abnormal for Russians, and ethnonationalism addresses the most painful problems of the new Russian identity being formed after the collapse of the Soviet Union.

The constituency of the project is very diverse and does not seem to have diminished between 1993 and 2000, although its political representation faded away, especially by 1999–2000, because of the inability of ethnonationalist political leaders to overcome differences between themselves and the lack of a strong leader. The ethnonationalist constituency includes some representatives of the intelligentsia (mainly from small and medium-size Russian cities, as well as from the countryside), the Cossacks, dislocated workers, and part of the new entrepreneurial class.

Walker Connor has argued that ethnonationalism was the only possible form of nationalism. He strongly opposed the tendency to equate nationalism with loyalty to the state, which he has called "patriotism."[12] On the other hand, Thomas Hylland Eriksen, among others, tended to acknowledge the existence of nonethnic nationalism.[13] It is hard not to agree with Eriksen when he contends: ". . . although it may be correct to talk of a general theory of nationalism . . . nationalisms on the ground are quite different."[14] In the Russian context, loyalty to the Soviet Union (the state that abruptly disappeared in 1991) and projects to restore it may be defined as one of the forms of nationalism. It is also known as neoimperialism or restorationism. Understanding the difference and interaction between ethnonationalism and neoimperialism is key to interpreting the new identity of the people and government policies toward the former Soviet republics.

• • • • • • • • • • • *Restorationalism* • • • • • • • • • • • •

After the breakup of the Soviet Union, several versions of restorationalism took shape in Russia.[15] In the Russian context, restorationalism is hardly distinguishable from imperialism or supraethnic nationalism. The most influential party that effectively backs restorationalism is the Communist Party of the Russian Federation. A less "Soviet" version of imperialism was formulated by former vice president Aleksandr Rutskoi, who drifted to a more ethnonationalist stand after 1993. The most extremist interpretation of this way of thinking in today's Russia can be found in the writings and statements of Liberal Democratic Party of Russia leader Vladimir Zhirinovsky.

The essence of this project is to restore a state within the borders of the USSR (in Zhirinovsky's vision, even to expand it). Such a project would be a solution to the diaspora question. Yet before it is achieved, its proponents advocate decisive assistance to the Russians in the near abroad—including economic sanctions and threats of military intervention. According to many restorationalists, the most important difference between the Soviet Union and the future state must be the abolition of ethnoterritorial units within the state and restoration of denationalized administrative *guberniyas.*

The political constituency for this project of state and nation building includes a considerable part of the Russian military and security agencies, the former Soviet nomenklatura, and ordinary Russians who miss the glory of the former empire and the superpower status enjoyed by the Soviet Union.

Unlike most ethnonationalists, restorationalists are modernizers. They favor a strong army and the development of industry in large urban centers. Vladimir Zhirinovsky, in his own distinctive style, dismissed the image of a Russia of "small villages, forests, fields, accordion player Pyotr and milkmaid Marfa" as a communist plot propagated by various "village prose" writers to partly compensate for the suppression of Russian nationalism.[16] His is the Russia of a historic might, world influence, and impressive richness. Zhirinovsky sided with artist Ilya Glazunov, who created images not of a country of drunken peasants, but

of an "empire with shining palaces of Petersburg, great historical traditions and achievements, thinkers of genius and the leading culture."[17]

The 1994–96 war in Chechnya significantly undermined the appeal
of the proponents of restorationalism. It became clear that any attempt
to implement their program might lead to a war for which Russia was
not prepared. Relative military success in the second Chechen war in
1999–2000 may revive restorationalist ambitions among some parts of
the elite.

• • • • • • • • *Hegemony and Dominance* • • • • • • • • •

The hegemony-and-dominance perspective might be viewed as very
similar to the imperialist approach. There is no clear-cut division between the two schools of thought, though the former has some distinctive features.

Antonio Gramsci was one of the first political scientists who wrote
on hegemony in international relations; this phenomenon found a
contemporary revival in the writings of Robert Keohane and others.[18]
According to Gramsci, a country usually becomes hegemonic because
other actors willingly or subconsciously defer to it, even if they wish to
do otherwise. The followers comply because they see both the leader's
policy position and its putative power as legitimate.[19]

Political scientists and international studies experts are divided on
whether hegemony and dominance are a description of the same phenomenon. Those who believe that it is plausible to make a distinction
claim that a country might involuntarily defer to an external power
without accepting the legitimacy of its policy.[20] The dominant power
does not necessarily seek to create an empire by absorbing dependent
political units; it can be quite satisfied with subjugation. But, unlike a
hegemonic leader, it might use more or less direct coercion to achieve
compliance.

Principles for a Russian policy of hegemony and dominance over
the near abroad were theoretically developed during the Yeltsin period
by Presidential Council member Andranik Migranyan.[21] In more policy-
oriented and moderate terms, this project was advocated by the former
chairman of the Committee for International Affairs and Foreign Economic Relations of the Russian Supreme Soviet, Yevgeny Ambartsumov.
Hegemony/dominance rhetoric was also present in some statements,

articles, and reports of Russian foreign minister Andrei Kozyrev during late 1992 and especially 1993.[22]

The essence of the project is state building within the borders of present-day Russia accompanied by subjugation of other successor states and the creation of a buffer zone of protectorates and dependent countries around Russia. Russian diasporas are viewed as a convenient instrument of influence and manipulation in the neighboring states.

From 1996 to 1999, the most vocal advocate of the policy of hegemony and domination was Yuri Luzhkov, the mayor of Moscow and leader of the Otechestvo movement. Luzhkov relied heavily on the political expertise of Konstantin Zatulin, his adviser and the director of the Institute of Diaspora and Integration. In 1997, a bold attempt was made to incorporate ideas of hegemony and domination into actual Russian policy in the Commonwealth of Independent States. On the eve of the May 1997 CIS summit, Zatulin's institute prepared a special report for the Ministry of Foreign Affairs.[23] The ministry rejected it and then–minister of foreign affairs Yevgeny Primakov immediately disclaimed any responsibility for the report because it did not reflect Russia's official stand, which respected the sovereignty of the newly independent states and promoted integration—principally economic—among them. According to Zatulin, however, the report made its way from the institute directly to the president, and some of its ideas were incorporated into Yeltsin's speech behind closed doors during the summit.[24] The main message of the report's explicitly hegemonic approach was to demonstrate that Russia's moderate policies toward the near abroad could be substituted with more assertive ones. In order to prevent the Soviet successor states' anti-Russian policies, Russia could encourage political instability and interethnic tensions in the region. In November 1998, Zatulin was elected chairman of the Derzhava movement, founded by Aleksandr Rutskoi in 1994. This event demonstrated that "dominators" had acquired a party base by taking over a restorationalist movement.

The political constituency for this project includes a considerable number of those who support imperialism. In their perception, dominance over the near abroad is the first step toward empire. The policy of hegemony and domination is also supported by a part of the Russian nomenklatura.

• • • • • • • • • • • ***Integrationalism*** • • • • • • • • • •

Integrationalism is a project embraced by those who call themselves Russia's political centrists; in some respects, they are intellectually close to Mikhail Gorbachev's circle. These forces included the amorphous Civic Union and its spin-offs, All-Russia's Union "Renewal," Sergei Shakhrai's Party for Russian Unity and Accord, and the Democratic Party of Russia. It is important to note that the project had wide support in other successor states of the former Soviet Union, its most active supporter being Kazakhstan's president Nursultan Nazarbaev.

The essence of the project is the promotion of economic reintegration, which could lead to similar coordination of defense and other policies. Some versions of integrationalism envisioned a sort of confederation of former Soviet republics. The project is very pragmatic, emphasizing economy and security and downplaying more abstract components, such as identity, ethnicity, and nationhood. Supporters of this school of thought maintain that diaspora issues will become obsolete when the post-Soviet space is integrated in terms of economics and security.

There have been several major visions of the future union in the integationists' views. They were developed in Nazarbaev's Eurasian Union program, in Shakhrai's plan for a confederation of three or four countries within the Commonwealth of Independent States, and in Grigori Yavlinsky's Economic Union program. The key common characteristic of all these versions is the claim of a need for some supranational institutions, controlled economic reintegration, and maintenance of major symbols of political sovereignty, accompanied by a high level of cooperation. Unlike the imperialist project, integrationalism claims to be a democratic program granting equal rights to all participating states.

Nazarbaev's idea of the Eurasian Union was the most well-advertised integrationalist project sponsored and supported at the highest level; it was sent to all CIS heads of state in June 1994, but met a lukewarm response. Recognition of territorial integrity and inviolability of borders was the cornerstone of the project, which stipulated economic integration of fully sovereign, independent states. The draft document stopped short of suggesting common or multiple citizenship; instead, it offered a moderate, pragmatic approach: free movement of citizens within the borders of the union. "When changing the country of residence within the [Eurasian Union], an individual automatically acquires citizenship of another country, if he or she desires to do so."[25]

The constituency of the project includes all those affected by the severing of economic ties among the former Soviet republics, especially in heavy and defense-related industries. Many former Soviet citizens not only miss the glory of the former superpower but are also nostalgic about the multinational country they used to live in and had loyalty to. They have had a hard time adjusting to their new, smaller, much more homogeneous homelands that lack the diversity and grandeur of the Soviet Union.

Though integrationalism is popular outside Russia, the difficulties of its implementation are immense. The most fundamental among them is the increasing incompatibility of the former Soviet republics' economies, which have been subjected to different types of reforms. Another obstacle is the position of a significant part of the Russian political elite, which fears the necessity of having to subsidize other Soviet successor states' frail economies. The strengthening of an influential energy-resources lobby from 1992 to 1996, which was directly connected to then–prime minister Viktor Chernomyrdin, also contributed to Russia's more isolationist posture because its economic interests do not stipulate integration of former Soviet republics as a priority. The fear of Russian domination disguised under an integrationalist veil, which is strong among the post-Soviet elites, and the U.S. policy of supporting Eurasian "geopolitical pluralism" are also significant barriers for integrationalist projects.

Political Parties and Nation Building

The Yeltsin regime's establishment in December 1993 of a republic in which tremendous power was granted to the president has not been beneficial for the development of a full-fledged party system. A weak parliament meant weak parties. To a certain extent, however, this was counterbalanced by an electoral law stipulating that half of the State Duma (the parliament's lower chamber) seats be filled by party electoral lists. Party politics has been evolving primarily in the Duma, while grassroots party organizations have been practically nonexistent, with the important exception of the communists. Many regions are domi-nated by local leaders—"the strongmen"—who might have loose party liaisons but in many cases act independently.

From 1993, Russia's political system was stabilized and based on the rule of law, to a greater or lesser extent. After the violent crisis of September–October 1993, the first post-Soviet Duma elected under the new constitution in December was an interim one and was in power for just a two-year term. The second and third Dumas were elected in December 1995 and December 1999, respectively, for four-year terms under much more normal conditions; these bodies are more represen-tative than the first Duma for the analysis of political trends, including those pertaining to the issues of nation building and diasporas.

The rest of this chapter is devoted to an examination of the parties' perspectives on nation building, and these political distinctions will be used as the major differentiating factor for a suggested typology of approaches toward diaspora issues. A secondary factor is the role of the parties in the political system. An examination of the parties' programs and other official documents, as well as their representation in the political arena as the result of 1995 and 1999 elections, is summarized in table 1 and may be illuminating for the assessment of the domestic political context of Russia's attitudes toward the Russian diasporas in the near abroad.

As seen in table 1, new state builders and imperialists were well rep-resented in both the second and the third Dumas. Four major parlia-mentary parties in 1995 and six in 1999 were split between these two perspectives on nation building. Those who represented a "new" Russia and an "old" Soviet Union were major political players, and their agendas were easily identifiable and comprehensible in election campaigns. However, it would be quite an oversimplification to reduce the nuances of political struggles from 1995 to 1999 to these two schools of thought. In their "pure" forms, ethnonationalists, integrationalists, and domi-nators were poorly represented in the Duma, but their influence on the politics of the major parties was significant and was getting stronger. The last three perspectives' strength was not so much in their direct representation in the Duma, but in intellectual influence across the entire Russian political spectrum.

The difficulties ethnonationalists faced in gaining much direct elec-toral support derived from their radicalism and exclusiveness. They could not reach out to non-Russians, mixed families, many intellectuals, and all whose identity may be defined as "Soviet." The weakness of Russian ethnonationalism was well demonstrated by the failures of this project in the political arena. Dominators and integrationalists also did not appeal to the general public because their ideas could hardly be wrapped up into catchy electoral slogans and put into the center of any campaign. However, it may be argued that ethnonationalism, integrationalism, and domination have been gaining much more influence by intellectually taking over the mainstream parties. This thesis may be proved by looking at the architecture of political alliances and rivalries.

Two important changes occurred in the Russian political arena during and after the December 1999 State Duma elections. First, the election campaign was dominated by loose and diverse electoral alliances, which united political forces and individuals whose perspectives on nation-building were fundamentally different from one another or were not concerned with these issues at all. The Unity bloc had no program or people who would be able or willing to develop one. Fatherland–All Russia included integrationalist/new state builder Primakov, dominator Luzhkov, and regional leaders who were interested in their parochial issues only. Second, those parties that had relatively consistent views of nation building—KPRF, Yabloko, the Union of Right Forces as an heir of Russia's Democratic Choice (DC), Common Course, and Forward Russia!—managed to preserve their representation in the parliament, though their real influence and visibility were diminished.

While nation-building issues played an important role in intellectual debates and some party programs, they were not divided along party lines during the December 1999 elections. This phenomenon was a reflection of nonideological personal power struggles within the Russian political class. The transition from loose Moscow-based election alliances toward more established parties with identifiable programs addressing important issues did not occur. As a result, the Russian parliament will not necessarily be the major arena for dialogue and competition among the different visions of nation building. The formation of ad hoc alliances and chaotic struggles among different factions within the parliament is much more likely. The issues of nation building may unexpectedly come to the fore in these struggles and reconfigure, at least temporarily, the political landscape of the legislature.

Table 1. Selected Political Parties, Movements, Associations, and Groups in 1995 and 1999*

Perspective on nation building	Parliamentary				Nonparliamentary			
	Major†		Other‡		Admitted to elections		Did not participate in elections	
	1995	1999	1995	1999	1995	1999	1995	1999
New state building	Our Home Is Russia, Yabloko	Unity, OVR, SPS, Yabloko	DVR,§ Democratic Russia, Common Course, Forward Russia!	Our Home Is Russia				
Ethnonationalism	(KPRF)‖ (LDPR)	(KPRF) (BZ)	(ROS) (KRO)	KRO	NRPR (Derzhava)	ROS DPS-RD	RNE, RP NBP	
Restorationalism	KPRF LDPR	KPRF BZ	Soyuz ROS		Smaller communist parties, Derzhava	Smaller communist parties, (ROS)		

Integrationalism	(Yabloko), (Our Home Is Russia)	(OVR), (Yabloko)	PRES, KRO, DPR, (Forward Russia!)	(KRO)
Domination	(LDPR)	(OVR)	(ROS)	(Derzhava)

*Those parties, movements, associations, and groups that have not been explicit enough on the issue of nation building or concentrated exclusively on the issues of internal federative structure of the Russian Federation (for example, the Agrarian Party of Russia, Women of Russia, Regions of Russia, Reforms–New Course, Party of Self-Government of Workers, Republican Party of the Russian Federation, Party of Pensioners, For Citizen's Worth, All-Russian Political Movement in Support the Army) are not included in the table. Marginal and nonrepresentative nonparliamentary parties and groups are also not included.

†The parties, movements, and associations that reached the 5 percent representation threshold in the party-list vote in 1995 and 1999 and were represented in the State Duma on the proportional system.

‡Parties, movements, and associations, whose members were elected into the State Duma from single-member constituencies, in the lists of the four major parties, or became ex officio members of the Federation Council.

§Abbreviations: DVR - Russia's Democratic Choice; KPRF - Communist Party of the Russian Federation; LDPR - Liberal Democratic Party of Russia; ROS - Russia All-People's Union; KRO - Congress of Russian Communities; NRPR - National-Republican Party of Russia; RNE - Russian National Unity; RP - Russian Party; NBP - National Bolshevik Party; PRES - Party of Russia's Unity and Accord; DPR - Democratic Party of Russia; OVR - Fatherland–All Russia; SPS - Union of Right Forces; BZ - Zhirinovsky Bloc; DPS-RD - Movement of Patriotic Forces–Russian Cause.

‖Parentheses indicate that the given perspective is present in the program of a party as a secondary issue.

Political Alliances and Rivalries

The five projects of state and nation building just summarized are more or less ideal types. Some party programs might include the features of several perspectives, and there is a natural affinity among some projects. On the one hand, these affinities might serve as the basis for coalition building. On the other hand, the parties that share similar views on the problems of nation building might be at odds with each other on different matters, such as economic policy. In addition, differences on tactical matters might drive apart political forces with similar strategic goals.

The forces that accept state building within current borders and advocate de-ethnicized nation building, different versions of integrationalism, or hegemonistic policies dominated the political arena from 1991 to 1999 by controlling the executive branch and exercising their influence in both chambers of the parliament. However, major opposition forces that act within the constitutional framework openly challenge the boundaries of the Russian political community and the meaning of the nation. These opposition forces, in turn, are divided between ethnonationalists and restorationalists. Yet the issue of the Russian diasporas consolidates the opposition. Most of the opposition parties agree on the crucial importance of the question of nation building and the necessity of adopting a more resolute policy toward Russians in the near abroad. However, communists view an overly assertive stance on diaspora issues, and especially support of irredentism (advocated by many nationalists), as detrimental to the prospect of using integration as a way to restore a united state on the territory of the former Soviet Union. For example, Ukraine as a whole is a more important issue for them than are the Russians of the Crimea.

Coalition building is possible not only within the restorationalist/ethnonationalist opposition, but also between certain segments of this opposition and those who are part of the ruling regime. For example, an opportunity for a coalition exists between new state builders and some restorationalists on the basis of integration. Upon agreeing to become a minister of cooperation with the CIS countries in Yeltsin's government, communist Aman Tuleev argued: "I took the pre-election program of our People–Patriotic bloc [a loose election coalition of communist and nationalist political parties and organizations], looked at the section on integration with the CIS countries, checked with the governmental program and decree of the president, and I saw that there were no differences."[26]

The diaspora issue undermined a temporary tactical alliance between new state builders and some ethnonationalists, which existed in 1989–91, when it was possible, for example, for prominent ethnonationalist Mikhail Astafiev to be an active member of the liberal Democratic Russia movement. While pushing Russia toward independence, the new state builders often used the slogans of ethnonationalists regarding the sovereignty of the RSFSR. By the end of the 1990s, ethnonationalists had become marginalized in the Russian political arena, as were their predecessors in the early twentieth century. The reason for this is more structural than purely political: it is the weak Russian ethnic identity.

Both hegemony/domination and restorationism imply a strong and assertive Russia. However, unlike the restorationist school, the hegemony/domination perspective does not adumbrate a change of borders. On this issue, restorationists are closer to ethnonationalists. There are other important common features between restorationalism and ethnonationalism. As a rule, a touch of ethnonationalism is present in most restorationalist programs in the form of a tacit understanding of the leading role of Russians (similar to the supraethnic policies of Nicholas I and the internationalist Soviet Union). Loyalty to the big state easily encompasses non-Russian ethnicity for most restorationalists. Both schools of thought take a rather paranoid view of history, in which Russia is portrayed as a permanent victim of evil coming from outside forces.

In line with nineteenth-century thinkers Konstantin Leontiev and Nikolai Danilevsky, the theme of geopolitical and spiritual battle between Russian and Western civilizations can be found in the writings of both Aleksandr Solzhenitsyn and Gennadi Zyuganov.[27] The one-dimensional view of history and the acknowledgment of a special role for ethnic Russians are the major themes of the section "The Ideology of Patriotism" in Zyuganov's book *Russia Is My Motherland: The Ideology of State Patriotism*.[28] According to Zyuganov: "Our enemies very well understand that Russia's people is the backbone of that great power that for centuries has been preventing the implementation of their hegemonic schemes."[29] His outline of the policy of "de-Russification," which was allegedly conducted by the Yeltsin regime, is very similar to Solzhenitsyn's narratives. Both of them point to Yeltsin's preventing political reunification of the three Eastern Slavic peoples and the Russians living compactly in the areas adjacent to Russia, promotion of Russo-phobic attitudes, and attacks against national consciousness.[30] Seemingly moderate Aleksei Podberezkin, chairman of the central council of the social and political movement Spiritual Heritage (close to the CPRF), has been even more ethnonationalist than Zyuganov, emphasizing the historical territory of the Russian ethnos and insisting on the term *russkii* instead of *rossiiskii* with regard to the nation.[31]

The Liberal Democratic Party's Vladimir Zhirinovsky is also a restorationalist, with some ethnonationalist overtones. Mark Yoffe, the author of the most sophisticated and accurate analysis of Zhirinovsky's views, was correct when he wrote:

> A detailed analysis of his writings shows that Zhirinovsky's use of the word "Russian" is purely generic. It serves as a substitute for the term "Soviet" and carries the same historical and ideological freight. . . . [H]e thinks of Russia not as a nation but as an empire. Geographically, his Russia is fully equated with the Soviet Union. Therefore, Zhirinovsky cannot be viewed as a true Russian nationalist, but is seen to be a Russian (Soviet-style) imperialist and expansionist.[32]

However, the ethnonationalist overtones in the rhetoric of Zhirinovsky and other prominent members of his party became stronger from 1995 to 2000. During parliamentary hearings in October 1996, Aleksei Mitrofanov, chairman of the State Duma's Committee on Geopolitics, argued that "it is necessary to acknowledge Russians as a divided people, which has a right for reunification."[33] The major theme of Mitrofanov's *Steps of New Geopolitics* is redrawing political boundaries all over the world along ethnic lines. He views Russia as a state within borders that are very similar to those outlined by Solzhenitsyn.[34]

There is a common theoretical inconsistency in most restorationalist projects. It is an attempt to combine the notions of a "divided Russian people" with claims that the Russian people is a sort of a "supranational super-ethnos." The coexistence of these seemingly mutually exclusive perspectives reflects the historical ambiguity over the membership and the boundaries of the Russian people. Only ethnonationalist extremists and leftist "proletarian internationalists" have been theoretically consistent in this respect. The mainstream communists and nationalists, who try to reach out to broader constituencies of the former "Soviet people" (for example, Gennadi Zyuganov and Sergei Baburin), seek to reconcile both narrow notions of Russianness, which are based on ethnicity, and broad, all-inclusive perspectives, which rely on the traditions of an all-encompassing "Russian idea" and the Soviet legacy. For example, Baburin wrote about the "strengthening and development of the supranational Russian super-ethnos" as a political task,[35] while his party program stipulated that "the restoration of the integrity of the Russian people, which is the founder and the core of Russia's statehood, and which was divided among several newly created states after 1991, is the priority issue of modern Russia."[36] The political declaration of Derzhava echoed the program of the Russian All-People's Union (ROS) on the issue of Russians as a divided people, reaffirming in exactly the same wording that "the Russian people is the founder and the core of Russia's statehood."[37]

There is evidence to suggest that ethnonationalist components in most mainstream restorationalist projects have been getting stronger. The issue of Russian diasporas has been the major factor pushing restorationalists toward an ethnonationalist position. Only the extreme left seems ingenuous in its desire to re-create the Soviet Union within its old borders, hoping for restoration of the "friendship of peoples." These movements include the All-Union Communist Party of Bolsheviks (VKPB), the Russian Communist Labor Party (RKPB), Working Russia, the Union of Communists, and the Russian Party of Communists (RPK).

Within the largest and the most influential communist party—the KPRF—there is a constant struggle between "national-patriotic" forces, led by Zyuganov, and more orthodox communists. The latter accuse Zyuganov of betraying the principles of "proletarian internationalism" in favor of "national-reformist" and Slavic Orthodox views. In 1997, hard-line communist ideologists launched a campaign to develop a concept of the KPRF's nationalities policy on the principles of Marxism-Leninism. They attacked Zyuganov for his flirtation with Russian nationalism,[38] criticized the idea of a *russkaya* republic within the Russian Federation, and cautioned against emphasizing Slavic unity, which could challenge the federation's friendship with Turkic and Islamic peoples.[39] Zyuganov himself seems to rely on several different perspectives, emphasizing proletarian internationalism to his fellow party members, while at the same time preaching great-power nationalism or ethnonationalism to the People's Patriotic Union umbrella organization.

In sum, ethnonationalism strengthened its position on the political arena in the 1990s not because of the rise of "pure" ethnonationalist groups, which remain relatively marginal, but as a result of the incorporation of their ideas by major opposition parties, namely the KPRF and LDPR, even though Zyuganov and Zhirinovsky remain more restorationalist. The alleged division of the Russian people and the issue of diasporas have been the driving forces behind the ethnonationalization of restorationalists. The background for this drift was formed by the growing acknowledgment that Russia's current weakness has made the country incapable of fighting an uphill battle for the restoration of the Soviet Union. Besides, there is the fear of an eventual dilution of ethnic Russians in a huge multiethnic state. Derzhava's political declaration openly stated:

> Currently, the Russian people, given its spiritual and historic demoralization, economic weakness, and demographic decline, is unable to keep the whole territory of historic Russia in its indisputable zone of state influence. That is why an attempt to restore the USSR in its old borders, even if all peoples state their intention to join it ... would, under conditions of direct, secret, and equal suffrage, inevitably lead to degeneration of the essence of the state in favor of other intensely growing peoples. .... The state, restoration and development of which would secure the preservation of the national historic existence of the Russian people, is precisely the one and indivisible Russia in its natural borders, defined first of all by the compact settlement of the Russian people.[40]

In the winter and spring of 1998, a bitter struggle unfolded between the major restorationalist factions—the KPRF and ROS, the latter headed by Sergei Baburin, the Duma's deputy speaker. It ended with Baburin's replacement as deputy speaker responsible for CIS issues by Svetlana Goryacheva, a communist. Differences in policy toward Russian diasporas led to this key personnel change, which immediately affected relations between Russia and other CIS countries. Baburin opposed treaties Russia had signed with Ukraine, Moldova, and Georgia and delayed their ratification, while the communists favored their immediate ratification. Baburin argued that those treaties did not sufficiently protect ethnic Russians in Crimea, Pridnestrovye, and Abkhazia. Even though the KPRF and ROS are both restorationalist forces, they differ significantly on tactical matters. KPRF policy contains noticeable integrationalist components, while an ROS leader is more inclined toward ethnonationalism. Though Gennadi Zyuganov is also prone to ethnonationalism, most communists see gradual economic integration and the building of close and friendly political relations with CIS countries as good ways to achieve a strategic goal, which they see in the restoration of some sort of union among former Soviet republics. Baburin, who shares this strategic goal with the communists, is more inclined to stress the grievances and aspirations of ethnic Russians in the near abroad and is less ready to compromise their well-being for the sake of an alliance with current regimes of the CIS countries, which he deems to be anti-Russian. Such a position might be partly explained by Baburin's evident attempt to become a leader of a coalition of Russian ethnonationalist parties and groups. In December 1997, he participated in the Fourth Congress of Russian Nationalists, which included such extremist parties as Russian National Unity and the National-Republican Party among the organizers, and said that he would be ready to head a "united national opposition."

Heated debates over ratification of the Treaty on Friendship, Cooperation, and Partnership with Ukraine in 1997–98 divided the Russian political arena and demonstrated that the issues of identity and nation building are intertwined with the questions of policy toward the near abroad. The negative attitude of the "restorationalist" ROS toward the treaty was shared by ethnonationalists, dominators, and some restorationalists. The most vocal among them were Yuri Luzhkov, Sergei Baburin, Vladimir Zhirinovsky, Aleksandr Lebed, and Konstantin Zatulin. On the opposite side, there were state builders, integrationalists, and, surprisingly, most restorationalists. This coalition's most articulate speakers were Yevgeny Primakov, Igor Ivanov, Gennadi Zyuganov, and Gennadi Seleznev. There was an evident consensus among Russian elites that Russia and Ukraine must draw closer, but they were divided on the issue of whether the treaty served that goal or, by acknowledging Ukraine's territorial integrity, stimulated the consolidation of the Ukrainian nation and assimilation of ethnic Russians living there.

In his report to the April 1997 KPRF congress, Zyuganov attacked those who raised the issue of disputed territories—Pridnestrovye, Abkhazia, and especially Sevastopol and Crimea—in relations between Russia and Moldova, Georgia, and Ukraine: "Those who deepen this division are trying to burn the bridges and close the road to reunification."[41] Evidently, this accusation was directed, above all, toward Baburin and Luzhkov. It is very telling that Zyuganov backed his position on this issue by referring to a broad vision of Russian nationhood and the boundaries of Russia: "In broad historical and cultural terms, Great Russia is the Soviet Union." Specifically on the issue of disputed areas, he said:

> After all, if you think about it, Sevastopol, and indeed Crimea as a whole, as well as such territories as, for instance, Pridnestrovye [the Dniestr Region] and Abkhazia, have "indefinite" status solely from the viewpoint of the Belaya Vezha Pushcha accords [which codified the dissolution of the Soviet Union]. From the viewpoint of the results of the 17 March referendum on the preservation of the USSR, there is nothing indefinite about it. It is necessary finally to dot the i's and cross the t's. There is historical statehood of Russia, and then there is its Belaya Vezha Pushcha statehood. What does this latter consist of? It consists of a rotten rung on a ladder leading downward—to Russia's final dismemberment into minor "principalities."[42]

This strict restorationist position, however, did not prevent Zyuganov from incorporating many ethnonationalist provisions into his vision of the boundaries and membership of the Russian nation, especially when he addressed the issue of the Russian diasporas.

On the opposite side of the Russian political spectrum, there are many differences in the positions of the new state building and integrationalist schools. However, they both favor civic identities, are moderate on diasporas, and tacitly acknowledge the fact that Russia simply has no strength for a more ambitious and assertive policy in the near abroad. Both new state builders and integrationalists advocate the preservation of current political borders. Characteristically, the programs of two important political parties in the Duma between 1995 and 1999— Our Home Is Russia and Yabloko—basically advocated new state building and contained provisions on the necessity of fostering economic integration among the CIS countries.[43] Smaller liberal parties —Democratic Choice, Democratic Russia, Common Course, and the Union of Right Forces—have been more consistent new state builders, sometimes implicitly advocating isolationism from other Soviet successor states. However, the programs of all liberal parties included provisions regarding the support of human rights and cultural needs of "compatriots abroad." Thus the political significance of the issue has been acknowledged, at least rhetorically, by both new state builders and integrationalists.

Some alliances, which were made during election campaigns between political forces with very different agendas, were based primarily on similarities of their nation-building visions. In 1995, some pragmatic administrators and economists (Yuri Skokov and Sergei Glaziev of the Democratic Party of Russia) made an alliance with much more ideological forces prone to ethnonationalism—for instance, Dmitri Rogozin of the Congress of Russian Communities, or KRO. As a result, two KROs coexisted. One was an international, nongovernmental umbrella organization of the Russian communities in the near abroad. The other was a Russian political movement that was created on the eve of the 1995 parliamentary elections and was not that much concerned with the diaspora issue.[44] The alliance infused the speeches of prominent integrationalists with ethnonationalist rhetoric concerning the "special role of Russians in the preservation of Russia's statehood" and the "necessity of the national awakening of Russians."[45]

The ideology of the Congress of Russian Communities, primarily formulated by Rogozin, can be easily labeled as ethnonationalist, but it is much more complex in reality. Its 1995 election campaign program emphasized integrationalism: "The Congress of Russian Communities is convinced that a really cardinal solution of the problem of Russian compatriots in the 'near abroad' is on the way of political, economic, and other integration of the former USSR republics."[46] However, the KRO's 1994 manifesto and Rogozin's 1998 book indicate that the long-term goal of the organization and its leader is building a sort of a nation-state around an ethnic Russian core.[47] Rogozin dismissed the concept of a "multinational people of the Russian Federation," which had made its way into the Yeltsin constitution of 1993. Instead, he suggested the concept of a "multi-people nation," where the Russian people plays the role of a backbone.[48] An attentive reader of Rogozin's writings might draw parallels between his ideas and the experience of nation building in Europe during the past several centuries, where nation-states were created around ethnic cores of, say, French or Germans. One may also find implicit allusions to the views of Pavel Milyukov. However, many neighbors of the Russian people have already perceived themselves as *nations* and would not easily and peacefully go back to the status of just *peoples*. This problem is not addressed in Rogozin's deliberations.

The political fate of the KRO is illustrative for a better understanding of the role of the diaspora issue in Russian politics. The party that made the most out of the issue had a poor showing in all elections, including the 1999 State Duma elections. Of course, the failures of KRO, as well as the successes of other parties, cannot be attributed solely to the shortcomings or the merits of the corresponding programs. Money, organization, and access to the mass media play a crucial role. It is evident, however, that the diaspora issue per se cannot mobilize the electorate if it is not combined with other important issues—namely, economics, social policies, and broad questions of state and nation building. KRO reoriented its profile away from being a single-issue party and became ever more preoccupied with the social, cultural, and economic problems of Russians in Russia.

Democracy in Russia made it possible to express antisystem sentiments in an electoral context.[49] Unlike in "mature" political systems, there is no consensus among the leading mainstream parties on the most fundamental issues. In Russia, the electorate is often forced to make a choice not simply among policies, but among proposed political systems and competing visions of the nation and its boundaries. This is a key feature of the unconsolidated Russian polity.

In many models of democratization, national unity and consensus on the country's boundaries are viewed as a precondition for the successful transition to democracy.[50] Much attention is usually paid in this regard to multiethnic states with strong separatist or national liberation movements, and the corresponding model of democratization assumes that claims for autonomy or independence must be settled in empires held together by force before success in democratization can be achieved. Though suffering such a problem, Russia's democratization has also been challenged by ardent claims of the need to expand its current borders—justified, in the view of some prominent political forces, by the necessity of unifying the Russian people. These claims are expressed in a democratic framework by legitimate political forces that acknowledge basic democratic rules. Even some dedicated new state builders in the government committed themselves to the extension of

Russia's political space in the form of dual citizenship for the diasporians. Must Russia address the interconnected problems of nation building and the issues of boundaries and diasporas first in order to succeed in its democratic transition in the future? To answer this question, it is necessary to look closer at the Russian diasporas themselves (chapter 4) and the Russian Federation's policy in the near abroad (chapter 5).

Russians outside Russia
before and after
the Breakup
of the Soviet Union

T HE ARGUMENT PRESENTED THUS FAR is that, in spite of extremely blurred ethnic boundaries and the predominance of an imperial tradition, Russian ethnonationalism could become a rising force under certain conditions. Such a force may lead to the formulation of policies that are aimed at the Russian state's reunification with its new diasporas. The discussion leading to these conclusions in the previous chapters was based on an analysis of Russian historical, intellectual, and political trends that have fostered ethnonationalism. Yet there is also another important contributor to Russian ethnonationalism: namely, the role of the new Russian diasporas themselves.

It seems logical to assume that the plight of the Russians in the near abroad might strengthen ethnonationalist sentiments in Russia. However, the present problem of Russians in the near abroad seems to be politically important but less intense in the Russian Federation than anyone would have predicted in 1990–1991. Though many in Russia perceive Russians as a divided nation, there have been no vigorous efforts to reunite Russia proper with the diasporas. Why is this the case? Will

moderation hold? To answer these questions, one must begin by analyzing the key features of the Russian diaspora communities. Are there
distinct boundaries that separate Russians from non-Russians in the
near abroad? What makes Russian communities different from titular
groups in Soviet successor states and from the "core" Russians in the
Russian Federation, as well as from one another? Finally, why do Russians
in different states choose different strategies—either migration to Russia
or adjustment to the "host society"?

There are two basic features that all Russians living in the near
abroad undoubtedly share: namely, the feeling of connection with the
Russian culture and the existence of an external homeland. However,
culture and a remote homeland are rather abstract categories, usually
detached from daily life. Significant intellectual and political efforts
must be undertaken by the elite in the homeland and by the leaders of
the diasporas themselves to have these abstract categories conceptualized and internalized by millions of people. Meanwhile, the differences between the Russian diasporas are numerous, and their concrete
situations—such as the degree of integration into the host country,
economic well-being, and political rights—vary considerably. Moreover, for analytical purposes it is practically impossible to separate
ethnic Russians from other Russian-speaking populations in the near
abroad. It can be argued that the important reasons for Russia's
unexpected moderation in its relations with co-ethnics in the near
abroad are the significant differences among the Russian communities
and the blurred ethnic boundaries between them and non-Russians.
It would be more appropriate to refer to them as different Russian
diasporas, rather than as a divided Russian nation or a single Russian diaspora.

This chapter will first address the issue of the blurred ethnic and
linguistic boundaries between Russians and non-Russians in the former Soviet republics. Second, it will analyze the differences among the
Russian communities in the former Soviet republics. Third, it will
highlight the problems of the transition from a supposedly privileged
position to the status of national minority. Fourth, it will outline various migration patterns among Russians. The analysis will be followed
by conclusions on the typology of the Russian diasporas and their future prospects.

Russians and Russian-Speakers

Drawing lines between Russians and non-Russians in the former Soviet republics is a much more complicated task than it seems at first glance. Self-reporting ethnic identification is the most evident criterion, and it has been widely used in the literature. The most recent reliable data in this area are contained in the last Soviet population census of 1989. However, the present work is based on the assumptions that identities are fluid and dynamic, that many people have multiple or changing identities, and that Russian culture has had strong universalistic components and that its influence in the former Soviet Union went well beyond the ethnic Russian core. An approach based on these premises requires attention to a variety of criteria for identifying the boundaries of the Russian communities in the newly independent states. Linguistic boundaries, in addition to self-reporting ethnic identity, may be illustrative in this regard.

German eighteenth-century Romantic thinkers Johann Gottlib Fichte and Johann von Herder argued that language played a crucial role in forming nations. Many modern scholars who belong to the constructionalist school of thought have been much more skeptical about this idea. Eric Hobsbawm contended: "It was always evident to all that language and people (however each was defined) did not coincide." He also argued: "Special cases aside, there is no reason to suppose that language was more than one among several criteria by which people indicated belonging to a human collectivity."[1] The perceptions of the elites in the former Soviet Union, however, have been traditionally more receptive to Germanic cultural definitions of nation than to the purely political ones prevalent in France or the United States.

The rise of nationalism in the former Soviet Union in the late 1980s was accompanied by policies of revival for titular languages in the Soviet republics. These policies were continued in the newly independent states. However, attempts to build new nations on the basis of a titular group's culture, including vigorous promotion of a titular language, have met serious difficulties in the Soviet successor states.[2] These problems are not just a result of the presence of ethnic Russian minorities, but numerous other groups that share the Russian language and are customarily referred to as the "Russian-speaking population." They include not only ethnic Russians, but all those nontitulars who prefer to speak Russian. Moreover, many titulars in Ukraine, Kazakhstan, and other countries effectively belong to these groups as well. The spread of the Russian language as the "native" one beyond ethnic Russian communities in the newly independent states did not necessarily signify making Russians out of non-Russians. It did, however, weaken ethnic identities and blur ethnic boundaries, especially among Eastern Slavs. Since the collapse of the Soviet Union, this process has probably stopped, if not reverted. However, the magnitude of the problem is often overlooked or underestimated by many outside observers.

The last Soviet population census provides illustrative information concerning the process of Russification, which in many cases blurred the lines between Russians and non-Russians before the breakup of the Soviet Union. The data presented below go beyond ethnic self-determination of the respondents and take into consideration linguistic self-identification, the latter determined by the self-reported identification of a native language.[3] The results of these calculations are based on the 1989 census data and are presented in tables 2–4.

Judging even from this statistical data, it is extremely difficult to draw clear-cut boundaries between Russians and non-Russians in most of the Soviet republics, which are now newly independent states. The influence of Russian culture in the form of proliferation of the Russian language in non-Russian republics went well beyond the Russian communities, and it is important to note that there are many more Russophones than ethnic Russians (36 and 25 million respectively) outside Russia.

Among other ethnic diasporas (nontitular non-Russians), whose native language is not the one of their native ethnic group, Russian is almost five times more popular than the titular tongue. In other words, an ethnic Armenian living in Uzbekistan, if he or she does not consider Armenian a native language, is much more likely to be a Russian speaker than an Uzbek speaker. Eleven million out of 19 million nontitular non-Russians in fourteen republics can be called a "Russian language–'leaning' population," which includes all those who name Russian as their native or second (after their own, but not titular) tongue. In almost all cases, these are nontitular non-Russians who feel closer to Russian, as opposed to the titular, culture. This group includes, for example, Russian-speaking Ukrainians or Jews living in Kazakhstan. If the number of ethnic Russians, the number of non-Russians who consider Russian their native language, and the number of nontitular non-Russians who name Russian as their second language (after their own) are added together, the overall figure is 42 million, or 30 percent of the population of the fourteen republics (all former Soviet republics excluding Russia). Still, this figure grossly underestimates the number of those who prefer Russian to any other language. Again, there are many millions of Russian-speaking titulars who report a titular language as their native tongue but prefer to speak Russian as a language of convenience.[4] The number of such people is especially high in eastern Ukraine and Kazakhstan, where up to 70 and 40 percent of the respective titular populations are Russophones.

There were significant differences in the patterns of Russification in the various Soviet republics. As seen in table 2, in comparison to ethnic Russians, the number of Russophones was particularly high in Ukraine, Belarus, Moldova, Latvia, and Kazakhstan. In Belarus, there were more Russophone Belarusians than ethnic Russians. In Latvia and Kazakhstan, nontitular non-Russian groups reported Russian as a native language more often than in other republics. In Ukraine, Belarus, and Moldova, significant segments of the titular populations claimed Russian as their mother tongue. In Central Asia (particularly in Uzbekistan and Tajikistan), Transcaucasia, and the Baltic states, titular groups were not significantly Russified in terms of linguistics. Such a distinction led to more distinct boundaries between titulars and ethnic Russians, resembling a classical colonial type of interaction between an indigenous population and settlers from the metropolis. Paradoxically, such a legacy might lead to better prospects for the survival of the distinct communities of those Russians who do not leave, while the blurred boundaries in countries like Ukraine provide an environment for the Ukrainization of Russians in the long run. However, the blurred boundaries between Russians and Russified nontitular non-Russians may remain a barrier for the consolidation of all post-Soviet states on a purely ethnic basis.

Many individuals belong to nontitular non-Russian groups in Uzbekistan, Kazakhstan, Ukraine, Tajikistan, Georgia, and Kyrgyzstan (from one to four million in each case; see table 3). An analysis of these groups' linguistic identifications and orientations shows that in some countries more than half of the persons belonging to them considered

Table 2. Russian and Russified Populations (Absolute Number and Percent)

Country	Total Population		Ethnic Russians		Russophones								
					Total		Russians		Titular		Others		% of total popu-lation
	thousands	%	thousands	%	thousands	%	thousands	%	thousands	%	thousands	%	
Ukraine	51,452	100	11,356	22.1	16,898	100	11,172	66.1	4,578	27.1	1,148	6.8	32.8
Belarus	10,152	100	1,342	13.2	3,243	100	1,311	40.4	1,560	48.1	372	11.5	31.9
Uzbekistan	19,810	100	1,654	8.4	2,152	100	1,652	76.8	64	3.0	436	20.3	10.9
Kazakhstan	16,465	100	6,228	37.8	7,797	100	6,224	79.8	89	1.1	1,484	19.0	47.4
Georgia	5,401	100	341	6.3	479	100	336	70.1	9	1.9	134	28.0	8.9
Azerbaijan	7,021	100	392	5.6	528	100	391	74.1	24	4.5	113	21.4	7.5

Lithuania	3,675	100	345	9.4	430	100	330	76.7	8	1.9	92	21.4	11.7
Moldova	4,335	100	562	13.0	1,003	100	557	55.5	120	12	326	32.5	23.1
Latvia	2,667	100	906	34.0	1,123	100	895	79.7	36	3.2	192	17.1	42.1
Kyrgyzstan	4,258	100	917	21.5	1,091	100	916	84.0	7	0.6	168	15.4	25.6
Tajikistan	5,093	100	389	7.6	496	100	389	78.4	16	3.2	91	18.4	9.7
Armenia	3,305	100	52	1.6	67	100	51	76.1	10	14.9	6	9.0	2.0
Turkmenistan	3,523	100	334	9.5	421	100	334	79.3	18	4.3	69	16.4	12.0
Estonia	1,566	100	475	30.3	546	100	469	85.9	10	1.8	67	12.3	34.9
TOTAL	138,723	100	25,293	18.2	36,274	100	25,027	69.0	6,549	18.1	4,698	13.0	26.2

Source: Calculated on the basis of data contained in *Itogi vsesoiuznoi perepesi naseleniya 1989 goda, tom VII: Natsional'nyi sostav naseleniia SSSR* (The results of the 1989 all-Union population census, vol. VII: The USSR population by nationalities) (Minneapolis: East View Press, 1993), passim.

Table 3. Non-Titular Non-Russian Groups by Language (Absolute Number and Percent)

Country	Total		Native Language, thousands		Command of Russian as a Second Language, thousands (3)	Russian Language–"Leaning" Population (1-2+3)	
	thousands	%	Russian (1)	Titular (2)		thousands	%
Ukraine	2,677	100	1,148	269	1,045	1,924	71.9
Belarus	905	100	372	293	357	436	48.2
Uzbekistan	4,013	100	436	171	1,312	1,577	39.3
Kazakhstan	3,702	100	1,484	25	1,781	3,240	87.5
Georgia	1,273	100	134	80	537	591	46.4
Azerbaijan	823	100	113	26	325	412	50.1
Lithuania	406	100	92	20	204	276	68.0

Moldova	978	100	326	18	473	781	79.9
Latvia	373	100	192	24	132	300	80.4
Kyrgyzstan	1,111	100	168	20	502	650	58.5
Tajikistan	1,532	100	91	17	403	477	31.1
Armenia	169	100	6	12	33	27	16.0
Turkmenistan	652	100	69	16	239	292	44.8
Estonia	128	100	67	10	48	105	82.0
Total	18,742	100	4,698	1,001	7,391	11,088	59.2

Source: Calculated on the basis of data contained in *Itogi vsesoiuznoi perepesi raseleniya 1989 goda, tom VII: Natsional'nyi sostav naseleniia SSSR* (The results of the 1989 all-Union population census, vol. VII: The USSR population by nationalities) (Minneapolis: East View Press, 1993), passim.

Table 4. Russian and Non-Russian Minorities (%)

Country	Total Non-Titular Population	Russians	Non-Russians
Ukraine	100	80.9	19.1
Belarus	100	59.7	40.3
Uzbekistan	100	29.2	70.8
Kazakhstan	100	62.7	37.3
Georgia	100	21.1	78.9
Azerbaijan	100	32.3	67.7
Lithuania	100	45.9	54.1
Moldova	100	36.5	63.5
Latvia	100	70.8	29.2
Kyrgyzstan	100	45.2	54.8
Tajikistan	100	20.3	79.7
Armenia	100	23.5	76.5
Turkmenistan	100	33.9	66.1
Estonia	100	78.8	21.2

Source: Calculated on the basis of data contained in *Itogi vsesoiuznoi perepesi naseleniya 1989 goda, tom VII: Natsional'nyi sostav naseleniia SSSR* (The results of the 1989 all-Union population census, vol. VII: The USSR population by nationalities) (Minneapolis: East View Press, 1993), passim.

Russian to be either their mother tongue or a second language (Ukraine, Moldova, the three Baltic republics—Estonia, Latvia, and Lithuania—Kazakhstan, Kyrgyzstan, and Azerbaijan). In Kazakhstan, Estonia, and Latvia this was the case for 80–90 percent of the nontitular non-Russians. In these three states, major linguistic divisions lie between the titulars and the nontitulars—not between the majority and a particular national minority. This fact prompts the Russian Federation to declare a policy of support for and defense of the "Russian-speaking population," and not only of ethnic Russians.

The growth of tensions along ethnically blurred lines between titulars and nontitulars has hindered the consolidation of Russian communities on a purely ethnic basis. In the late 1980s and early 1990s, some ethnic Russians and the Russified groups in the former Soviet republics tried to organize politically in the so-called Interfronts to defend the Soviet order; these organizations collapsed after the defeat of the hard-liners' coup in August 1991. It remains to be seen whether the ethnic factor will play a more important role in the attitudes of these groups, for whom ethnicity has been subordinate to political affiliation with the USSR, which they considered to be a giant "melting pot" of nations. The ethnonationalism of titular groups may cause more ethnically defined attitudes as a sort of a reactive ethnonationalism among the nontitulars, including Russians.

In sum, there are three major forms of Russian cultural influence in the newly independent states: First, the presence of ethnic Russians. Second, Russification of the part of titular population that occurred in the Soviet period and was particularly mass-based in Belarus, Ukraine, and Moldova; in some other cases, the cultural influence was mainly socially selective Russification of the titular urban elites, particularly true in Kazakhstan and Kyrgyzstan.[5] Third, Russification of many nontitular non-Russian groups; together with ethnic Russians, they serve as a barrier to ethnonationalization (nation building on an ethnic basis) in the newly independent states, and it is an important factor in Ukraine, Moldova, Kazakhstan, Kyrgyzstan, and the three Baltic states.

Significant groups in all former Soviet republics culturally represent fragments of a collapsed Soviet Union. Ethnicity has played a less important role for their identity, as these groups contain both ethnic Russians and non-Russians. The titulars, even if they are Russian speakers, seem to differ from other Russian-speaking groups in their feelings on the situation: They became more comfortable with new political realities and changes in linguistic policies after their respective republics acquired independence. The rest of the Russian-speaking population shows little differentiation between ethnic Russians and nontitular non-Russians in many of the republics. There are significant differences between the newly independent states and the linguistic, cultural, and political situations that ethnic Russians and Russian speakers found themselves in after the collapse of the Soviet Union.

The Diversity of Russians and Russified Groups

Russians and Russian speakers have their own distinct features in each of the former Soviet republics. Most available statistical data reflect the features of ethnic Russians only. The ethnic Russian communities differ in size: in 1989, they varied from 11.4 million in Ukraine to 52,000 in Armenia. They grew by 10.2 percent in Estonia between 1959 and 1989 and shrank by 8.7 percent in Kyrgyzstan during the same period. They constituted different percentages of the population: from 1.6 percent in Armenia to 37.8 percent in Kazakhstan in 1989. The general trend in the 1960s to 1980s was an increase in their absolute and relative numbers in the European Soviet republics and a relative decrease in all eight southern republics.[6] Russian communities are very different in their lifestyles and the level of integration into their "host societies." In 1989, the percentage of Russians who knew as a second language the titular language of the republic they lived in varied from more than 30 percent in Ukraine, Lithuania, and Armenia to 1 percent in Kazakhstan and Kyrgyzstan. Russians constituted more than 70 percent of those employed in the sciences in Kazakhstan and Kyrgyzstan, while the same indicator for Armenia was only 6 percent.[7]

In a similar vein, indigenous peoples vary significantly in their command of Russian as a first or a second language: from 23 percent in Uzbekistan to about 80 percent in Belarus in 1989.[8] The differences in the level of integration into host societies are reflected in the rates of mixed marriages between Russians and non-Russians in the former Soviet republics.[9] Thus it may be argued that even before the dissolution of the Soviet Union, Russian communities, while displaying some common features, varied significantly in their patterns of interaction with host societies in the former Soviet republics. Moreover, the very term "host society" is hardly applicable to the situation in, say, Belarus or Ukraine, where Russians were an integral part of the societies. At the same time, Tajikistan and Lithuania, for example, were indeed perceived as host societies by many Russians who lived there.

The collapse of the Soviet Union made pre-existing differences among the Russian communities much more dramatic. Unique conditions and the policies of each newly independent state sharpened these differences, so that they became major influences in the evolution of these communities. A. Susokolov, Paul Kolstoe, and David Laitin came to similar conclusions, stipulating that the most likely outcome of the collapse of the Soviet Union for the Russian communities might be the formation of new identities.[10] These identities probably will be unique in each of the newly independent states. As a result, a Russian-Estonian identity will be very different from, say, a Russian-Uzbek one. According to Kolstoe:

> there is no reason to believe that the final outcome of the identity formation of the Russian communities in the Soviet successor states will be the creation of a single diaspora identity. Not only is the cohesion within the Russian ethnos at large—between the core and the periphery—being weakened, it is also true of the cohesion within the diaspora itself. The social, political, economic, and cultural conditions under which the diaspora is living differ greatly. Rather than one diaspora identity, we should expect the formation of several new identity types.[11]

History is the most fundamental factor of differentiation of the Russian diasporas in the newly independent states. They settled in different periods of time and under different conditions and circumstances. After the collapse of the Soviet Union, the key factors in the further differentiation among the Russian communities are the differences in economic conditions in the post-Soviet states, the presence or absence of armed conflicts, the weakness or strength of mass-based nationalism among the titular groups, the compactness or dispersion of Russian settlements, and the inclusiveness or exclusiveness of the newly independent states' policies toward Russians.

Economic conditions vary from satisfactory to catastrophic throughout the former Soviet Union. The relatively better-off countries are the three Baltic states, Belarus, Russia, and Ukraine. Although some countries in this group, notably Ukraine and Belarus, have experienced deeper declines in their gross domestic product and have lagged behind in terms of economic reforms, all six might be called comparatively developed, industrialized, and urbanized (see table 5). They also have a comparatively low infant mortality rate, which is a representative indicator of modernization. Nevertheless, in many of these countries, especially in Estonia (the leading country of this group of states), Russians found themselves stuck in industrial enterprises that were often defense-related and previously linked directly to Moscow; as such, they inevitably became victims of restructuring economies. Transcaucasia and Central Asia are comparatively less developed, and their prospects for rapid improvement of social indicators in the near future are gloomy, although some of them, notably Uzbekistan, demonstrate relatively stable economic growth and little social discontent.

Armed conflicts in Georgia, Armenia, Azerbaijan, Tajikistan, and Moldova have made Russians feel particularly vulnerable in these countries. Although in none of these conflicts were they singled out as targets of violence, most Russians living in these countries have perceived their environment as dangerous and hostile in recent years.

Mass-based nationalism in the former Soviet republics is another factor that can aggravate the conditions of the Russian minorities. The Baltic states, Georgia, and Armenia are the countries where the intensity of indigenous national consciousness is probably the highest; however, titular groups' nationalism does not necessarily take an anti-Russian expression. In Armenia and Georgia, popular anti-Russian sentiments have not been the issue, whereas in the Baltics, national liberation movements against the imperial center contained a significant anti-Russian component. Such anti-Russian sentiment has become apparent in light of recent policies of these newly independent states. Initially, in the late 1980s and early 1990s, national, anti-imperial, and anticommunist protests in these states seemed to be primarily democratic in character. Later on, however, the leadership of these national-democratic movements consisted mainly of hard-line nationalists, concerned primarily with the well-being of the titular ethnos, rather than of democrats, who favored individual human rights and civil liberties.

The concentration of the former Soviet republics' Russian settlements is also an important factor in their social and political development after 1991. Northern Kazakhstan, northeastern Estonia, parts of Ukraine, and Pridnestrovye in Moldova are major areas of concentration for Russian populations. This factor provides the basis for potential political ambitions to establish autonomy and, possibly, to pursue irredentist claims. In most other areas, Russians are dispersed in cities and thus can strive only toward cultural rather than territorial autonomy.

Differences in state policies toward Russians in the former Soviet republics manifest themselves in citizenship and language issues. Latvia and Estonia are the only two countries of the former Soviet Union

Table 5. Selected Socioeconomic Indicators of the Soviet Successor States

Country	GNP per capita, $ (1998)	GDP growth rate, % (1997–98)	Employment in agriculture, % (1994 or 1995)	Urban population, % (1998)	Infant mortality per 1,000 births (1997)
Estonia	3,390	6*	...	74	10
Lithuania	2,440	6	24	74	10
Latvia	2,430	0*	18	74	15
Russia	2,300	–6	15	77	17
Belarus	2,200	–22*	20	73	12
Ukraine	850	–24*	23	72	14
Kazakhstan	1,310	–3	22	61	24
Georgia	930	–28*	30	60	17
Uzbekistan	870	3	46	42	...
Azerbaijan	490	9	31	57	20
Armenia	480	3*	34	69	15
Moldova	410	–22*	46	54	20
Kyrgyzstan	350	4	42	40	28
Tajikistan	350	–15*	55	33	30
Turkmenistan	...	...	44	45	40

*1994 data.
Source: World Development Report 1996: From Plan to Market (Washington, D.C.: The World Bank, 1996), 172; *Statistical Handbook 1996: States of the Former USSR* (Washington, D.C.: The World Bank, 1996), 10; *Entering the 21st Century: World Development Report, 1999–2000* (New York: Oxford University Press, published for The World Bank, 2000), 230–33.

where citizenship was not automatically granted to all legal residents. In Estonia in the mid- to late 1990s, ethnic Russians totaled approximately 29 percent, and non–ethnic Estonians as a whole totaled some 37 percent, of the population of slightly less than 1.5 million. Approximately 400,000, or 28 percent of the population (almost exclusively Russians and other Eastern Slavs), remained as noncitizens in the late 1990s, with up to 40 percent of them born in Estonia. Between 1992 and 1998, 105,000 people were naturalized in Estonia. While 120,000 persons obtained Russian citizenship, the Russian embassy declined to supply the Estonian government with the list of these individuals, and there may be quite a few "dual citizens" in the country now. In Latvia, ethnic Russians total approximately 33 percent, and all non–ethnic Latvians 45 percent, of the more than 2.5 million registered residents of the country. About 690,000, or 27 percent of the population, were still noncitizens in the late 1990s, 86 percent of them being Eastern Slavs. Only 11,000 people were naturalized between 1992 and 1998.[12]

Russian political leaders have been particularly hurt by Estonian and Latvian citizenship policies that neglected the January 1991 signing of treaties on the foundations of interstate relations between the RSFSR and these two other former Soviet republics, agreements that played an important role in dismantling the Soviet Union. The treaties' parties granted mutual recognition of sovereignty and agreed to grant the right for all USSR citizens residing in the respective republics to choose citizenship according to their wish. Later on, however, the governments of Latvia and Estonia reneged on their earlier promises and preferred an ethnonationalist path to building multicultural societies.

Language policies differ widely in the Soviet successor states. In some countries (the three Baltic states and Georgia), language politics have played an important role in the drive for independence since the late 1980s. In Belarus, however, few have opposed linguistic Russification. Following a 1995 referendum, Belarus is so far the only country that has upgraded the status of Russian to that of an official state language. This policy was a reaction against attempts on the part of the Belarusian elite to construct a new state on the heels of the USSR's dissolution, despite the low level of ethnic consciousness within the country and the lack of popular support for independence. More than 80 percent of the voters who participated in the May 1995 referendum approved the change of status for the Russian language.

Several other countries, including Moldova and Kyrgyzstan, established transitional periods or delays in enforcing certain provisions concerning the Russian language after they faced difficulties in implementing new legislation because of the significant linguistic Russification of the titular population and Russians' lack of knowledge of titular languages. Nevertheless, the use of the Russian language for official and educational purposes has been limited in the former Soviet republics since 1990, when language laws promoting a titular tongue were adopted everywhere but Turkmenistan. Russian is still widely used for communication between people of different nationalities, but the general trend leans toward switching to the titular languages.[13] Opinion polls show that Russians in the newly independent states perceive language policy as one of the major factors worsening their social, career, and educational opportunities. In 1994, this was the opinion of 97 percent of urban Russians in Moldova and 68 percent of urban Russians in Kyrgyzstan.[14] The behavior of Russians under these circumstances varies from rapidly learning local languages (Latvia) to being reluctant to do so and choosing emigration (Central Asia).

The most critical linguistic situation exists in Ukraine and Kazakhstan, where the Russification of titular nationalities prompted nationalists in these countries to adopt assertive policies that affected not only Russians but the titular Russian speakers as well, and there have been active internal political struggles over these issues in the two countries. In Ukraine, the issue of the status of the Russian language is part of both local and state politics. Some local governments use their authority to further decrease the legal status of Russian, while others do exactly the opposite.[15] Despite the protests from Russian officials, Kazakhstan passed a law in 1997 that did not favor the use of the Russian language. One of the new law's most controversial provisions proclaims that all television broadcasting, irrespective of the station's ownership, must be equally divided between Russian and Kazakh languages. In a situation where the audience is predominantly Russian speaking, irrespective of ethnicity, and where there are not enough journalists capable of working in Kazakh, the legislation seemed inappropriate to many Kazakhstani citizens.[16] Similarly, one of Ukraine's major linguistic battles has centered on radio and television. A 1997 conference in Ukraine, in which government officials participated, recommended ensuring a complete switch by all state- and private-owned stations to the Ukrainian language because "the negative consequences [of using a non-state language] are no less a threat to national security than are violence, prostitution, and various forms of anti-Ukrainian propaganda."[17]

In addressing the means by which the population of a state can be turned into a nation, Canovan suggested that it can usually be done by "mobilizing them for struggle, preferably against their former rulers."[18] In such a struggle, culture and language are the usual points of contention. From this admittedly narrow perspective, the populations of Kazakhstan and Ukraine can hardly fit into a definition of a modern cohesive civic nation.

It may be argued that the formation of the Russian people was not completed before the empire began to grow; that is to say, the Russian people is a product of empire building. This perspective reflects, among other things, the diversity of a large people spread over a vast territory that assimilated and included into itself many other groups that began to identify themselves as Russians. Following the dissolution of the Soviet state, which united not only different peoples but also different subgroups of the Russian people, the pre-existing distinctions among Russians could become stronger. Thus it can be said that the cohesiveness of the Russian people has been seriously challenged by the collapse of the Soviet Union. However, there are several long-term "structural" factors that can facilitate consolidation of the Russian diaspora communities and make the shared common culture an important basis of their unity. These factors are the urban way of life, good education, and a negative dynamic in their social status (in comparison to that of the indigenous people), leading to a strong feeling of deprivation and reactive nationalism.

"The Law of Colonial Ingratitude" in Eurasia

Hugh Seton-Watson asserted that "opposition arises not when an imperial power brutally suppresses a conquered people, but when it brings them material improvements and opportunities for education and social mobility." He called this phenomenon "the law of colonial ingratitude."[19] The Soviet Union was not exempt from this law, and the Russians living in Soviet republics felt its effects long before the collapse of the state.

The Russians in the former Soviet republics, in comparison with the indigenous groups, possessed some important advantages: among them, urban residency and better education. With the important exception of northern Kazakhstan, Russians have been highly concentrated in cities.[20] In all former Soviet republics, excluding Kazakhstan and Kyrgyzstan, the percentage of Russians living in urban areas ranged between 85 and 92 percent, and they have been concentrated primarily in the capital cities of the republics.[21] Because of the process of indigenization in non-Russian republics throughout the Soviet period, the number of cities that became republican capitals with a predominantly indigenous population increased from a surprising two in late Imperial Russia (1897) to a still low six (out of fourteen) in 1989.[22] Russians continued to dominate in industrial and professional occupations.[23]

Analysis of the 1989 Soviet census shows that Russians were better educated than the indigenous peoples in all former Soviet republics but Georgia (see table 6). This trend cannot be attributed to the fact that Russians were predominantly urban dwellers, whereas indigenous groups lagged behind because of their significant rural presence. Even in urban areas, the percentage of people with postsecondary (higher and "special secondary"[24]) education was higher among Russians than among the indigenous populations in all republics, with Georgia again being the only exception. The gap was particularly wide in Tajikistan, Turkmenistan, Kazakhstan, Uzbekistan, Moldova, and Belarus. In these republics, with the exception of Belarus, Russians were particularly hurt after the dissolution of the Soviet Union, when state policies became much more favorable to the indigenous peoples at the alleged expense of the better-educated Russians. The gap was not so wide, but was nevertheless present, in the Baltic states and Kyrgyzstan.[25]

Possessing such evident advantages as better education and urban residency, the Russians in the former Soviet republics nevertheless felt deprived of many privileges allegedly enjoyed by titular nationalities. It is important to emphasize that these feelings started to develop long before the dissolution of the Soviet Union: In the last decades of the USSR's existence, significant changes occurred in the status of Russians living in the non-Russian republics and, even more important, in their perceptions of themselves. By the 1980s there was a widespread feeling among Russians that they had become the victims of Soviet nationality policy in the non-Russian republics. Emigration of Russians from the non-Russian republics, which began in the 1970s and accelerated in the 1980s (see the next section of this chapter), was a dramatic reflection

Table 6. Percentage of people over 15 with postsecondary education, 1989

Country	Russians	Indigenous	Urban Russians	Urban Indigenous
Belarus	47	26	50	33
Armenia	45	35	45	40
Turkmenistan	45	18	45	26
Uzbekistan	44	22	45	30
Moldova	43	19	46	31
Lithuania	42	31	44	38
Tajikistan	42	16	44	25
Azerbaijan	40	25	42	35
Ukraine	40	27	42	35
Georgia	39	40	41	51
Estonia	37	31	38	35
Kyrgyzstan	36	23	40	36
Kazakhstan	34	28	54	37
Latvia	34	28	37	32

Source: Calculated on the basis of data contained in *Itogi vsesoiuznoi prepesi naseleniya 1989 goda, tom VII: Natsional'nyi sostav naseleniia SSSR* (The results of the 1989 all-Union population census, vol. VII: The USSR population by nationality) (Minneapolis: East View Press, 1993), 60–133.

of the change in their status. Additional evidence is suggested by the fact that in the 1980s, children from mixed marriages in the republics began to choose the indigenous nationality, while previously they would have been more likely to identify themselves as Russians.[26] These developments unfolded simultaneously with the "awakening" of the indigenous groups demanding fuller control over their republics.

In the 1990s, a great deal of research was done on the process of nation building in the former Soviet republics during the Soviet period.[27] This research suggested that nation building fostered the growth of indigenous non-Russian nationalism.[28] Two sets of developments shaped this process. First, a critical mass of well-educated, indigenous elites capable of articulating nationalistic aspirations had formed in most Soviet republics by the 1980s. A type of ethnicity-based "affirmative action" that gave preferences to the indigenous peoples in their respective republics was an important part of Soviet nationality policy. (This was a manifestation of Vladimir Lenin's idea of overcoming "actual inequalities among Soviet nationalities" and a favorite topic for the vast apologetic Soviet literature on the "success of Lenin's nationality policy."[29]) This policy furnished important changes by the 1980s, including a larger number of indigenous students in institutions of higher education,[30] an increased presence of intelligentsia among the non-Russians in both the non-Russian republics and the autonomous republics of the RSFSR,[31] and growth in the number of non-Russians in prestigious occupational slots in most republics.[32] However, Russians did not give up their domination in important industrial enterprises and republican branches of state ministries. Party representation and leadership was a more complex affair; native cadres often occupied more visible—but not necessarily more powerful—positions.

Second, the institutional structure of the Soviet Union facilitated the increasing domination by the non-Russians in their home republics. When the iron grip of Stalinism was released, the indigenous populations began to take advantage of opportunities given to them by the ethnic-based structure of the USSR, and the process of granting decision-making authority to the indigenous elites in their home republics gained momentum during the Brezhnev era. This phenomenon has been called a "two-tier system" by Robert Kaiser or a "displacement of nationhood to substate level" by Rogers Brubaker.[33] The Soviet Union remained a supranational entity in which Russians nevertheless dominated in holding key positions in all-Union institutions and enjoying cultural rights throughout the whole country, a fact that was often pointed out by non-Russians. As a rule, Russians also occupied such key positions in each republic as the second secretary of the party organization, commander of the military district, and head of the republican branch of the KGB. In the non-Russian republics, however, the indigenous peoples were engaged in an intense process of their own nation building. For the Russians in the republics, the Moscow-based all-Union structures that were dominated by their ethnic kin were of more symbolic than practical significance, while the republican institutions dominated by titular groups affected their daily lives much more directly.

Thus the feeling that Russians were strangers in other peoples' midsts outside Russia began to intensify slowly in the two decades before the dissolution of the Soviet Union. After the breakup of the USSR, this perception became even more intense as Russians found themselves in what they saw as the "national states" created by and for other ethnic groups. Of course, this is a rough generalization that overlooks huge differences between, for example, eastern Ukraine, where such feelings have not been so strong and, say, Latvia, where the Russians' sense of alienation from the local population has increased dramatically. Paul Kolstoe correctly notes that in the newly independent states, the new governing structures display "civic" as well as "ethnic" elements: "In country after country, one finds these rival conceptions of nationhood dwelling in an uneasy cohabitation."[34] The proportion of these elements in each newly independent state varies, thus creating different levels of alienation for local Russians.

All former Soviet republics have adopted ethnopolitical myths identifying the state as a homeland of a specific, "indigenous" people.[35] This trend is reflected in the names of the new states, their flags, anthems, political emblems, official histories and holidays, pantheons of national heroes, and language policies. Walker Connor's generalization concerning the impact of such developments upon diasporas is quite applicable to the current environment in most Soviet successor states. In his opinion:

> Diasporas are viewed at best as outsiders, strangers within the gates. They may be tolerated, even treated most equitably, and individual members of the diaspora may achieve the highest office. Their stay may be multigenerational, but they remain outsiders in the eyes of the indigenous people, who reserve the inalienable right to assert their primary and exclusive proprietary claim to the homeland, should they so desire. Moreover, in a number of cases, what superficially might pass for the peaceful acceptance of a diaspora has been due to the lack of means to purge the homeland of an alien presence.[36]

The independence the Soviet republics acquired in 1991 has been interpreted by many indigenous ideologists, politicians, and intellectuals, as well as by some Western scholars specializing in a particular republic, as the establishment of "peoples'" control over their fate. However, it may be argued that independence was achieved primarily in the name of a particular ethnic group and not in the name of the multicultural population living in each republic. According to Kolstoe, "the titular ethnos is everywhere becoming 'the state-bearing' nation."[37] Intellectually, this conceptualization of independence has relied on the Romantic historicist tradition, claiming that humanity could be divided neatly into nations, stipulating that culturally or ethnically defined nations possessed sacred rights, and therefore downplaying individual human rights and due respect for minorities.[38]

Analysis of the newly adopted constitutions in the post-Soviet states might provide some important insights into the legal and ideological environment and the official attitudes toward Russians as a nontitular people in the newly independent states. The preambles of most of these new constitutions stress historical traditions of statehood of their titular peoples (Armenia, Azerbaijan, Belarus, Georgia, Lithuania, Ukraine, Uzbekistan), thus making an explicit link to the pre-Soviet and pre-Russian periods, when the titular people allegedly enjoyed independence. In Armenia, for example, the restoration of the sovereign state is perceived in the constitution as a fulfillment of "the sacred message of their freedom loving ancestors."[39] Reconstruction of the past is usually based on the assumption that a titular ethnos is a continuous and unchangeable entity that can be easily traced many centuries back. In this context, Russians, as well as any other minorities, may be perceived as recent settlers, outsiders with no historically justifiable claims to a titular group's homeland.

The most significant constitutional provision, which sets a framework for the status of Russians in the newly independent states, is the distinction between the "indigenous" groups and the rest of the population; it is explicitly drawn in Estonia, Kazakhstan, Kyrgyzstan, Lithuania, Moldova, and Ukraine. In the preamble of the Ukrainian constitution, which is one of the most civic in spirit, there are nevertheless references to both "the Ukrainian nation" and "all the Ukrainian people."[40] In the post-Soviet context, where the term "nation" has a decidedly ethnic connotation, this distinction signifies the separation between ethnic Ukrainians and others. Article 11 of the constitution declares that "the state promotes consolidation and development of the Ukrainian nation, of its historical consciousness, traditions and culture; and also the development of the ethnic, cultural, linguistic and religious identity of all

indigenous peoples and national minorities of Ukraine."[41] In such a
way, the state views promoting the national consciousness of different
ethnic groups, with an evident emphasis on ethnic Ukrainians, as
an important task, while nothing is said about consolidating the new
civic nation.

The constitution of Kazakhstan emphasizes that the state has been
created "on the ancient *(iskonny)* Kazakh land." At the same time, Russians living in northern Kazakhstan claim that they came there at least
four hundred years ago and founded all the country's major cities. In
Kyrgyzstan, the state seeks to "secure national revival of the Kyrgyz." In
Moldova, the constitution rather vaguely states that "while growing into
a nation the Moldovan people has given strong evidence of the historical and ethnic continuity in its statehood." In Turkmenistan, only a
Turkmen may become president.[42] In Estonia, the state will "guarantee
the preservation of the Estonian nation and its culture throughout the
ages."[43] Besides, the Estonian constitution contains numerous provisions that curb civil and political rights of noncitizens and stateless
persons (who are overwhelmingly Russian), which is very unusual for
a basic law.[44] In Lithuania, only ethnic Lithuanians are considered the
"people" entitled to the advantages of statehood because "the Lithuanian
people . . . having preserved its spirit, native language, writing, and customs . . . approves and declares this Constitution."[45] Many post-Soviet
constitutions seem to confirm the following observation of Michael
Walzer: ". . . bring the 'people' into political life and they will arrive,
marching in tribal ranks and orders, carrying with them their own languages, historic memories, customs, beliefs, and commitments."[46]

Citizenship policy in the newly independent states also highlights
the status of the Russian minorities in these countries. As a manifestation of membership in the state, citizenship can serve as a powerful
vehicle for forging the new civic identities that may rival (and eventually replace) the old ethnic ones. Apart from the discriminatory citizenship policies in Latvia and Estonia, the ethnic factor has a legal dimension in some other newly independent states as well. For instance, in
Armenia, Kazakhstan, Kyrgyzstan, and Turkmenistan, it is easier for a
person who belongs to the titular nationality to acquire citizenship by
"admission."[47]

To a certain extent, the collapse of the Soviet Union meant the inter-
ruption of the trend toward universalism and signified a return to

parochialism. These developments led to "self-victimization" of the Russian minorities, whose members traditionally perceived themselves as bearers of "progress" and "internationalism."[48] However, these Russian communities have thus far failed to create vocal elites capable of formulating their interests and demands on the political arenas of the newly independent states, with the partial and controversial exceptions of Crimea and Pridnestrovye.[49] One of the main reasons for this failure has been the lack of a tradition of organizing along ethnic lines; the ideas of ethnonationalism have never served as an instrument for Russian political mobilization. Since the period of industrialization, Russians have been closely connected to cosmopolitan cities, large-scale industrial production, and a big multinational state. Small-scale community networks have been much less characteristic of Russians than of many titular groups. Such grassroots ties have been crucial for forging ethnic solidarity among many smaller ethnic groups in the former Soviet Union. Russians, especially outside Russia, feel like fragments of the collapsed state, abandoned by everyone, including their alleged homeland. These people have not overcome the psychological shock of the breakup of the Soviet Union. Discontent and disillusionment are widespread, and these feelings and attitudes are reflected in the process of migration.

Migrants and Refugees: "Our Country Is No More, But We Still Exist"

International migrations in the territory of the former Soviet Union have had a significant impact on the development of all Eurasian states, as millions of people change their residency, jobs, social environment, and lifestyles. Being ethnically specific, such migration has changed the composition of the populations of these countries. The International Organization for Migration's Technical Cooperation Center for Europe and Central Asia emphasized in its first annual report: "With 4,207,000 persons, repatriants (defined as persons returning voluntarily to the country of their citizenship or origin for the purpose of permanent residence) constitute by far the largest migrant group in the CIS region. ... The overwhelming majority of the Russian-speaking repatriants are

Russians and are directed toward the Russian Federation."[50] This migration trend has led to a gradual shrinking of the collective Russian diaspora and has made the Russian Federation, by dint of sheer numbers, more ethnically Russian.

Several different forms of population movement between the former Soviet republics and Russia can be identified, including refugees fleeing the horrors of armed conflicts and direct violence; forced migration of people suffering ethnic discrimination and hostile attitudes; movements occurring because of gloomy economic, career, or educational prospects in host societies; and temporary labor moves. The "push" factors are characteristic of the first two types of migration, while a combination of "push" and "pull" motivations prompts the third and the fourth types of moves. A survey conducted by Hilary Pilkington suggests that push factors outweigh pull factors by almost nine to one.[51] Refugees and forced migrants, whose age composition is very similar to that of the general population, come to Russia because of urgent necessity. As a rule, younger individuals with relatively higher education and labor skills who hope to improve their social and economic status can be found among the last two types of migrants. "Regular" resettlers who buy a one-way ticket to Russia and "guest" workers who move temporarily represent a long-term phenomenon, shaped by relatively better economic prospects in selected regions of Russia. By coming to Russia, such migrants hope to eliminate the ethnic factor in determining their opportunities and are ready for the inevitable temporary difficulties involved in resettling.

These four categories of migrants are, of course, ideal types, which may be suitable for certain academic purposes, but they can by no means reflect all the complexities of post-Soviet population movements. Pilkington, for example, has challenged the traditional dichotomy between economic (voluntary) and political (involuntary) migrants that is found in academic literature and state practices. Her field interviews among refugees in Russia confirmed that it was a constructed dichotomy used primarily for institutional purposes. Analyzing the reasons for migration cited by respondents led Pilkington to conclude that "a minority of respondents had 'fled' their homes, while the vast majority articulated their motivations for migration in a way which clearly illustrated that ethnic issues were inextricably entwined with socioeconomic and political dissatisfactions."[52]

Pre-1991 (interrepublic) and post-Soviet (interstate) migration changed the composition of "the Russian people" and the proportions of the "core" community within Russia and its "sister" communities in the near abroad. From 1926 to 1979, the number of Russians living outside RSFSR increased from 5 to 24 million (or from 6 to 17 percent of all Soviet Russians), the result of population redistribution stemming from industrialization, World War II, the "Virgin Lands" development program, and so on. Intermarriages and state subsidies for the economic development of the relatively "backward" peripheral areas of the Soviet Union also contributed to this trend.[53] There is a belief, especially popular in the Baltic states, that the Soviet authorities consciously conducted the policy of Russification of the non-Russian republics by sending significant numbers of Russians to work and live there.[54] This assumption has not been seriously substantiated by archival research, which fails to show whether it was a deliberate state policy, a consequence of economic considerations, or both. Moreover, classic migration studies explain most population moves in the former Soviet Union by individual rational choice and job and lifestyle opportunities. According to Robert Lewis and Richard Rowland, migration in the USSR was primarily voluntary and unorganized.[55]

The historic pattern of Russian migration within the former Soviet Union (from Russia to other republics) changed dramatically in the late 1970s. Starting in this period, Russians began migrating back to Russia in greater numbers than they were emigrating out. The dissolution of the Soviet Union did not trigger but, rather, accelerated the process. The absolute numbers of Russians began to decrease in Georgia in the 1960s, in Azerbaijan in the 1970s, and in Armenia and Turkmenistan in the 1980s.[56] Also in the 1980s, there was a net outflow of Russians from all Central Asian republics, Kazakhstan, and Moldova.[57] The Baltic region was the last to join the trend. Starting in 1989, there has been a moderate net outflow (several tens of thousands annually) from all three countries into Russia.[58]

After the dissolution of the Soviet Union, Russians emigrated primarily from zones of armed conflicts. Between 1989 and 1995, Armenia lost more than 50 percent of Russians registered there, while Tajikistan lost 48 percent; Azerbaijan, 42 percent; and Georgia, 39 percent.[59] Overall, non-Slavic countries of the former Soviet Union lost 17 percent of their Russian populations between 1991 and 1996.[60] According to the State Statistical Department of Russia, less than 23 million ethnic Russians remained in the near abroad in 1996.[61] In light of Russia's natural population decline, immigration from the former Soviet republics became the only source of Russian demographic growth in the 1989–1996 period. In 1995, Russia (together with Turkmenistan) became one of only two post-Soviet states with a positive net migration rate.[62]

The total annual number of immigrants to Russia between 1989 and 1995 varies from 700,000 to 1.1 million people, depending on the method of calculation used.[63] Immigration became more ethnically pronounced after the disintegration of the Soviet Union: the percentage of Russians in overall immigration increased from 46 percent in 1989 to 61–66 percent in 1992–1995.[64] In the 1990s, the major sources of migration to Russia were the five Soviet successor states with predominantly Muslim populations: Kazakhstan (738,000 in 1991–1995), Uzbekistan (420,000 in 1991–1995), Kyrgyzstan (225,000 in 1991–1995), Azerbaijan (211,000 in 1991–1995), and Tajikistan (191,000 in 1991–1994).[65] Migration has been the major factor contributing to the changes in the nationality composition of most post-Soviet states (see table 7).

Ethnic conflicts and tensions are cited as major incentives for migration to Russia from the newly independent states. This was the case for 70 percent of migrants from Azerbaijan, 64 percent of migrants from Tajikistan, 63 percent of migrants from Georgia, 53 percent of migrants from Lithuania, 51 percent of migrants from Uzbekistan, and 50 percent of migrants from Armenia.[66] In some of these countries, migration was triggered by the armed ethnic conflicts between the non-Russians, while in others, tensions between Russians and the titulars stimulated population outflow.

After a peak in 1994, when approximately 1.1 million people moved to Russia, a downward trend in immigration to Russia was registered in 1995–1998. In 1995, 842,000 people immigrated to Russia; in 1996 the number was 700,000.[67] In 1997, the number dropped to 490,200 immigrants, and in 1998 to 439,400.[68] The decrease in the number of migrants is attributable to the lower rate of emigration from many countries, especially Kyrgyzstan, Uzbekistan, and Georgia. This unprecedented decline surprised even the authoritative *CIS Migration Report,* which forecast 700,000–900,000 people per year in 1997–1998.[69] The new trend can be explained by several factors. Most Russians who had the

Table 7. Russians in Selected Former Soviet Republics, 1989 and 1995

Country	Thousands		Percent		Change (2–1), thousands	Change (5/1*100), percent
	1989	1995	1989	1995	1989–1995	1989–1995
	1	2	3	4	5	6
Kazakhstan	6,228	5,783	37.7	34.7	-445	-7.1
Kyrgyzstan	917	720	21.4	16.1	-197	-21.4
Latvia	906	820	34.0	32.8	-85	-9.4
Lithuania	344	311	9.4	8.4	-34	-9.7
Russia	119,866	123,070	81.3	83	3,204	2.7

Source: Tim Heleniak, "Migration and Population Change in the Soviet Successor States," (paper presented at the 28th National Convention of the American Association for the Advancement of Slavic Studies, Boston, Mass., November 14–17, 1996), table 8.

means to move from war-torn areas had already done so. The tremendous difficulties that the newcomers faced in Russia, where they lacked governmental support and usually found jobs well below their skill level, discouraged those who lived under less than extreme circumstances. Agreements on simplified methods of obtaining citizenship that Russia signed with Kazakhstan and Kyrgyzstan provided relief for those who decided to wait and see rather than to move in a hurry. However, Kazakhstan was the only country of the CIS where the number of emigrants to Russia increased slightly. Almost half of all migrants to Russia come from Kazakhstan now.[70]

Although population shifts occurred between Ukraine, Belarus, and Russia from 1992 to 1997, the net flows were relatively insignificant. Nevertheless, in 1994, the net migration to Russia from Ukraine and Belarus began to increase, primarily because of the outflow of ethnic Russians. Migration between these three countries seems to be based primarily on economic and personal considerations. In the fall of 1991, interethnic tensions were cited as a reason to move to Russia by only 4 percent of migrants from Ukraine and by 2 percent of migrants from Belarus (an average of 46 percent of resettlers from other former Soviet republics cited this reason for migration).[71]

Temporary work force migration is another phenomenon contributing to population shifts from Ukraine and Belarus to Russia. At any given moment, about 300,000 people can be found in Moscow and several other major Russian cities working as temporary drivers, construction workers, and so forth.[72] Migrant workers from these two countries make up more than 70 percent of the total number of foreign workers in Russia.[73] The reason for this phenomenon is the relative economic well-being of some of Russia's regions that allows migrant workers to earn higher wages. In Moscow, for example, Ukrainian construction workers earn seven to ten times and drivers three times more than at home.[74] Between 1989 and 1993, the share of ethnic Russians in the total number of migrants to Russia increased from 49 to 63 percent in Ukraine and from 43 to 61 percent in Belarus, while the share of Ukrainians and Belarusians in outflows from Russia to the respective countries grew from 38 to 46 percent in both cases.[75] It is still unclear whether these numbers represent a strengthening trend of ethnically selective migration between the three Slavic states of the former Soviet Union. If that is the case, it might mean that the processes of ethnic "unmixing" that are currently unfolding in Eurasia now include these three states as well.[76]

From 1992 to 1997, refugees and forced migrants made up one-third of all newcomers to Russia.[77] In 1995, 21 percent came from war-torn Tajikistan, followed by refugees from Uzbekistan, Kazakhstan, Georgia, Azerbaijan, and Kyrgyzstan.[78] Most refugees and forced migrants settle in the areas of Russia adjacent to their exodus points, such as the Urals, Volga, and the Northern Caucasus regions. In the beginning of 1997, the total number of registered refugees was approximately one million.[79] In 1996, ethnic Russians constituted 76 percent of the refugees and forced migrants in the country, while they made up only 58 percent among all immigrants from the CIS and the Baltic states. As *CIS Migration Report* noted, "Such a discrepancy can be attributed either to the fact that Russians experience greater pressure in the countries of origin as compared to other nonindigenous groups, or that they are more sensitive to such pressure, or else that they are registered more easily."[80] Probably, the interplay of all three factors can explain this phenomenon.

In many cases, the process of social adaptation in Russia is extremely difficult for the newcomers. As well-known writer Svetlana Alexievich put it, "there are two Russias now—one lives in Russia itself, and the second one is beyond it, without time and place."[81] In this vein, one could say that migrants move from one Russia to another. They are often viewed as competitors for scarce resources or as aliens with different lifestyles and attitudes. As Pilkington's survey suggested, more than 70 percent of local respondents in the city of Ul'ianovsk, for example, associated the arrival of migrants from the former USSR with the aggravation of a housing shortage in their region, and 55 percent with the rise of unemployment.[82] Local Russians often refer to migrants as "Tajiks," or "Kyrgyz" —that is, by the name of their place of origin. They are considered to be the "other Russians," as pointed out by writer Boris Ryakhovsky.[83] The low level of ethnonational consciousness and the lack of traditions of ethnic solidarity are some of the reasons for the difficulties that Russian migrants experience in Russia. Alexievich quoted a Russian nurse who fled the horrors of war in Tajikistan only to find no better place to settle than an abandoned, radioactively contaminated zone close to Chernobyl:

> We are left without a homeland. We belong to nobody. All the Germans have left for Germany, Tartars went to the Crimea, but nobody needs the

Russians. What should we hope for? What should we wait for? Russia never
rescued its people, because it is big, limitless. We are always miserable, not
taken care of. Frankly, I do not feel that Russia is my homeland. We were
raised differently: our home was the Soviet Union. Now you do not know
how to save your soul. Nobody is ready to shoot here, and this is good
at least.[84]

Another Russian migrant, who also ended up in a contaminated
zone, provided the following dramatic account:

We used to have a motherland, and now there is none. Who am I? My mom
is a Ukrainian, my dad is a Russian. I was born and raised in Kyrgyzia and
married a Tartar. Who are our kids? What is their nationality? We are all
mixed, our blood is mixed. My kids are registered as Russians in our passports, but we are not Russians. We are the Soviets. But the country where I
was born does not exist anymore. There is neither the place we used to call
our motherland nor the time, that Soviet time which was also our motherland. . . . Our country does not exist anymore, but we still do. People flee.
Run. All Russian people. Soviet people. Nobody needs them. . . . Nobody
waits for them. . . .[85]

Neither these two women nor the author of the article seemed to
notice that the families had moved from Central Asia to Belarus and not
to Russia. For the "Soviet people," it does not make much difference.

The "unmixing" of the population along ethnic lines is taking place
in the former Soviet Union, though not with dramatic speed.[86] Russians, of course, are not the only ethnic group that is involved in this
process on the Eurasian continent. However, there are important differences between Russians and other groups. In addition to their significant absolute size, Russians are distinct from other peoples because (as
noted earlier) their "non-core" communities are dispersed throughout
the entire former Soviet Union, while other diasporas, as a rule, reside
in one or two neighboring states. Overall, about 2.4 million Russians
came to Russia from the near abroad from 1990 to 1996.[87]

It is important to note that Russians migrate mostly from the
regions where there are more cultural differences between themselves
and the indigenous population (for example, Central Asia and Transcaucasia). At least one million out of a total of four million Russians
who lived in these countries (excluding Kazakhstan) have already left.
Conversely, Russians remain in the states where they are less distinct
from titular nationalities (for example, Belarus and Ukraine) or are more

likely to be assimilated in the long run (for example, the Baltic states, excluding recent immigrants to these countries).

In spite of ethnic Russians' natural demographic decline, migration has stimulated the growth of the ethnic Russians' share in the population of Russia from 81 to 83 percent in the period 1989–1994.[88] This moderate change indicates a radical shift from the old trend, in which the percentage of Russians was diminishing in both the Soviet Union and RSFSR following World War II. However, there is no reason to believe that most Russians will "return" to their "historic homeland." Many Russians consider Ukraine, Belarus, Kazakhstan, or the Baltic states to be their homeland because several generations of their ancestors lived there. Besides, there are other powerful factors restraining migration, such as a lack of adequate affordable housing in Russia. Therefore, one may conclude that Russian diasporas will remain an important feature of all newly independent states of Eurasia for the foreseeable future.

The widely used term "repatriation"[89] may be very misleading when applied to the migration of Russians from the near abroad "back" to Russia. The term reflects an attempt to automatically apply the model of a fragmenting empire to the post-Soviet situation and a tacit assumption that common ethnicity always produces feeling of solidarity. Another popular term, "historic homeland" (used to describe the Russia to which migrants return) is also based on a primordialist perspective and an assumption that national identity is tied to a "bounded" territory and rooted in history.[90] These terms and perspectives are challenged by a postmodernist view of national identities as multiple and dynamic, constructed in the process of interactions between individuals and states. Pilkington's survey suggested that most Russians who have moved to Russia feel more like "Soviets" than ethnic Russians or Russian citizens. Two-thirds of the respondents expressly said that they did not consider their move to Russia a return to the homeland: Their true homeland, the Soviet Union, has been disembodied.[91] The notion of a native land has been uncertain, and simplistic models of postimperial "repatriation to a historic homeland" do not fully grasp the realities of post-Soviet transnational diasporas and the cultural complexities of a highly urbanized, industrialized, and mobile society. However, redefinition of migrants' identities will probably turn from a primarily Soviet into a Russian identity, so the question is whether "Russian" will take on civic or ethnic significance.

Typology of Russian Diasporas and Future Prospects

As suggested previously, Russian communities in the near abroad developed along different paths and can hardly be described by a single paradigm. In fact, it is probably more appropriate to delineate four major types of situations confronted by the Russian diasporas.

The first group consists of Russians intermingled with other Eastern Slavs;[92] the group includes Russians living in Belarus and parts of Ukraine.[93] They are very similar to Belarusians and Ukrainians in their social conditions, culture, and political orientations. Therefore, there are no significant out-migrations from these countries. Russians hardly constitute separate, well-defined communities in these countries, with the exceptions of Ukraine's Crimea and Galicia regions.[94] Hence, there is little basis for Russia to pursue a special policy toward them.

In Ukraine, about 12–15 percent of all marriages are between Ukrainians and Russians. Many people in this kind of marriage shift their self-identification from census to census, proving that cultural identities are somewhat fluid in Ukraine.[95] Fifty-six percent of Russians in the Russian Federation believe that Russians and Ukrainians are "one people."[96] In Ukraine, regional rather than ethnic differences have been the greatest problem. Both ethnic Russians and Ukrainians living in eastern Ukraine (unlike the Ukrainians of western Ukraine) are predominantly Russian speaking, vote in a similar way, and hold positive attitudes toward Russia. According to survey data gathered by the Kiev International Institute of Sociology, in 183 cities and villages of eastern Ukraine between 1991 and 1994, 82 percent of the population used Russian as their language of convenience, 61 percent wanted to have it as an equal "state" language along with Ukrainian, 49 percent thought that Ukraine and Russia should unite into one state, and 72 percent of ethnic Ukrainians were Russophones.[97] One of many manifestations of these attitudes was the move by legislators in the Kharkiv and Donetsk provinces to grant the Russian language the same status as Ukrainian in late 1996 and early 1997, a move supported by both local Russians and Ukrainians who spoke Russian as their first language. Indeed, the "gray area" of intermingled Ukrainians and Russians serves as a good buffer for both Ukrainian and Russian nationalists and diminishes tensions in and around Ukraine.[98]

In Belarus, the environment for Russians is shaped primarily by the fact that Belarusians have probably the weakest national consciousness in the former USSR. The majority of Belarusians hardly feel as though they constitute a nation separate from Russia, with its own distinct language, culture, and history. Russian and Belarusian citizens of Belarus have no trouble communicating with each other. The problem the Belarusian government faces is how to build a state that lacks a unique historical or ethnic background.[99]

In sum, it is misleading to talk about Russians in eastern Ukraine and Belarus, where they have lived for centuries, as a nonindigenous people or a minority, because they are not separated from titular groups by any identifiable characteristic. This situation hinders an active policy of the Russian Federation toward the Russian diasporas in these countries.

The second group of Russians in the near abroad consists of Russians living in compact communities in northern Kazakhstan, Crimea, northeastern Estonia, and Pridnestrovye. The presence of Russian communities in these areas potentially could result in calls for separatism or claims of ethnoterritorial autonomy. Pridnestrovye Russians have many features of the first group, because their regional identity is probably a more important factor than ethnicity. The difference is that, unlike in eastern and southern Ukraine, regionalism in Moldova has been much more explicit, having well-defined historical and geographic boundaries.[100] According to a 1993–1995 survey conducted by an international team of researchers headed by Jerry Hough and David Laitin, less than a quarter of the Russian respondents in Estonia, and less than half of respondents in Kazakhstan and Ukraine felt that they did not have the right to territorial autonomy, while more than 70 percent of Latvian Russians, who live primarily in big cities, shared this view.[101] Demands for territorial autonomy were first raised in the Crimea and Pridnestrovye in 1990, and in northern Kazakhstan and Estonia in 1992–1994. The governments of the newly independent states are well aware of the challenges they might face from compact Russian areas of settlement, and they constantly try to reduce any potential for separatism or drive for territorial autonomy. Kazakhstan has planned the most determined steps in this direction, developing a comprehensive territorial reform that envisions a radical change of ethnic composition in the country's administrative regions. At the center of the reform plan are the fusion of predominantly Russian regions with those where Kazakhs are in a majority and the encouragement of ethnic Kazakhs to move north.[102] In support of the plan, ethnic Kazakhs who repatriate from China and Mongolia are now settled in the country's northern regions.

Dispersed Russian communities constitute the third group, which includes Russians of Central Asia and Transcaucasia. In these regions, the cultural and educational differences between Russians and the host populations are significant, and Russians rapidly migrate to Russia in the face of armed conflicts, economic collapse, potential threats to their security, and dim prospects for higher education or promising careers for their children. Though officially there are no restrictions on political rights for Russians in these states, they are seriously underrepresented in the political arena; titular nationalities have monopolized the top positions and dominate representative political bodies through traditional kinship networks. For example, the titular group in Kazakhstan made up less than half of the population in 1994 but controlled 62 percent of the seats in the parliament; in 1995, it held 81 percent of senior positions in state agencies.[103] In most countries of this region, politics consists primarily of the struggle between indigenous clans, while the Russians remain political outsiders.

Finally, there are the Baltic Russian diasporas. Compared with other Russian communities, their situation better resembles the classic definition of a diaspora. Because the Baltic states are not CIS members and have stringent visa requirements, Baltic Russians are separated from Russia proper to a great extent. They are challenged by discriminatory citizenship laws in Latvia and Estonia but, surprisingly, do not flee to Russia at rates comparable to those of Central Asia or Transcaucasia. This phenomenon is attributable to three basic factors. First, there are no immediate threats to their security, as in areas of armed conflict and general political instability. Second, many of them (particularly in Latvia) have adopted behavior typical of a diaspora by starting business enterprises, primarily in trade and financial operations, and are therefore thriving economically; about 48 percent of Russian respondents in Latvia agreed that the best future for them would be to assimilate.[104] Third, those who work in failing industrial plants and factories (there is a greater proportion of this kind of Russian worker in the Baltic states, especially in Estonia, than in many other regions of the former Soviet Union) are simply less mobile and do not see any brighter prospects in Russia, where their qualifications are even less in demand.

Ukraine, Kazakhstan, Latvia, and Estonia are the "key" states, where "the Russian question" is crucial to security, political stability, success of the nationalization process, and construction of viable nation-states. Strong nationalist strains in the policies of these states may indicate the absence of cohesive nations. Ukraine, where Russians are not fundamentally separated from ethnic Ukrainians, and Kazakhstan, where the community of six million Russians lives compactly in the area adjacent to the Russian border, are extremely important for the self-perceptions of all Russians, the redefinition of "Russianness," and nation building, not only in these two countries but in Russia itself. Russians in Latvia and Estonia, who constitute significant minorities and are for all intents and purposes actually excluded from nation building, might become important actors in or, rather, instruments of geopolitical games (especially in the light of eventual North Atlantic Treaty Organization expansion into that area). For various reasons, the Russian question is not as internationally important in other regions of the former Soviet Union.

Robert Kaiser has developed a well-articulated theory linking the importance of a territorial homeland and the rise of national consciousness and self-awareness of the peoples of the former Soviet Union.[105] While Kaiser's theory provides a good framework for the analysis of nationalism in many of the former Soviet republics, this perspective has been the least applicable to the Russian people. A nebulous sense of homeland and the undefined boundaries of the Russian nation made the Russians one of the least consolidated nations by the time the USSR dissolved. Prior to 1991, the Russians' alleged homeland reached well beyond the area where Russian culture, language, religion, and traditions held sway. But after the collapse of the Soviet Union, the Russian state no longer occupied the entirety of this domain. According to polls conducted by the Russian Academy of Sciences' Institute for Ethnic and Anthropological Studies, from half to three-quarters of Russians in Lithuania, Kyrgyzstan, and Moldova named the Soviet Union as their "motherland" in 1992–1993.[106]

No longer hidden under an imperial veil, Russian ethnic identity has become more salient to Russians in both the Russian Federation and other Soviet successor states. Alternately, the emergence of fifteen

independent states has led inevitably to the weakening of political connections among Russians. This attenuation of political ties has ruptured
the centuries-old tradition of Russians grouping themselves around
the state. Sooner or later, these two trends may start to contradict each
other, which could result in one of two different directions. First, as has
happened many times in the history of Europe, a well-articulated common culture may come to be defined as the ideal political boundary,
leading to strong claims for all Russians to reunite under one political
roof. Second, Russians might disintegrate into a bunch of poorly connected communities within the successor states, while the core group
forms a new nation, together with other peoples, within the boundaries
of the Russian Federation. A primordial basis—in the form of a common culture and language, belief in sharing a common past from time
immemorial, and a sense of common origin and connection—does
exist in the minds of many Russians, irrespective of their current citizenship. But the social construction of the nation could take any form,
inclusive for all ethnic Russians or exclusive only for citizens of the
Russian Federation. So far, the second option seems more plausible.
Nevertheless, any political catastrophe in Russia—which cannot be
ruled out entirely—could shift the trend.

Some Russian diasporas in the former Soviet Union have developed a
dual attachment: loyalty to the political unit—the newly independent
state where they find themselves after the breakup—and a sense of
affiliation with the ethnic community, the "Russian people." They
receive various social rewards from the new state, while they retain their
emotional bond of kinship with fellow Russians. Many people have
tried to combine the claims of citizenship with the demands of ethnic
solidarity. Many historic diasporas (Jewish, Armenian, Greek, Irish)
extended their ethnic attachments to other ethnic fragments in other
states and to the core ethnie in an external homeland.[107] The Russians,
thus far, have demonstrated a limited ability and desire to build such
interstate networks. They have also demonstrated little loyalty to the
Russian state, which, in their view, abandoned them.[108] However, the
idea of the "Russian people," one and united, could be ascendant in the
coming years.

Russian ethnonational consciousness may become stronger in the
Russian communities outside Russia than in Russia itself. This is typical for the periphery of most nations, where there is more intensified

interaction with the neighboring peoples in building a stronger common identity.[109] However, without Russia's support, these communities can hardly unite under a single political roof on the basis of their common culture. It is safe to assume that the near abroad policy of the Russian Federation, if indeed there is one, is the key potential factor for raising the Russian diasporas to international significance, a factor addressed in the next chapter. These communities are poorly organized and have almost no links to one another. Thus if Russia decides to move toward uniting and mobilizing the Russian communities, it will have to appeal to Russian nationalism, which is a very abstract notion at best. While there has been little evidence of Russia's desire to take such action so far, the possibility of future attempts should not be discarded.

Policy of the
Russian Federation
toward the Russian Diasporas

ONTRARY TO THE BELIEF that Russian policy in the near abroad has
been imperialistic and aggressive over the issues concerning
the new Russian diasporas, Russian policy has instead been
reasonably moderate in some of its features and tremendously ineffective
in others. Indeed, in those undertakings that could destabilize the whole
region, Russian policy has been particularly ineffective. As a result of such
moderation and ineffectiveness, a great discrepancy exists between the
boastful, assertive rhetoric of Russia's leaders and the actual policy of
Russia in its relations with the Russian diasporas. Of course, other factors also contribute to the stability of the region, including: (1) restraint
exercised by other actors, primarily by the governments of the newly
independent states; (2) the political weakness and lack of organization
of Russian communities in the near abroad; and (3) Western support
of the sovereignty and territorial integrity of Eurasian states. These factors could recede in light of an aggressive Russia, however, just as Serbia
ignored analogous constraints in a similar situation. It is the very fact
that Moscow has chosen not to ignore these constraints that needs to
be explained.

The argument regarding moderation and ineffectiveness of Russian
policy can be supported by analyzing three Russian policies toward
Russian diasporas in the near abroad: (1) Russia's lost battle for dual citizenship, (2) the adoption of a very moderate governmental program

and its actual conversion into the cornerstone of the official perspective of the Russian state, and (3) multilateralism as a restraining factor in relations among the Soviet successor states. All three of these policies are recent manifestations that fully surfaced only from 1995 to 2000; they belie generalizations about contemporary Russian policy that are based on the rhetoric and aspirations of the 1993–94 period.

Dual Citizenship

After the disintegration of the Soviet Union, many who found themselves in other successor states looked upon Russia as a destination of possible migration or as a power that might help to ensure their rights and interests. Their bonds with Russia, however, were not always clear. For some, these bonds were ties of ethnicity. For others, Russia was a place of birth and long-time residence. And for many Russified intellectuals of non-Russian origin, Russia represented the center of "Soviet civilization." These people viewed Russia as the successor of a culturally diverse Soviet Union that was very different from the more ethnically oriented newly independent states. In most cases, nostalgia for communism had little to do with this viewpoint.

Recent demographic trends illustrate the pull of Russia for so many citizens of successor states. As was shown in chapter 4, more people now migrate into than out of Russia. More people in the near abroad want to establish some sort of cultural, business, or political relations with Russia than do residents of Russia with the other former Soviet republics. Moscow and other large Russian cities are full of cosmopolitan businesses, criminal organizations, cultural elites, political dissidents, and opposition activists from every former republic of the Soviet Union.[1] It should be noted, however, that most of those who immigrate into Russia are ethnic Russians, and most of those who seek to establish some sort of secure ties with Russia, while residing permanently in another state, are also ethnic Russians.

The Russian government has felt the tension between the concept of a Russian state within the allegedly arbitrarily drawn borders of the

RSFSR on the one hand, and the actual domain of Russian culture, language, and national consciousness on the other. The idea of dual citizenship was originally perceived as something of a panacea for all the problems associated with this discrepancy between the boundaries of the newly emerging state and those of the newly emerging nation. Seizing upon this idea, the Russian government decided to grant Russian citizenship to all Russians in the near abroad, as well as to people of other nationalities who had some sort of historic tie with the territory of Russia. Such a conferral of rights was to be a supplement to a local citizenship granted by another independent state. From the perspective of international law, it was an ambiguous idea. Most countries of the world discourage dual citizenship because they are apprehensive about split loyalties, especially in times of war. The Universal Declaration of Human Rights established the right for only one nationality per individual. However, more than forty countries around the world have recognized, though sometimes reluctantly, dual citizenship as a fact of life.[2]

In the opinion of officials in the Russian government, the advantages of dual citizenship for Russians in the near abroad seemed to be threefold. First, such a policy looked much more "civilized" (a favorite term of the Russian political elite in early 1990s) than the establishment of some sort of "special relationship" with coethnics abroad. It stressed the civic, not ethnic, nature of the Russian polity and policy and thus held the promise of protecting the Russian nation without exacerbating ethnic conflict. Indeed, in his memoirs, Andrei Kozyrev wrote in precisely such terms: "We cannot put an ethnic factor in the foundation of our policy. It would lead to conflicts among nationalities like those in Yugoslavia."[3]

The second perceived advantage of dual citizenship policy was that it could help to curb an uncontrolled flow of migrants to Russia by providing them with some sort of security and peace of mind in their host state. Given the immense financial drain, Russia could not easily accommodate the newcomers. Both the Russian elite and the public are even less inclined to be dragged into wars to annex diaspora territories. Abdulakh Mikitaev, then chief of the Citizenship Directorate of the Presidential Administration and chairman of the Presidential Commission on Citizenship, candidly expressed the sentiment in an interview with a journal published by the Russian government: "One of the major tasks of state policy, in my view, is the prevention of a mass exodus of people from the states of the former Union."[4]

The third advantage of dual citizenship was geared more toward self-aggrandizement than to conflict avoidance. The policy could serve as a convenient source of leverage and influence on the neighboring states and as an instrument for implementing a Russian policy of domination and hegemony. The protection by a powerful state of its citizens abroad has become normal practice in modern international relations; such a policy has often been used by the United States in Latin America and by France in Africa. If Russia could maintain millions of its citizens in neighboring states, no one would be able to challenge its absolute and unrestrained domination in Eurasia.

Actually, the idea of dual citizenship replaced an earlier policy that was less attentive to the interests of Russians in the near abroad. In 1992, Russia adopted a strategy of new state building, defined as the creation and stabilization of new state institutions within the borders of RSFSR, establishment of the inviolability of borders between former Soviet republics, and development of relations with neighboring states as equal, fully independent entities.[5] This official policy lasted only about a year; indeed, it stood in tension with the supplementary political rhetoric of top officials, who boasted of their willingness to defend "compatriots abroad."[6] In April 1992, only four months after the Belaya Vezha agreements, which put an end to the Soviet Union, Boris Yeltsin declared in a speech at the Sixth Congress of People's Deputies: "Twenty-five million of our compatriots in these countries must not and will not be forgotten by Russia."[7] In another speech at the same congress a few days later, he admitted: " . . . we still defend our compatriots poorly."[8] But in 1992, these sentiments remained at the level of rhetoric.

In 1993, the idea of dual citizenship as an effective tool for the defense of compatriots started to take shape, and President Yeltsin took the lead. The concept then found supporters in the Supreme Soviet and was promoted by Foreign Minister Kozyrev, as well as by the Presidential Commission on Citizenship and, significantly, the Ministry of Defense. The new Russian military doctrine adopted in 1993 identified abuse of "the rights, freedoms, and legal interests of citizens of the Russian Federation in foreign countries" as an "external danger,"[9] and the creation of such a category of citizens served as a precondi-tion for subsequently justifying the Russian military's intervention in their defense. Thus, with his usual ham-handed grace, General Pavel Grachev entered the arena of discourse and inadvertently undermined the initiative by showing Russia's neighbors all possible consequences of the new strategy.

The results of the December 1993 parliamentary elections strengthened the assertive, nationalistic trends in official policy. In January 1994, Foreign Minister Kozyrev organized a conference of Russian ambassadors to the countries of the Commonwealth of Independent States and the Baltics. Also participating were the Russian interior minister, deputy defense minister, and other high officials. In his speech to the conference, Kozyrev declared that protection of the rights of "compatriots" in the near abroad was "the main strategic task of Russia's foreign policy" and that dual citizenship was the major instrument for fulfilling that task. This was the first time that the issue of dual citizenship was elevated to such a high place on Russia's foreign policy agenda.[10]

Also in 1994, substantial support for the idea came from the Federal Migration Service (FMS), an agency of the Russian government. According to the Federal Migration Program, adopted by presidential decree in August 1994, " . . . it is necessary to strive for recognition of dual citizenship by these states."[11] The reason for support of the idea from this quarter was clear: According to the FMS forecast, the projected minimal number of forced migrants from the near abroad to Russia was more than 800,000 during 1994–1996.[12] Their intermediate variant projected 2–3 million; the maximal projection was 4–6 million. Yet the Federal Migration Program was financed to accommodate only 400,000 people, or half the minimal forecast. Accordingly, the position of the Federal Migration Service is easy to explain: it hoped that dual citizenship would keep many potential migrants to Russia at home.

By 1994, a strong coalition for dual citizenship had formed. It included the major branches of the Russian government, significant constituencies within Russia that refused to accept the notion that Russians outside Russia had suddenly become foreigners, and Russian communities in the near abroad. The latter were the most passionate supporters of dual citizenship. According to opinion polls, three-quarters of the Russian respondents in Tashkent, 85 percent of respondents in Moldovan cities, and 58 percent of respondents in Kyrgyzstan's cities supported the idea of dual citizenship.[13] Citizenship in a newly independent state has been much less valuable for ethnic Russians than for titular groups. For example, only 37 percent of Russians expressed pride in being citizens of Uzbekistan, while 87 percent of Uzbeks had this feeling in 1993.[14]

The coalition was opposed by the governments of all other successor states, which feared that dual citizenship would undermine their nation-building efforts. Citizenship has played an important role in forging new identities in the former Soviet republics, and the leaders of these successor states did not want any split loyalties among citizens in difficult times; they saw dual citizenship as an attempt to create an instrument of Russian domination, masked behind rhetorical concern for fellow Russians. The non-Russian population of the new Eurasian states was also suspicious of the idea. It was unclear by what criteria Russia intended to confer Russian citizenship on persons who, in most cases other than Latvia and Estonia, were already citizens of other countries. The selection process might contradict the principle of equal rights regardless of ethnicity, religion, or language. In spite of vigorous promotion of the idea of dual citizenship by Boris Yeltsin, Andrei Kozyrev, Abdulakh Mikitaev, and others, all bilateral talks with their counterparts from the Soviet successor states achieved virtually nothing. The only significant results of the attempts to use this "major instrument" in fulfilling "the main strategic task of Russia's foreign policy" have been agreements with Turkmenistan, signed in December 1993 (Boris Yeltsin was solemnly granted a Turkmen passport in Ashkhabad), and Tajikistan, signed in September 1995.[15] Yet it is noteworthy that Russian diasporas in Turkmenistan and Tajikistan are among the smallest in the former USSR. Aside from the agreement to acknowledge the individual right to obtain second citizenship without revoking the first one, there was an attempt to reconcile legal contradictions arising from noncoincidence between citizenship and residence in these two treaties. An individual acquired his or her rights and duties in full in the country where he or she was a permanent resident. In other words, a concept of a "dormant" second citizenship was adopted.[16]

Between 1992 and 1994, Kyrgyzstan president Askar Akaev publicly stated on several occasions that he also supported the idea of a treaty on dual citizenship with Russia. He argued that Kazakhstan's negative attitude to the issue was natural because of a shared border with Russia. For the same reasons, Akaev opposed dual citizenship with regard to Uzbekistan. As there could be no border disputes between Kyrgyzstan and Russia, Akaev was ready to grant the right of dual citizenship to ethnic Russians in the hope that it would give them peace of mind and prevent mass emigration from Kyrgyzstan. He faced strong parliamentary opposition, however, and was forced to alter his position later.[17]

Four developments that took place in 1995 were indicative of the failure of Russian policy on the issue of dual citizenship. First, Ukrainian president Leonid Kuchma took a firm stand against dual citizenship, despite his presidential campaign pledges made in 1994. In February 1995, after talks with President Yeltsin in Moscow, Kuchma said that he would not sign any agreements with Russia if they so much as mentioned dual citizenship.[18] Later that year, this position was confirmed at meetings between Russian and Ukrainian experts on citizenship issues.[19] Disagreement on dual citizenship was one of the reasons that postponed the signing of the comprehensive treaty on relations between Russia and Ukraine until May 1997. The main reason for postponement, however, lay elsewhere—namely, the disputes over the status of the former Soviet navy's Black Sea Fleet, stationed at the major Ukrainian port city of Sevastopol. The Treaty on Friendship, Cooperation, and Partnership between the Russian Federation and Ukraine did not contain any provision that mentioned citizenship, which was Russia's major concession in the light of its position prior to 1995.[20]

Second, an analogous comprehensive treaty with Belarus was signed in February 1995 but contained no provisions on dual citizenship.[21] Russia was never persistent in its dealings with Belarus on the matter of dual citizenship, perhaps because leaders anticipated some sort of reintegration with that country, did not see any need for creating an additional instrument of influence over it, and did not perceive any threats to the rights and interests of Russians there. This was a case of exceptional flexibility in Russia's efforts to promote dual citizenship. In all other cases, the idea was given a universalistic meaning, and its applicability to all successor states was presumed.

Third, after Russia's long, persistent, and desperate pressure on Kazakhstan regarding dual citizenship, Yeltsin's government retreated and signed two documents that contained no provisions on this issue.[22] Instead of dual citizenship, these documents offered easier acquisition of the new citizenship with simultaneous loss of the previous one.[23]

It is worth bearing in mind that 75 percent of new Russian diasporas reside in the three countries just discussed: Ukraine, Belarus, and Kazakhstan. The failure to achieve progress on dual citizenship with all three countries signified the practical collapse of Russia's strategy.

The fourth indicator of failure was a policy document signed into law by President Yeltsin in September 1995.[24] This document did not contain a single word regarding dual citizenship. Instead, it outlined different and, in most cases, much less effective measures for establishing relations with the Russian diaspora. It called for smooth adaptation by Russians into their host societies, preservation of their culture, and the use of trade sanctions in case of serious violations of their rights.

The State Duma Committee on CIS Affairs and Relations with Compatriots, headed by Konstantin Zatulin, was one of a few state agencies that stood firm on issues of dual citizenship in 1995. The committee stated that it would oppose ratification of any treaty with newly independent states if there was no provision with regard to dual citizenship.[25] Yet even this threat was muted when it clashed with reality. Thus, the committee's level of activity was low during the second half of 1995, marked by a heated election campaign. Its last achievement was to establish a Council of Compatriots, an analytical-consultative body of the State Duma charged with representing the interests of *rossiyanye* residing abroad (that is, of Russian citizens and their descendants who acknowledge culturally "belonging" to Russia). It is noteworthy that there was no mention of dual citizenship in the council's "Declaration of the Constituent Congress." Instead, it called for reintegration of former Soviet republics and Moscow's benevolence toward compatriots living in the near abroad.[26]

After the evident collapse of attempts to impose dual citizenship treaties on the newly independent states, Russia began to pay more attention to the status of Russian citizens residing in those states. By 1995, treaties on the legal status of such individuals and the citizens of respective countries who were residents of Russia were signed with Georgia, Turkmenistan, and Kazakhstan.[27] This new bilateralism suggested a significant shift in Russian policy: In accordance with international norms, Russia constitutionally acknowledged that dual citizenship could exist only in the context of a special treaty relationship with a particular state. In the absence of such a treaty, Russia, like many other states of the world, treats an individual de facto possessing a citizenship in addition to the Russian one as a Russian citizen only; but at the same time, it does not object to or deem this possession as a legal violation.[28]

The current law on citizenship is a good indicator of the nature and evolution of Russia's policy toward Russians living abroad.[29] The citizenship law is very friendly to those former Soviet citizens who reside in other successor states and wish to move to Russia and become Russian citizens. Indeed, all changes and amendments to the law since its initial adoption in November 1991 have made it progressively easier to obtain Russian citizenship by broadening the categories of individuals who can obtain such citizenship automatically upon moving to Russia by registration and not through an application process.[30] In 1995, the period for obtaining Russian citizenship through registration for former Soviet citizens was extended until the year 2000.[31] In 2001, the Duma planned to decide whether to extend the eased citizenship process for CIS countries to 2006.

Though facing strong opposition from virtually all its neighboring states, Russia effectively extended the same rights to those who preferred to stay in their host state. The Russian consulates in the former Soviet republics granted Russian citizenship to stateless persons on the spot almost immediately and sent the documents on to Moscow for its approval if the applicants held citizenship of a host state.[32] Unlike the initial versions of the citizenship law in 1991 and 1992, the Russian legislation of 1993–1995 did not require relinquishing the citizenship of the country of residence to acquire Russian Federation citizenship.[33] This is a fundamental legal provision that allows the growth of de facto dual citizenship without the consent of other newly independent states. The law permitted easy acquisition of Russian citizenship by registration until the year 2000. Most of those in Central Asia and the south Caucasus who obtained Russian citizenship moved to Russia afterward (up to 80 percent), while in the Baltic states people in the same situation have usually preferred to stay.[34]

Especially vigorous protests against the Russian consulates' practice of issuing passports to the citizens or residents of respective countries were filed by the authorities of Estonia and Ukraine. In 1994–1995, Russian consulates issued an undisclosed number of passports in northeastern Estonia and the Crimea. In March 1995, a particularly tense situation developed in Simferopol, where a special consular group from Russia began accepting applications for Russian citizenship without asking for documents that validated relinquishing Ukrainian citizenship. After ultimatums and threats from the Ukrainian side, the consular group returned to Russia.[35]

In 1997, the President's Commission on Citizenship and the Ministry for Foreign Affairs advocated new amendments to the law on citizenship that would make it even easier for citizens of other Soviet successor states to obtain Russian citizenship without losing citizenship in the other state. Deputy Foreign Minister Yuri Zubakov, a particularly close associate and former intelligence colleague of then–foreign minister Yevgeny Primakov, stated during the official meeting: "In the opinion of the Russian Federation's Foreign Ministry, the desire to obtain Russian citizenship by those individuals who are related to Russia by birth, descent, language, and culture, irrespective of having a citizenship in the country of residence, is natural and legitimate, especially if they move to Russia to reside. Our current legislation is very liberal in this area."[36] Zubakov argued for granting Russian consulates in the near abroad the right to issue citizenship without the formal approval of Moscow.

Apparently, the Russian government came to the conclusion by early 1997 that after the failure to introduce dual citizenship in multilateral or bilateral agreements, it was time to act unilaterally. Zubakov attacked the previous policy of concluding agreements on simplified acquisition of citizenship after change of residence (such agreements were signed with Kazakhstan and Kyrgyzstan in 1995–1996, and a similar multilateral framework convention was concluded with CIS member states[37]) as "dubious" for Russian interests and legally meaningless. He argued that these agreements did not add anything to already existing internal Russian legislation on citizenship. He especially disliked the CIS countries' insistence on including provisions for relinquishing previous citizenship after acquiring a new one.[38]

Though obtaining Russian citizenship either by registration or application was rather easy,[39] relatively few people from the near abroad dared obtain it at the price of losing citizenship of the state in which they resided. Until 1997, there were no reliable statistics on this issue; however, the number of voters in the near abroad registered for the December 1995 Russian State Duma elections can serve as an indirect indicator. Only 200,000 people, or less then 1 percent of Russians residing in the near abroad, were registered; this figure corresponded to the estimate of Abdulakh Mikitaev.[40] However, even at that time, it was evident that some "illegal" dual citizens, who obtained Russian passports without revoking their previous ones, would not want to expose themselves by registering as voters. In 1997, the State Statistics Committee provided a significantly higher figure of 900,000 Russian citizens residing in the near abroad who had obtained such citizenship between 1992 and

1996;[41] this figure was confirmed by O. E. Kutafin, chairman of the Russian Federation's Presidential Commission on Citizenship, during a February 1997 official meeting.[42] One can only speculate how many of those 900,000 individuals have another citizenship in addition to the Russian one. Yet it is safe to say that dual citizenship has become a reality in the post-Soviet environment, "even if the respective national laws persisted in denying the phenomenon of formally recognized status and regardless of whether or not Russia had succeeded in concluding a corresponding treaty with the state concerned."[43] Although it seemed premature when this assertion was written in 1994, by 2000 it had proven to be more accurate. There is enough evidence to believe that there are quite a few de facto dual citizens who are not in a hurry to report their status to any authorities.[44]

Some leaders of the newly independent states indicated their extreme displeasure toward those who carry two passports. Kazakhstan's Nazarbaev effectively threatened dual citizens when he said: "What will be the attitude toward an individual with two passports? Most probably, he will not be hired for a job connected with state secrets or appointed for an executive position: this person is somewhat alien, of the 'second class.' The best laws will not save the situation."[45] Authorities in Latvia and Estonia tried to base their permission for establishing ballot stations to allow Russian citizens residing in these states to vote in the 1996 Russian elections on the condition that they receive lists of those Russian citizens. Russian residents of these two Baltic states were alarmed by such a prospect.[46]

In sum, de jure introduction of dual citizenship in Eurasia, once elevated as a strategic task of Russian foreign policy, began to disappear from the political and diplomatic agenda as an issue in bilateral or multilateral relations by 1995. Despite the Russian government's energetic efforts, a very important instrument of the Russian policy of hegemony and dominance has not been created within the framework of international law. When Moscow encountered determined resistance from other governments on this issue, it simply backed off. However, the poorly controlled process of multiplying citizenships continues on the Eurasian continent, and Russian officials will do little to stop it. Moreover, there is enough evidence to believe that by early 1997, the Russian government opted for a unilateral policy of encouraging de facto dual citizenship in the near abroad. The pursuit of dual citizenship in bilateral and multilateral frameworks had the potential of integrating the post-Soviet states, as well as fostering Russian hegemony. As a unilateral policy, however, it looks more like implementing the strategy of domination over the territory of the former Soviet Union.

The governments of the newly independent states have been successful in their resistance to the official introduction of dual citizenship approved by treaties and other instruments of international law. If they had agreed to conclude such treaties, the number of dual citizens probably would have been much greater than 900,000. On the other hand, Russia turned to an unchecked unilateral policy absent these agreements. In short, the newly independent states have lost any control over the increasing number of dual citizens on their territories.

It would be premature to argue that the spread of de facto dual citizenship will lead to Russia's obtaining unquestionable leverage in relations with neighboring states. The newly independent states do not acknowledge dual citizenship and simply regard individuals with two passports as their citizens. There is a significant difference between an individual's possession of two passports and governmental acknowledgment of this individual's dual citizenship.[47] This difference creates a legal deadlock for any Russian attempts to protect these dual citizens or intervene on their behalf from the perspective of international law, as codified by the 1930 Hague Convention.[48] For Russia, it is much easier to justify protection of those Russian citizens who reside in a Soviet successor state and do not have local citizenship. However, the proliferation of de facto dual citizenship creates some additional prerequisites for Russian preponderance vis-à-vis the Eurasian states.

The Concept of "Compatriots Living Abroad"

In 1994, the Russian government decided to supplement the idea of dual citizenship with a broader strategy of building special relations with Russians living abroad, and it officially endorsed the concept of "compatriots" (fellow countrymen). Abdulakh Mikitaev claimed that it was he who persuaded President Yeltsin to adopt a special government program to this effect.[49] Andrei Kozyrev reported in his memoirs that he was proud of the fact that his Ministry of Foreign Affairs initiated the program.[50]

According to Mikitaev, there are three categories of residents of the neighboring states who qualify as "compatriots": (1) Russian citizens residing in the near abroad; (2) former Soviet citizens who have not obtained new citizenships (apatriates, or stateless persons, most of whom live in Latvia and Estonia); and (3) those who obtained citizenship of the host country but wish to maintain their own culture and ties with Russia.[51] From this perspective, compatriots form a much broader circle, with Russian citizens residing abroad as its core. Russia's ties with this broader entity were envisioned to be a bit looser than those with Russian citizens.

On August 2, 1994, President Yeltsin signed a decree that called for the government to formulate the major components of this policy, and on August 31, 1994, the government adopted such a program.[52] This document defined the "strategic line of Russia's policy toward the compatriots" as promotion of their voluntary integration into host states in a way that both adapted to local culture and preserved their own distinctive culture. The program read like a manifesto of multiculturalism, yet it avoided any indication that it had been designed for ethnic Russians alone, and it spoke for all nationalities whose roots lay in the territory of Russia.

According to this program, the Russian government's primary means for defending the rights and interests of compatriots must be diplomatic and economic. It suggested the use of international human rights instruments and, in extreme cases, economic pressure. It called for strengthening cultural ties with compatriots by broadcasting Russian-language television in the neighboring states, supporting other Russian-language mass media, assisting cultural centers, and so on. It also called for the promotion of economic ties between Russia and those industrial enterprises in the near abroad in which most employees were compatriots.

Generally, the structure, language, and style of the program were reminiscent of documents designed by the CPSU Central Committee; there was a great deal of abstract terminology, lack of clarity about implementation, and poor guidelines for coordination among governmental bodies. It read as if decision makers in the government did not truly believe that the program would ever be fully implemented. Many provisions required financial resources the government obviously lacked in light of severe budget constraints. For example, Russia effectively ceded its positions in the post-Soviet information space because of a lack of money for the retransmission of Moscow television and radio broadcasts by local companies in many of the newly independent states. To be sure, the real significance of the program seemed to be in its spirit, reflecting the strategy of state building within the borders of present-day Russia and supplemented by moderate support for compatriots in the near abroad. The primary aim of this support was defined in the program as preventing the mass immigration of those compatriots into Russia.

It took almost two years to develop and adopt more concrete guidelines of support for compatriots to be implemented by Russian governmental agencies. On May 17, 1996, then–Russian prime minister Viktor Chernomyrdin signed a "Program of Actions to Support the Compatriots Abroad," a compendium of assignments for Russian federal institutions.[53] The "Program of Actions" actually acknowledged that Russia was still forming the mechanisms of interaction with its diaspora. It was the first official document in which the term "diaspora"—in addition to "compatriots"—was widely used. It also stated for the first time that "newly independent countries are being formed as national states of self-determined titular nations" with negative consequences for the nontitulars. Unlike all previous official documents, this program emphasized that the composition of the Russian diasporas and the situations that they face are very different in the various states. The program called for legislative confirmation of the legal status of compatriots, negotiations with the newly independent states on the elevation of Russian to the status of a second state language, establishment of bilateral human rights commissions, and ratification by the CIS countries of the Convention on the Rights of Individuals Belonging to National Minorities.[54]

Ironically, it took two more years to prepare the "Concept of the Russian Federation's State Policy toward the Compatriots Abroad," a document designed to provide a conceptual foundation for the policy adopted earlier.[55] The fact that it was prepared by the Governmental Commission on the Affairs of Compatriots Abroad in 1997 (after the 1994 "Basic Directions" and the 1996 "Program of Actions") suggests that the Russian government tried to implement certain policies prior to—or, at best, simultaneous with—any effort to grasp the problem conceptually.

The "Concept" provided a newly refined definition of compatriots, who are "understood to be all individuals who live outside the Russian Federation and consider themselves to be connected to Russia by historical, ethnocultural, and spiritual links, and who wish to maintain these links irrespective of their citizenship, ethnicity, language, religion, social, and economic status."[56] It also differed from previous official documents in its tougher assessment of the situation compatriots face in their host states, characterized as "discrimination," "forceful assimilation," "pushing out," "ethnic isolation," and "growth of ethnic and cultural distance."[57] Yet the suggested policy was still rather moderate, stressing that it would be the newly independent states' responsibility to provide the compatriots' individual and collective rights and adequate social conditions. Nonetheless, the "Concept" stipulated that Russia would try to influence the respective governments; in addition, it would extend organizational help to compatriots in order to achieve equal status, political representation, access to material resources, and conditions for cultural development.[58] In other words, assistance for the political organization of compatriots was proclaimed as one of the aims of the Russian Federation's state policy.

The "Concept" was scheduled to be adopted in the spring of 1998, but a reshuffling of the government delayed, if not buried, the initiative. The commission responsible for developing the "Concept" was absent from the Russian Federation's list of governmental bodies in 1998 and resumed its work only in the spring of 1999.

Programs of assistance to compatriots have been underfinanced since 1995, when they became a separate item in the federal budget. That year, only 60 percent of the money was allocated; in 1996, 40 percent. The situation improved in 1997. In 1998, the government planned to spend 50.2 million rubles (approximately U.S. $8.4 million), twice as much than in 1997.[59] However, this money was not released by the Ministry of Finance that year. In the same year, the authority to disperse the money was transferred from the Ministry of Nationalities and Federative Relations to the Ministry of CIS Affairs, a move that prompted protests from the former. This administrative squabbling over meager (and often virtual) resources strengthened the position of those who suggested a concentration of all functions for maintaining the relationship with compatriots into one powerful and well-financed governmental agency.[60] However, such propositions did not seem plausible in the volatile context of Russian politics. In 1998–1999, the problem of compatriots remained institutionally marginal for the executive branch of the government, in spite of all the rhetoric of politicians and high officials.

According to Vladimir Chernous, the key governmental official in the Governmental Commission on the Affairs of Compatriots Abroad, there have been three major reasons for poor implementation of the governmental programs in this area: insufficient attention to the problem within the government, regular reshuffling of deputy prime ministers responsible for this issue, and the absence of political pressure from compatriots or constituencies within Russia—government officials have not considered diaspora issues a particularly "prestigious" assignment.[61]

Once the attempt to introduce de jure dual citizenship began to fail, the program became the primary framework for Russian policy toward Russians in the near abroad. Designed originally as a supplement to the more assertive strategy of dual citizenship, this program came to be the heart of Russian policy. De jure dual citizenship had the potential to be converted into a very strong instrument of domination within the Eurasian region; the program of aid to compatriots, by contrast, lacks that potential. However, addressing the problems of the Russians in the near abroad, not only in terms of national minorities but also in terms of compatriots, has provided Russia with a basis for unilateral policy in this area. Conceptualizing the situation along a "Russia/compatriots" dimension has allowed the Russian Federation to address the problems of diasporas as an internal matter and not exclusively as a subject of interstate relations. This way of thinking has led to several legislative initiatives in the Russian parliament.

The first attempt to draft legislation on the compatriots dates to early 1993, when the Russian Supreme Soviet Presidium's Commission on the Affairs of Russians Abroad asked the Russian Independent Institute for International Law to prepare a concept document and a draft bill on the state policy toward compatriots, but the dissolution of the parliament in September 1993 stalled the process.[62] The next step was taken on December 8, 1995, on the day of the fourth anniversary of the Belaya Vezha agreements, when the State Duma approved the "Declaration on the Russian Federation Support of Russia's Diaspora and on Protection of Russia's Compatriots."

In 1996–1998, the State Duma held extensive hearings on the issue, and members of its Committee on CIS Affairs and Relations with Compatriots (headed by Georgi Tikhonov) prepared a draft bill of the "Federal Law on the State Policy toward the Compatriots Abroad." Vyacheslav Igrunov, deputy chairman of the committee, drafted an alternative bill—the "Federal Law on the Support of Russia's Diaspora, Protection of Russia's Compatriots, and Repatriation." The first draft was mainly a communist and procommunist undertaking, while the second was the initiative of a prominent member of the liberal party Yabloko. Surprisingly, there were few differences between the two documents, which indicates a relatively broad consensus in the State Duma on the major principles of policy toward the Russian diasporas.

The differences between the two drafts could be collapsed into two major points. First, Tikhonov's draft emphasized ethnic Russians and other "indigenous" nationalities of the Russian Federation in its definition of compatriots. Igrunov's draft was more inclusive, suggesting a purely subjective approach. For example, if ethnic Armenians living in Armenia identified themselves as Russian, they would be considered in Russia as "compatriots." Second, Tikhonov's draft stipulated material support, trade privileges, and other favorable terms of economic interaction with compatriots and their businesses.[63] Igrunov preferred direct support of cultural activities only.[64]

After the usual three hearings in the Duma, the bill based on Tikhonov's draft was unanimously adopted by the lower chamber of the parliament on November 13, 1998. Coming as no surprise to the lawmakers, the Yeltsin administration undertook vigorous efforts to prevent the bill from reaching the president's desk for his signature. In fact, the executive branch expressed its negative attitude toward the adoption of the law at all stages of the legislative process. Its objections were mainly twofold.

First, the Ministry of Foreign Affairs preferred to draw a strict line between Russian citizens and the citizens of the newly independent states. While promoting dual citizenship, Russian diplomats were strongly against granting compatriots any Russian-issued identification cards. The Ministry of Foreign Affairs realized that this provision would be strongly opposed by most of the newly independent states. Identification cards issued by a foreign state to some of the citizens of the former Soviet republics would theoretically mean that they had special rights and privileges in relation to this state. Evidently, Russian diplomats could try neighboring states' tempers for the sake of obtaining an internationally recognized right to support the holders of Russian passports in the near abroad, but they did not want to provoke irritation by merely issuing dubious identification cards.

Second, many officials in the government were afraid that self-identification as a Russian compatriot with the receipt of an identification card by the citizens of neighboring states could lead to extensive material claims on Russia. In sum, the executive branch of the government held the view that the adoption of the law would be detrimental to the interests of both the Russian state and the compatriots themselves, who could face additional problems with the authorities of the newly independent states as a result. Wary of the executive's position, the Duma made sure that it did not legally require the executive branch's opinion on the draft: Special Provision 2103 ("State Support of Compatriots Living Outside the Russian Federation") already existed in the federal budget, and under Russian law, the official opinion of the executive branch on the bill was not needed in such a case. The bill also suggested incentives for cooperation with companies that were owned by compatriots or those in which compatriots constituted a majority of employees. It also called for promoting joint ventures with such companies and stimulating compatriots' investing in Russia.

The Russian parliament's upper chamber, the Federation Council, was more attentive to the recommendations of the Ministry of Foreign Affairs and raised serious objections to the bill. A reconciliation commission was formed in the parliament in late 1998, and the bill underwent some changes. For example, an article providing for financial support of local governments, national cultural "autonomies," and nongovernmental organizations of compatriots was removed. President Yeltsin vetoed the bill, nevertheless. In March 1999, the Federal Assembly overrode the veto, forcing Yeltsin to sign the bill into law on May 24, 1999; the law went into force on June 1.

Any tax breaks, economic privileges, or state-supported foundations for compatriots were definitely a hot issue in Yeltsin's Russia. The scandal around a fund for the support of the compatriots is illustrative in this regard. On April 13, 1996, the president signed a decree "On Creation of 'Rossiyane,' the Fund for the Support of the Compatriots Abroad" and gave the fund the status of a "state-public foundation."[65] Aleksandr Kazakov, Yeltsin's former first deputy chief of staff and later chairman of the board for the energy conglomerate Gazprom, became president of the fund. Valery Grebennikov, the State Duma deputy, member of the progovernment Our Home Is Russia parliamentary faction, and vice-president of the firm OLBI, became Kazakov's deputy. In 1998, there were media reports that about 5 billion rubles (approximately U.S. $1 million) were transferred from the accounts of the Rossiyane fund to the accounts of the private Voskhozhdenie fund. Grebennikov was the president of Voskhozhdenie. According to the newspaper *Moskovskii komsomolets*, the budget money earmarked for support of compatriots disappeared indefinitely.[66]

Under current conditions of extreme weakness of state institutions, lack of financial resources, rampant corruption of the elite, and public apathy, Russian legislation and governmental programs cannot function properly. This is also true with regard to policy instruments aimed at supporting the compatriots. At the end of the Yeltsin era, there was administrative chaos in this field. However, by conceptualizing the problem and adopting relevant programs and laws, the government has established preconditions for steps to be taken in this area that might lead to a more meaningful policy in the future. The conceptual and legal structure for a more interventionist policy has been created.

Multilateralism

The third component of Russian policy in the realm of ties with the Russians in the near abroad were efforts undertaken within the multilateral framework of the CIS. In his memoirs, Andrei Kozyrev, a dedicated neoliberal in his views on world politics, assumed that the problems of the Russian-speaking population could not be addressed as a bilateral issue in relations between Russia and other Soviet successor states. Instead, he wrote, "Russian diplomacy seeks to make the defense of human rights and the rights of ethnic minorities one of the major policy directions of the Commonwealth." He also admitted: "I will tell you straight: the human rights dialogue is not proceeding easily. There are still misgivings that Russia will use it to interfere in the domestic affairs of its neighbors."[67] As a result of such misgivings, the Russian Foreign Ministry later came to the conclusion that the defense of Russians' rights in the near abroad can be more effectively addressed in bilateral relations. At April 1997 parliamentary hearings, Deputy Foreign Minister V. S. Sidorov called the bilateral level "more preferable and effective" for pursuing these policies.[68]

Thus far, no document adopted within the framework of the CIS has directly addressed the issue of the Russian or any other diasporas. Nevertheless, in 1994–1995 several important declarations and agreements connected to the issue were signed. The "Declaration on Observing the Sovereignty, Territorial Integrity, and Inviolability of Borders"[69] and the "Memorandum on the Maintenance of Peace and Stability in the CIS"[70] were among the first multilateral CIS documents that strongly and unconditionally condemned separatism and any support of separatism. By supporting these principles, Russia actually sent a message against irredentism to the Russian diasporas in Kazakhstan, Ukraine, Moldova, and the other newly independent states.

In 1993–1994, some politicians and officials within Russia were hoping to promote the idea of a CIS convention on the rights of ethnic minorities. The only CIS country that actively backed the idea was Kyrgyzstan, which was desperately trying to stop the emigration of the largely skilled non-Kyrgyz population that has devastated the state's industry. In 1994, the Convention on the Rights of Persons Belonging to National Minorities was signed by the presidents of Azerbaijan (with concurrent opinion), Armenia, Belarus, Georgia, Kazakhstan, Kyrgyzstan, Moldova, Russia, Tajikistan, and Ukraine (with respect to Ukrainian legislation). Theoretically, this convention was open to the Baltic states as well, but they evinced no intent to join. Conceptually, the convention was based on the ideas of the 1992 UN Declaration on the Rights of Persons Belonging to National or Ethnic, Religious, and Linguistic Minorities and was also concurrent with the work on the Council of Europe's Framework Convention for the Protection of National Minorities, which was open for signing in 1995.

The CIS convention contained a minimalist approach to the rights of minorities, providing for their equality with the dominant groups in terms of nondiscrimination. In terms of recognizing their special rights and rendering certain positive services by the state (what is termed "affirmative action" in the United States), the convention provided nothing. Instead, it was supposed to open the way for obtaining assistance from abroad in the field of minorities' cultural, educational, and religious activities (Article 9).[71] CIS members were apprehensive about such obligations. Evidently, the presidents of the CIS states who signed the convention had no intentions of implementing it. The convention was not ratified by their parliaments, including the Russian State Duma. The latter stayed firm on the nonrecognition of the Russians in the near abroad as minorities. Instead, they perceived the Russian diasporas as parts of "the divided Russian nation": "minorities" are elements of their respective states; parts of a divided nation belong to their historical homeland. On this particular issue, the Russian executive, especially the Ministry of Foreign Affairs, was much more in line with the traditions of international law than the legislature by recognizing Russians in the near abroad as minorities.

In May 1995, the adoption of the CIS Convention on Human Rights and Fundamental Freedoms was yet another indicator of Russian policy's moderation.[72] Nonetheless, half of the CIS members (Azerbaijan, Kazakhstan, Turkmenistan, Uzbekistan, and Ukraine) have not signed the document, even though its recommendations are nonbinding. Notably, this convention addressed all problems of human rights as individual rights, not as collective or group rights. True, Article 21 declared that persons belonging to ethnic minorities shall not be denied the right to express, maintain, or develop their distinctive ethnic, linguistic, or religious culture; however, this simply echoed Article 27 of the 1966 UN International Covenant on Civil and Political Rights. This right, in the particular wording of the United Nations Covenant, is an individual right and is attributed to "persons belonging to . . . minorities," not to communities.[73] This means that no "affirmative action" is required on the part of the state. The only obligation of the state is to not prevent individuals from enjoying their distinctive culture. Article 27 of the 1995 CIS convention confirmed this principle by stating that each participating state must "respect the right of parents to provide their children with education and teaching that corresponds to their own beliefs and national traditions." The convention, following the 1966 UN Covenant, is much more conservative and limited than the approach of the Organization for Security and Cooperation in Europe (OSCE), which includes an acknowledgment of the group rights of ethnic minorities.

The 1995 CIS convention provides almost no basis for governments to support ethnic minorities living abroad. Instead, it creates a legal framework for multilateral support of individual human rights. This is not exactly what Russia is seeking if it intends to bolster its instruments of domination in the region. Nevertheless, Russia was a driving force for adoption of the convention. Immediately after the signing of the document, Russia began to lobby for the establishment of a CIS Commission on Human Rights to monitor compliance with the convention by all parties. The commission was never created, and the convention itself was ratified by only three states: Russia, Belarus, and Tajikistan.

The result of all these developments has been an ambiguous situation wherein multilateral instruments of the CIS are oriented toward individual rights, while unilateral Russian policy is aimed at supporting the rights of collectivities in the form of compatriot communities. If they are consistently implemented and enforced, the multilateral agreements and regimes may serve as an important obstacle to using the issue of diasporas as an instrument of Russia's hegemony or dominance across the Eurasian continent. Multilateralism may help the newly independent states to prevent such a situation, which is influenced by Russia more than by others. Paradoxically, however, these agreements have been promoted and supported by Russia and have met lukewarm support at best in most other former Soviet republics. In the absence of adequate international regimes, or if they are weak and nonenforceable, Russia will face the newly independent states one by one if it overcomes its current extreme weakness. In such a scenario, Russia may have much more leverage in imposing its will and the ability to play the compatriot-protection card exclusively for its own benefit.

Nationalist Rhetoric and the Imperatives of State Building

The evidence adduced thus far suggests that the most assertive policy toward Russian diasporas (introduction of dual citizenship acknowledged by respective countries) has been a failure, while two other policy initiatives (strengthening ties with compatriots and the creation of multilateral instruments within the CIS) have been very modest and moderate in content. Let us now turn to the forces opposing these moderate initiatives in today's Russia.

From 1992 to 2000, the opponents of moderation urged the adoption of three highly assertive policies: (1) trade sanctions against Latvia and Estonia as punishment for their citizenship policies toward Russian speakers; (2) pressure for the elevation of the Russian language to the status of a second official language in states with a significant Russian-speaking population (Ukraine, Kazakhstan, Belarus, Moldova, Latvia, and Estonia);[74] and (3) pressure for self-governance of Russian communities within the near abroad.[75] In the chaotic years that followed the disintegration of the USSR, some high-ranking members of the Russian government actually sided with the opposition on the issue of relations with Russian diasporas. This was the case especially during the period between December 1991 and December 1993, through the forcible dissolution of the Supreme Soviet and the adoption of a new constitution. For example, former vice president Aleksandr Rutskoi and Yeltsin's adviser, Sergei Stankevich, were much tougher on this issue than the rest of the government, suggesting that Russia should recognize Crimea and Pridnestrovye as sovereign entities because the large majority of their populations were Russian.[76]

Although none of these hard-line measures was adopted by the Russian government, there has been plenty of tough rhetoric on the issue. The gap between rhetoric and action has been large throughout the period of Russian independence, especially in 1992–1995. Thus in 1992, a tough-looking, tough-sounding Boris Yeltsin made an explicit link between the treatment of Russian minorities on issues of citizenship in Latvia and Estonia and the withdrawal of Russian troops from those countries. Yet this statement in no way affected the schedule of troop withdrawals.[77] Since 1992, Kozyrev had been threatening to implement "forceful methods" to protect Russians in the near abroad. In 1995, he went as far as to state at a session of the Council for Foreign Policy of Russia: "There may be cases when it is necessary to use armed force to defend our citizens and compatriots abroad."[78] However, no such scenario has unfolded.

What, then, explains the gap between policy and muscular rhetoric? First, the current regime views defense of the rights and interests of Russian minorities as an instrument, not a goal, of domination throughout the territory of the former Soviet Union. That instrument has been consistently compromised for the sake of other policies that are considered to be of higher priority.[79] Yet the regime has found it convenient to keep the issue alive. But the gap cannot be explained by reference to a general lack of will or capacity to dominate. In some other areas, Russia has been more successful in establishing its regional hegemony through: (1) the dependency of many new states on Russia's energy resources; (2) success in wringing concessions from certain neighbors on the retention of Russian military bases on their soil; and (3) joint patrolling of the former Soviet borders with Armenia, Belarus, Georgia, Kazakhstan, Kyrgyzstan, Tajikistan, and Turkmenistan.

Second, and these successes notwithstanding, there remains a large gap between Russia's ambitions of domination in the entire Eurasian region and its current limited ability to meet this goal. Facing deep economic crisis and tremendous social problems, having a significantly weakened and disorganized army, and being politically unstable, Russia hardly matches the portrait of a regional hegemon. It is only Russia's potential, combined with the extremely frail condition of most neighboring states, that provides some basis for its stated aspirations. But that potential cannot be realized until Russia has gone through at least several years of stabilization.

The third reason for the gap between rhetoric and policy relates to the contradictions between the principles espoused by Russian officials and the realities of Russia's internal federal structure. For example, if Russia officially supported Crimean demands to join Russia, or even significantly elevated its level of autonomy from Ukraine, serious repercussions could arise for the nature and legitimacy of regional demands within the Russian Federation itself. While working hard to strengthen the integrity of Russia and the Russian state, Yeltsin's regime could not afford to prevent other newly independent states from consolidating their own statehood.

Stephen Sestanovich suggested a thoughtful parallel between France of the 1960s and Russia of the 1990s, relying on a three-decade-old analysis of President Charles de Gaulle's leadership by Henry Kissinger.[80] According to Kissinger, de Gaulle attempted to revive the glory of France with the help of tough, nationalistic, often anti-American rhetoric that resonated in a humiliated country that was experiencing a crisis of identity. Contemporary Russia has even fewer resources than de Gaulle's France to back up its rhetoric, but what is common between the two cases is the therapeutic effect of words: They help to heal wounds and, when they are not backed by aggressive policies, they need not destabilize international relations. Russian rhetoric concerning the protection of compatriots might help psychologically to offset the shock of division of the Russian nation after the breakup of the Soviet Union. Such rhetoric can help to ease the tensions engendered by a policy of state building within Russia's current, artificial borders, which reflect neither historical experience nor the perceptions of Russians regarding the spatial distribution and formal subordination of their nation. Thus far, verbal imperialism in the form of rhetoric may have helped to prevent a real imperialist policy. In 1992, Russian policy toward Russian diasporas was entirely rhetorical. During 1993–1994, there was an attempt to back up the rhetoric with some assertive measures, including the advocacy of dual citizenship. After the failure of this undertaking, only a combination of moderate policy and tough rhetoric have remained. Of course, discourse can have real, and often dangerous, consequences.[81] Yet discourse in Russia has played a moderating role so far. It remains to be seen if inflammatory language makes its way into actual policy in the future.

Contemporary Russia is neither a nation-state nor an empire. Rather, it is in the process of becoming a hegemonic regional power. The thrust of its policy is to combine state building within its current borders with the creation of a zone of formally sovereign but effectively dependent countries around it. Analysis of one of the key components of this policy—building special relations with the new Russian diasporas— has demonstrated that this is no easy task. It has also shown that, whatever their ideal aspirations, Russian policymakers have adjusted their policies to real-world constraints, while compensating for the adjustment with boastful rhetoric.

Future Prospects

Will the issue of Russian diasporas remain in its current dormant form? There are many reasons to believe that the situation will not change as a result of assertiveness on the part of the diasporians themselves. First, there are no noticeable horizontal ties among Russian communities, and few prospects that they will be constructed.[82] As a result, without Russia's involvement, problems arising within the diasporas are likely to remain local issues. Moreover, differences in the characteristics of these communities bode ill for the development of such ties. In chapter 4, it was argued that these communities are very different in size, lifestyles, and level of integration into their host societies. They do not have a common enemy or a single vision. Second, each of the Russian communities is very poorly organized. Political or other mobilization, solidarity, and cooperation along ethnic lines are entirely new concepts for the formerly dominant people.

Third, there is a widespread belief in Eurasia that only the existence of Russia can prevent the Russian communities from repeating the historical experience of some other notable diasporas—Jewish, Greek, and Armenian among them. This belief gains support from comparative perspectives on the fates of diasporas. As the late Ernest Gellner wrote: "The disastrous and tragic consequences, in modern conditions, of the conjunction of economic superiority and cultural identifiability with political and military weakness, are too well known to require repetition."[83] In most cases, Russian diasporas are unable to prevent unfavorable developments in the near abroad without the assistance of Russia.

In sum, the diasporians themselves are unlikely to force a change in their status. The governments of Soviet successor states, by endorsing or initiating persecution of the Russian diasporas, could well trigger a backlash by the Russian government. Short of that, what are the chances that the Russian government will more actively use its preponderance of power vis-à-vis the near abroad to protect the interests of Russian diasporas or manipulate the issue in order to create leverage against the governments of those states? This analysis of Russian policy has shown that Moscow has thus far been restrained and moderate, especially when facing resistance. However, the issue of diasporas, and Russia's alleged responsibility over their fate, have been injected into theoretical discussions of state and nation building that have helped to shape Russia's political agenda.

Current Russian policy concentrates on state building within the Russian Federation, but we should not assume that current policy will necessarily prevail over ethnonationalist sentiments. How can ethnonationalist ideological currents make their way into real policymaking? Thus far, the issue of diasporas has been kept mainly behind the front lines of Russian policies; yet under certain conditions, it can be dragged to the forefront. For example, studies of nationalist movements in other parts of the world led James Mayall to the conclusion that irredentist claims "are available to governments as a mobilization instrument, a means of securing popular support at times when, for whatever reason, such support seems particularly desirable."[84] In Russia, the issues connected to diaspora problems, including irredentism, potentially can be used to generate popular support by defining them as a major concern of national interest and security.

But when are circumstances most propitious for credibly floating such ideas? In his analysis of political leadership in post-Soviet Russia with relation to the decision to invade Chechnya, George Breslauer identified a circumstance that catalyzes unexpected military adventures of the Russian government:[85]

> In contrast to leaders in more strongly institutionalized (or constitutionalized) regimes who may seek only "minimal winning coalitions" on policy, both Soviet and post-Soviet leaders have felt the need to over-insure themselves. This may explain why they all embraced programs that promised a great deal to almost everybody, and therefore proved impossible to fulfill. In the presence of dashed promises, the insecurity of tenure becomes ever more salient and the leader becomes ever more sensitive to a glowingly hostile or skeptical climate within the political establishment. When threats to fundamental state interests at home or abroad coincide with this stage of an administration, the conditions sufficient for brinkmanship or military intervention have crystallized.

Furthermore, the Leninist legacy provides justification for subordinating current problems to urgent political tasks. This practice could facilitate the efforts of a Russian leader who, for reasons of state or personal authority, decides to declare the continued division of the Russian people as unacceptable.

In sum, there are many conditions within Russia and the Russian polity that could undermine the current policy of restraint. Much will depend on the direction taken by the ongoing redefinition of the Russian nation. Much will also depend on the kinds of political institutions that will develop and their implications for the maintenance of political authority. There are enough organized political forces and ambitious political entrepreneurs that may try to mobilize public opinion in the Russian Federation and among the diasporas in order to present themselves as "saviors of the Russian nation." At present, "integrationalism," or the expanded economic reintegration of the former Soviet republics that leads to some sort of a voluntary political union, may be the only viable alternative to isolationist state building and ethnonationalist or imperialistic programs, which are destabilizing and threatening to peace in Eurasia. These programs have not made their way into the realm of state policies, but the Yeltsin government did not present an effective alternative to them. Indeed, some sort of integration of former Soviet republics would have an additional virtue of decreasing the political salience of the issue of Russian diasporas and reducing the chances that these diasporas would become pawns in some sort of opportunistic— and potentially bloody—political game.

Conclusions
and Implications

WHAT ARE THE IMPLICATIONS for American foreign policy of the main ideas and arguments presented in this book? They are threefold.

First, policymakers should probably rethink some theoretical assumptions underlying U.S. strategy toward Russia and other successor states of the former Soviet Union. On the one hand, it would be unwise for policymakers to become hostages of a theoretical framework based on the Wilsonian worldview and allow the "anti-imperial" concepts currently popular among some analysts and policymakers to become an ultimate "value" and dominate Western strategy in the region; it is always tempting, yet dangerous, to conflate analysis and moral vision. On the other hand, it would be counterproductive to view Russia through an exclusively "Realist" lens as the scion of a hostile anti-Western Soviet Union, a source of instability and various dangers from proliferation of nuclear weapons to organized crime. Both the inflexible "idealist" and "Realist" approaches dictate a one-sided suspicious view of the Russian diasporas as instruments of sinister plans aimed at restoring a Russian hegemony in Eurasia that is unfriendly to Western interests.

Second, it is critical that the United States understand that Russia could respond in a variety of ways—some of them dangerous, some quite constructive—to the challenge presented by the emergence of the Russian diaspora. It is probably beyond American power and desire to control and shape Russian policy in this area. However, the United States

may encourage benign Russian responses and help to create a favorable international climate for constructive Russian policy.

Third, a new approach toward the prospects of regional integration
in Eurasia may be appropriate in view of the problems associated with
Russian diasporas and the Russian Federation's attitudes toward them.

Rethinking the Theoretical Framework

Mainstream Western Sovietology has concentrated almost entirely on
the Soviet Union as a whole, paying little attention to particular nationalities. Such a paradigmatic lens prompted Alexander Motyl to accuse
Sovietology of "traditional Russocentrism."[1] Motyl's assertion is especially illustrative for reconceptualization of the most basic premises in
Soviet studies, which occurred in the late 1980s and early 1990s. In ret-
rospect, many scholars equated "Soviet" with "Russian" during this
period. Policies of the communist regime, especially in non-Russian
regions, were uncompromisingly declared "Russian." However, the relationship between "Soviet" and "Russian," though of course intimate
(especially in the view of many non-Russians), is very complex. Many
Russians, for example, believe that the Soviet regime was first and foremost anti-Russian. In fact, for political scientists studying the Soviet
Union as a whole, the framework of analysis was not Russocentrism
but, rather, the neglect of all ethnic groups, including Russians.

In the late years of perestroika, the problems of nationalities within
the Soviet Union dominated the agenda of scholars and policymakers
alike.[2] Many volumes on newly emerging or re-emerging non-Russian
nations have been published since then. The constructs of imperial
collapse, self-determination, newly acquired independence of free-
dom-loving peoples, nation building, and resistance to imperial Russia
have dominated neoliberal academic and strategic thinking about the
Eurasian states. Again, many of these constructs represent the Wilsonian
worldview and historically look back, not forward. Such a view ignores
some rather pressing contemporary realities, of course. First, this approach ignores new trends in the economic and political development

of the world, usually conceptualized as "globalization." Second, the traditional framework of analysis ignores deeply ingrained perceptions about Eurasia, the Soviet Union, and post-Soviet developments held by many people living in that region. These perceptions may be conceptualized as "civilizational identity."

The future belongs to economic, political, and security interdependence, regional integration, transnational populations and multicultural states, open borders, and multiple identities. Nation building in the newly independent states of Eurasia is occurring in an entirely different context than in Central Europe in the wake of World War I. A new global condition brings new challenges to peace and security and does not promise a problem-free world and prosperity to all. The issues of a new Russian identity and diasporas, as well as the policy options in this area, should be soberly addressed in the context of the most recent trends in international development—namely, the formation of an interdependent world.

Thus far, there has not been an explicit conceptual link between globalization and political processes in Eurasia in American policymaking in the region. From the perspective that pays appropriate attention to globalization, diasporas may be seen not as simply an unfortunate leftover from the imperial past, but as an important ingredient of a transnational future. Economic and political integration of the former Soviet republics may be viewed not only as a manifestation of Russian imperial ambitions, but also as a natural modern development. Nation building on an ethnic basis in the newly independent states and the rupture of traditional ties with neighboring states may be perceived as a counterproductive trend not to be encouraged by the West. President Clinton questioned the usefulness of the nationalist projects in the era of globalization in his speech at Mont Tremblant on October 9, 1999. National independence, he warned, is often "a questionable assertion in a global economy where cooperation pays greater benefits in every area than destructive competition."[3] This approach provides a good prism for assessing developments not only in North America.

It is important for the West to be attentive to the perceptions of the Russian elite and the public regarding Russian identity, diasporas, and Eurasia. A newly emerging Russian nation is too easily associated with a new Russian state by American foreign policymakers. The difference between the two is also too often ignored. As is the case with most scholars, U.S. foreign policymakers have concentrated on the Russian *state*, not the *nation* or *civilization*. On the one hand, this focus on the state is quite normal, because international relations are primarily concerned with interstate relations. On the other hand, ignoring the non-state dimensions of world politics could result in serious misjudgments and leave policymakers unprepared for new challenges. It is important to understand that, as yet, there is no congruence between states and nations in the former Soviet Union. Compared with their studies of other former Soviet nationalities, political scientists have lagged behind in studies of Russians as a "people," or as a "nation," in the post-Soviet context.[4] The civilizational approach also has not been adequately applied to post-Soviet realities. The concept of civilization may be particularly helpful for the inclusion of Russian diasporas in analysis and policy recommendations.

Throughout several centuries, Russian identity has been formed by the interplay of ethnic and nonethnic factors. The latter may be defined in many different ways. Politically, these factors are imperial. In Dostoevsky's tradition of universalistic humanitarianism, they are *panhuman*. From the comparative cultural studies perspective, they may be called civilizational, if one engages the ideas of Arnold Toynbee and Samuel Huntington on civilization as the highest cultural grouping of people. One may also argue that Russian civilization was long diluted in the Soviet one, though the latter represented much more than simply the continuation of Russian imperialism.[5]

Many Russians felt that they belonged to some entity that was bigger and more important than just an ethnic group. Russian intellectuals tended to define their national distinctiveness not in terms of peculiar songs, dances, or food, but in terms of a special set of values and attitudes that manifested themselves in the so-called Russian idea. For a century and a half, the elite has tended to define Russia in opposition to Europe as a whole, not to particular European peoples, for example Germans or French.

Of course, not all non-Russians in the empire and the Soviet Union considered themselves members of this civilization, but many did. If we look not at the cores of ethnic groups or their ideal types, but at their margins, boundaries, and mixed entities, we will find, particularly in the Soviet period, tens of millions of individuals who were Russian speakers, ethnically mixed, or living outside their putative homelands. Often having a relatively weak ethnic identity, they were more receptive to de-ethnicized Soviet—in this context, civilizational—trends. For some non-Russians, that meant linguistic and to some extent broader cultural Russification and thus expansion of the Russian civilization. For Russians, it was fulfillment of their peculiar self-imposed manifest destiny to "civilize" all of Eurasia and to assert themselves as prime bearers of a distinct civilization.

Russians' perception of their culture as a civilization has historically presented itself in two different ways. On the one hand, there is the tradition of Danilevsky and Leontiev, with the emphasis on the separateness from and hostility to the West. On the other hand, there is the influential tradition of Dostoevsky and Solovyov, with its attempt to present "the Russian idea" as a set of moral values of openness and universality. "Russianness" in this case had primarily a civilizational connotation and could be perceived as an umbrella category for many nationalities. Later on, this approach was further developed by Eurasianists, who wrote about multinational civilization.

Imperial Russia and then the Soviet state collapsed. Disintegration of the respective civilization is still under way. On the individual level, a crisis of identity is particularly profound among those who have found themselves outside their putative homelands or who simply have difficulty in defining one. Post-Soviet diasporas are fragments of a shattered civilization. Will ethnic components of their identities become stronger and gradually fill up the vacuum left by vanishing civilizational elements? Or will "Russian-speakingness" assert itself as a new national form, as David Laitin suggested, and thus continue its quasi-civilizational existence as a conglomerate of ethnically mixed (Russian and non-Russian) minorities of a very special sort?[6] Or will they simply assimilate to the titulars and wither away as distinct entities? The crux of this book has been that the new Russian state will play the crucial role in shaping the answers to these questions. At the same time, the very existence of diasporas is playing an important role in forming a new collective identity in the Russian Federation itself.

It may seem axiomatic to say that the civilizational approach, as is suggested here, emphasizes the past. However, it also may be illuminative for the future because it goes beyond the current scholarly and political preoccupation with ethnicity, self-determination, and nation building. Intellectual and political discourse often shapes social reality,

which is especially true for the formation and redefinition of identities
in the post-Soviet context. On the one hand, there are many factors that
may strengthen ethnonationalist sentiments in modern Russia and
among Russian-speaking diasporas. On the other hand, Russians and
Russian speakers in the newly independent states may be viewed not
only as leftovers of an imperial past but also as ferments of a transnational future.[7] As has been pointed out here, politicization of diasporas may be a destabilizing factor in international relations if it
occurs on an ethnonationalist basis. In a more benign context, diasporas may act as important elements connecting civil societies in
Eurasia. Different elements of the post-Soviet states participate differently in cross-border interactions. Russian-speaking professional
urban dwellers are much more connected in various ways to people in
other post-Soviet states than many other segments of their respective
societies; they represent a strong pro-integration constituency in Eurasia. Diasporas can play a positive role, from the perspective of international security, if they facilitate links among civil societies and voluntary regional integration. Russian heritage, like that of any nation,
has many different faces, including imperialistic and humanistic ones.
If the latter is properly engaged in a new context, Russia can play the
role of a legitimate leader in Eurasia as a center of cultural, economic,
and political gravitation. However, the current international environment has not been favorable for such a result. Nation-state building
on an ethnic basis seems to be the only game in the Eurasian arena
thus far. How has Russia responded to these developments and what
are its future options?

Understanding Possible Russian Responses to the Challenges Presented by the Diasporas

Interaction between Russia and the Russian diasporas is a transnational
relationship between state and nonstate actors. This relationship has
been incorporated into the Russian foreign policy agenda and reflects
an attempt of the Russian state to address "the Russian question" as it
was shaped by the collapse of the Soviet Union. It has not been the

driving force of Russian foreign policy toward the newly independent states, but it has the potential to become so and to reshape the Eurasian geopolitical landscape if (or, as some would argue, when) Russia takes a more nationalistic path. U.S. foreign policymakers are so preoccupied with putative Russian imperial ambitions in Eurasia that they fail to recognize other challenges to peace and security on the continent. Russian ethnonationalism is among the most significant threats to security in Eurasia, and stimulation of nation-state building, as well as politicization of diaspora issues, could lead to an explosive process of redrawing state borders along ethnic lines. However, Russian policy toward its diasporas is not at all destined to be imperialistic or to become ethnonationalist.

Across the political spectrum, there is a consensus that Russia does have some responsibility to those people who identify themselves as Russians or Russian speakers and who live in the Soviet successor states. It is important that the United States understand the deep sense of obligation shared by many citizens of the Russian Federation in this matter. There is broad agreement among both the Russian elite and ordinary citizens that they must not abandon the diasporas. U.S. policymakers need to understand that it is politically impossible for even the most liberal Russian politician not to express some concern for the fate of those Russians. That is why the programs of all the significant political parties, from communist to liberal, contain provisions on this issue. Every government during the Yeltsin era expressed, at least rhetorically, its commitment to protect compatriots in the near abroad.

Russia's future attempts to help the Russians in the near abroad could range from neo-imperialistic ambitions to efforts to ensure their human rights. It might facilitate a peaceful resolution of the problem if U. S. policymakers considered that Russia could respond in a variety of ways—some of them quite constructive. The tendency today is to assume automatically that any talk about the Russians in the Soviet successor states is potentially aggressive, but this is not necessarily the case. So, the best option for the United States is not to ring alarm bells when Russians talk about their diasporas, but to encourage Russia to take steps in the direction of protecting human rights in the neighboring states.

On the imperialistic side—much feared by international observers as well as by leaders of the Soviet successor states—it is possible that

Russia could use the Russian populations to help re-establish its domination, perhaps turning the successor states into protectorates or semi-independent entities in a buffer zone around Russia. In countries where the diasporas are directly adjacent to Russia, Russia could stir up the Russian populations to form breakaway regions that would reunite with Russia. Politicization of the diasporas and efforts to redraw state borders along ethnic lines are among the most significant potential threats to security in the region.

It is also possible that Russia will pursue a constructive and humanistic course. Such a path might include helping Russians in the diasporas maintain their distinct culture, for example, by helping to develop educational institutions, cultural centers, or periodicals. Or it might include efforts to protect Russians' human rights by acting within the framework of existing international institutions designed for the protection of both individual human rights and the rights of minorities, such as the Council of Europe and the OSCE.

Russia and the neighboring states might also rely on recent western European experience in creating the Eurasian analogues to the so-called Euroregions. In January 1996, France, Germany, Luxembourg, and Switzerland signed the Karlsruhe Agreement, which opened the way for border-transcending cooperation among the communities, cities, and regions of the signatory nations. The treaty allowed regional entities to conclude direct agreements and carry out common ventures without the involvement of central governments. Establishment of special transfrontier regions, cultural and territorial autonomy, and protection of bilingualism may be among many tools to protect the interests of the diasporas.[8]

Russian foreign minister Igor Ivanov recently emphasized that Russia would concentrate on helping compatriots living abroad in solving their cultural, educational, and social problems. He pointed to the importance of providing textbooks to Russian-language schools, educating the teachers, and supporting Russian-language newspapers within the existing laws of respective countries. He also underlined the necessity to work within the Council of Europe and OSCE frameworks in the field of protecting the human rights of Russian speakers.[9]

U. S. foreign policymakers would be wise to support Russian leaders in their efforts along these lines, in part because that might deter the latter from taking more extreme measures. Nonetheless, some observers still fear that Russia will use human rights issues as a cover for interfering in the domestic policies of the Soviet successor states. While Russia does aspire to be the dominant power in the region, currently it is in no position politically, economically, or militarily to pose a serious threat to the new Eurasian states. The real danger is the possibility that the international community might overreact to some Russian politicians' rhetoric about protecting the interests of the Russians in the near abroad and not notice the attempts to protect human rights and the desire to work within international institutions.

In his first short address on general priorities of his government made to the lower chamber of the parliament on August 16, 1999, then–prime minister Vladimir Putin deemed it necessary to promise in very resolute and assertive terms to defend the interests of the Russians abroad. However, it is significant that Putin mentioned diplomatic measures only. He said that "we do not have a right to allow violation of our compatriots' rights and keeping them as humans of the second class. . . . Our diplomacy must act more energetically and aggressively in this area."[10] It is doubtful that Putin had any concrete program or ideas on this issue just several days after his unexpected appointment as premier. However, he decided to include these passages into his first public address in his new capacity. It was a strong indicator of the political importance of the issue for both parliamentarians and the public.

What will the policy of President Putin toward compatriots abroad look like? Should we expect any significant transformations in this field in comparison with the Yeltsin era? It is evident enough that policy toward the Russian diasporas will be a function of broader national security and foreign policy strategies of the Russian Federation under new leadership in the new century. President Putin has vowed to rebuild the Russian state and restore Russia's standing in the world. He has declared that he will lead Russia to regain its strength, its sense of national pride and purpose. Analysis of Putin's background, his first steps in the presidency, and his early statements and interviews suggest that he is first of all a new state builder, much like his predecessor. His rhetoric also includes some elements of domination and integration strategies, but they are hardly ideologies of ethnonationalism or restorationalism. How may Putin's strategic goals and perception of the tasks of state and nation building in Russia influence more concrete policies toward the diasporas? It may be plausible to suggest that the diaspora issues will remain instruments, not the goals, of Russian policy in the near abroad. In this sense, there will be no radical departure from Yeltsin's course. The question of Russian compatriots in the near abroad per se rarely will be elevated to receive serious presidential attention. Rather, they will be addressed by the president primarily in the context of interstate relations with the newly independent states, which will be driven by "economic pragmatism." That means that diaspora issues will be handled mainly by the governmental bodies that were created in the Yeltsin era and concerned primarily with human rights, cultural, and educational issues. These bodies include, first of all, sections in the Foreign Ministry and Ministry for Nationalities Policy, the Governmental Commission on the Affairs of Compatriots Abroad, and the Duma Committee on CIS Affairs and Relations with Compatriots.

Of course, a violent crisis directly involving Russian diasporas could dramatically change Russia's pragmatic, cautious, and benign policy. Judging by Putin's handling of the second Chechen war in 1999–2000, his response may be immediate, decisive, and forceful. Russia's National Security Concept, adopted by presidential decree on January 10, 2000, stated that the foreign policy of the Russian Federation should be designed, among other purposes, "to protect the lawful rights and interests of Russian citizens abroad through the use of political, economic, and other measures."[11] The Military Doctrine of the Russian Federation, approved by a presidential decree on April 21, 2000, went further and named discrimination and suppression of rights, freedoms, and legitimate interests of the citizens of the Russian Federation in foreign countries among the main external threats.[12] However, the scenario of Russian military intervention to protect Russians in the near abroad is very unlikely. First, the countries where Russian minorities play important roles (Ukraine, Kazakhstan, Latvia, and Estonia) are relatively stable, and prospects for violence there are low. Second, in the unstable countries of the south Caucasus and Central Asia, Russians are not important actors or potential targets of violence. Third, the leaders of all newly independent states are well aware of the possible consequences of a crisis involving Russian diasporas and would certainly try to prevent any use of force against them.

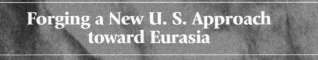

Forging a New U. S. Approach toward Eurasia

The Clinton administration tried to implement a policy of engagement toward a new Russia. It encouraged Russian integration into the world economy and its democratic transition. It supported Russia's effort to transform its political, economic, and social institutions. At the same time, an important task of U.S. policy in Eurasia has been to ensure that the collapse of the Soviet Union is irreversible.[13] The United States has also shown determination to block any Russian attempt to develop as a regional hegemonic power. The goal of American international leadership is incompatible with giving regionally dominant powers a free hand in their "zones of influence." This is the area where the question of the diasporas, if they are viewed as an instrument of Russia's hegemonic ambitions, might become an issue in Russian-American relations.

Much of American geopolitical and strategic thinking about Eurasia has been informed by the historic (and well-grounded) fear of Russian imperialism and an attempt to prevent its revival. Zbigniew Brzezinski, whose views of course do not represent the entirety of American perceptions but were influential in the Clinton administration's national security team and are highly regarded in Washington's academic community, has contributed significantly to this approach, warning U.S. policymakers about Russia's designs to revitalize "a regionally hegemonic Russia . . . to become again the strongest power in Eurasia. Unlike the old centralized Soviet Union and its neighboring bloc of satellite states, the new arrangements would embrace Russia and its satellite states (within the former Soviet Union) in some kind of confederation."[14] Instead, Brzezinski suggested another, much smaller, confederation when he wrote about the desirability of "a loosely confederated Russia —composed of a European Russia, a Siberian Republic, and a Far Eastern Republic."[15] In other words, Russia, even in its present borders, is too big for Brzezinski's taste. Only a marginal, confederated Russian state on the periphery of Europe in the future may be included into the Euro-Atlantic system envisioned by Brzezinski. Russia in its present form is seen as a force that can obstruct American geopolitical goals of determining the course of events in Eurasia.[16]

"Democratic, national, truly modern, and European Russia" fits the goal of America's primacy in the Euro-Atlantic community much better than Russia with imperial ambitions, according to Brzezinski.[17] Paradoxically, two positive components of this formula—namely, *national* and *European*—may be destabilizing and counterproductive if interpreted as broad goals of Western policy toward Russia. What has not been noticed is the important fact that "national Russia," in the view of the country's elites and many ordinary Russians, includes all the Russian diasporas in the near abroad and thus spreads well beyond the borders of the Russian Federation. Abstract notions of nation-state are mechanically applied to the region, which has not had any relevant historical experience and where "national" means primarily "ethnic." Building "national Russia" may also alienate non–ethnic Russians within the Russian Federation. This fact makes calls for a "national Russia" extremely dangerous for regional and global security.

Paradoxically, thinking of Russia as a potentially European state may slow its integration into international institutions and security arrangements. The size of the country, its diversity, nuclear arsenal, instability on its southern borders, economic problems, the existence of multi-million-member diasporas, and peculiarities of national identity make Western countries very cautious when discussing the admission of Russia into European or transatlantic institutions. Recognition of Russia as a significant and important other, on the contrary, may ease building a constructive partnership with it.[18]

Former U.S. secretary of state James A. Baker III thoughtfully suggested an approach that recognizes the fact that Russia is indeed different and that there are limitations to outsiders' attempts to transform it into an entity that is well known to the European or American experience. Still, this does not mean disengagement in the international arena. As Baker argues: "A peaceful, democratic, and prosperous Russia is strongly in our national interest. . . . We must recognize that Russia will develop on her own terms and in her own way. . . . Our efforts to help Russia meet her challenges can only have a modest impact on a country that vast and complex. But that impact in itself is well worth our time and resources."[19] Russian policy toward its sister communities in the near abroad is exactly the area where U.S. efforts may have only a modest impact. However, if Western policy does not have ambitions to change the historical identity of Russians but limits it to efforts to help Russians solve their problems peacefully, within international law and in cooperation with international institutions, it is worth the time and resources.

Recognition of Russia as a country, which deserves a much more sophisticated policy than simply the suggestion that an instant European nation-state be created on the ruins of an empire and that the United States must stimulate this process, has led some analysts to rethink a standard moralistic vision of imperialism. Anatol Lieven even suggests that the West must not fear some kind of restrained Russian imperialism and that such imperialism may block the development of a "real threat." He has been one of very few Western observers who make a clear distinction between imperialism and ethnonationalism and who point to the greater danger of the latter to international security. When analyzing options for Western policy in the "triangle" of Ukraine, Russia, and the West, he argues:

> The great threat is not that Russia will retain certain "imperialist" attitudes and seek a sort of sphere of influence among its neighbors, for this is inevitable. The West's task must be to see that it does so in a restrained and civilized manner, without either force or subversion.
>
> The real threat, on the contrary, is that perceiving itself isolated from the West and threatened by its neighbors, Russia will develop a form of narrow, bitter, ethnic nationalism resembling that of the Ukrainian radical nationalists. In my view, for Russia to swing from its present mild and highly constricted "imperialism" to such a form of nationalism would be no gain for Russia, for its neighbors, for Europe, or indeed for humanity—and it is precisely this outcome that would be risked by a misguided strategy of using Ukraine as a weapon against Russia.[20]

This conclusion is probably applicable not only to Western policy toward Ukraine, but also toward Azerbaijan, Georgia, Uzbekistan, or the Baltic states. Lieven's framework of analysis is an important step forward in shaping a new policy toward Eurasia as it brings the threat of Russian ethnonationalism into the equation. However, limiting alternatives to imperialism, even restrained, is ignoring another option, namely that of integration.

In sum, it is important for U.S. foreign policymakers to go beyond the dichotomy of "imperialistic Russia" or "Russia as a nation-state."

Thinking exclusively within this framework is using eighty-year-old concepts. Rather, it would be helpful to pay attention to a different pair of options—namely, "ethnonationalist Russia" or "Russia as a leader of regional integration." Encouragement of nation building may lead to endorsement of destructive ethnonationalism. Paralyzing fear of imperialism may lead unintentionally to a situation in which modern, positive trends of integration are mistakenly perceived as signs of imperial ambition. Ethnonationalism and globalization, including regional integration, characterize the modern world, and the issue of Russian diasporas must be addressed in the context of these trends. Policy recommendations cannot ignore the threats accompanying ethnonationalism and the inevitability of growing cooperation among nations, which usually starts with building bridges among neighbors.

While the theme of Russian neo-imperialist ambitions in the near abroad dominates American discourse on security and foreign policy issues in Eurasia, the topic of economic and political integration in the region is mainly ignored. Many analysts have failed to see that there are not only neo-imperial or nation-state options for Russia, but also an alternative policy to both of these scenarios—namely, integration. The latter may prevent the rise of a militant, revanchist Russian ethnonationalism.

Indeed, in conjunction with a focus on human rights, Russia and the surrounding states might also be encouraged to advance their economic integration and maintain open borders. If people can move about freely, and if the countries can work together to resolve cultural identity issues, there would be no point in staging a bloody process to redraw borders, as happened in the Balkans. The integration would resemble Europe's and thus might also lead to some form of voluntary political association similar to the European Union.

In the former Soviet Union, integration may be the only peaceful alternative to the rise of ethnonationalism and the claims that Russians are a divided nation and must reunite under one political roof. However, U.S. foreign policymakers tend to perceive even talk about integration of the former Soviet republics as a disguised attempt to reinstitute Russian domination, if not to restore the Soviet Union. It would benefit everyone if they could begin to consider the constructive aspects of integration in the region. The positive effect of regional integration on a peaceful solution to the diasporas issue cannot be overestimated.

Meanwhile, the challenge to Russian policymakers presented by the diasporas has not as yet been included into mainstream American strategic analysis of the perils and opportunities of integration on the territory of the former Soviet Union.

Within the internationalist option, there are several alternatives. In a groundbreaking study of integration and disintegration processes in the former Soviet Union, Terrence Hopmann, Stephen Shenfield, and Dominique Arel make an important conceptual distinction between four likely scenarios in the realm of integration: coercive integration under Russian domination, voluntary cooperative integration, chaotic unregulated disintegration, and cooperative independence. The authors come to the conclusion that

> the West must be cautious about interpreting Russian efforts to promote integration within the CIS as an inherently neo-imperialist effort by Russian leaders to exert hegemony over former Soviet territory. In particular, the West must distinguish clearly between coercive attempts by Russia's leaders to use integration as a guise to dominate other countries, which the West should oppose, and other more cooperative efforts to integrate, toward which the West should adopt a more sanguine attitude. In fact, many experts [in Russia and some other newly independent states] argue that the West should aid integration within the CIS region, as the United States did in Western Europe through the Marshall Plan after World War II. Integration based on common historical and cultural ties, comparative economic advantage, existing infrastructure, and other common interests is not only natural, but in fact serves the long-term security interests of Western Europe, North America, and indeed the entire world.[21]

Whether U. S. foreign policymakers' desired outcomes for the region want it or not, a significant and influential part of the Russian elite strongly believes that the Western attitude toward economic, defense, and political integration among the former Soviet republics is negative. This was the main theme of the 1994 Russian External Intelligence Service special report "Russia and the CIS: Does the Western Position Need to Be Corrected?" It was very unusual for the Russian intelligence service to make a public statement on an issue of international politics; the report reflected a strong conviction that the issue was extremely important and probably indicated divergence between the intelligence community and Kozyrev's Foreign Ministry. The report directly linked the fate of the Russian diasporas to the prospects of economic integration among the former Soviet republics: "Creation of a common economic space in the CIS is the only way to reduce tension in the relations between the Soviet successor states arising from the fact that millions of ethnic Russians and Russian speakers remain in the 'near abroad.'"[22] The report was prepared under the supervision of Yevgeny Primakov, then the director of the External Intelligence Service. In 1999, Primakov, the most popular Russian politician at that time, asserted in his memoirs that the Russian intelligence service had obtained documentary affirmation from a very reliable source that the U.S. Central Intelligence Agency was interested in preventing grouping of the sovereign CIS countries around Moscow. Analysis of the materials led him to the conclusion that the leaders of some Western countries acted to undermine rapprochement between Russia and other CIS countries.[23]

Of course, Russian foreign policymakers well understand that the Western position may play an important but secondary role in the failures of CIS integration. The prime reasons for failure are lack of consensus among Russian political and economic elites on this issue, coupled with the extreme weakness of state institutions and the difficulties of implementing any foreign policy or domestic decisions. However, Russians can point to concrete Western policies aimed at preventing integration among former Soviet republics and at limiting Russian influence. They include a negative attitude toward a pro-Russian regime in Belarus (though human rights violations have not been any worse there than in many other post-Soviet states) and the proposed Belarus-Russia union; vigorous attempts to keep a distance between Russia and Ukraine; readiness to spend considerable political capital to help build alternative pipelines for Caspian oil that would bypass Russia; joint military exercises involving the United States and the Central Asian nations; and discussions of eventual inclusion of the Baltic states into NATO. American financial assistance to Ukraine and Georgia to demarcate their new state borders and to equip checkpoints along those borders has been particularly symbolic for the policy of building walls, not bridges, in Eurasia.

These policies may be perceived as anti-Russian by the Russian elite not only because they could weaken the country's preponderance in Eurasia, but also because they block solving "the Russian question" on the methods of integration. They stir up anti-Western sentiments even among otherwise quite liberal parts of the Russian elite. Many Russians fail to realize that U.S. policies are often not part of an anti-Russian conspiracy but simply reflect other domestic and international concerns of the United States. Many U.S. policies can be attributed to a desire to have a pro-Western regime in the country (Belarus) that now borders NATO members, support of Turkey as the key ally in the Middle East (pipeline routes), and domestic pressures of émigrés from the borderlands of the Russian Empire and their descendants. The problem is that these concerns are often not balanced by due consideration of other factors, including those related to specific features of Russian identity and the existence of multiple millions of Russian diasporians.

The problem of Russian diasporas to some extent structures the whole of Eurasia and ties many former Soviet republics together. In the near abroad, there remain about 23 million ethnic Russians, an additional 11 million Russophones, and many more non-Russians who live outside their putative homelands and prefer to speak Russian. Combined, they total about 30 percent of the entire population of non-Russian Soviet successor states. Joined with the geopolitical preponderance of the Russian Federation in Eurasia, it makes Russia not simply a marginal *national* European state, but a potential center of a revived, distinct *civilization*.

It has been correctly pointed out that the popular Russian view of integration or reintegration as an inevitable outcome is "more faith than strategy."[24] Indeed, Russia has lacked a well-developed strategy and consistent policy in the near abroad. However, the faith in integration is based on a long historic tradition and objective (or perceived as objective) facts. In this context, musings about the current weakness of Russia as an obstacle to its playing a special role in the region seem unconvincing if long-term factors are taken into account. It would be unwise for U.S. foreign policymakers to try to restructure Eurasia according to geopolitical schemes that ignore the existence of Russian diasporas and the civilizational aspects of Russian culture. Recognizing Russia as a central element of complex ties among Eurasian countries does not contradict the aim of strengthening the statehood of newly independent states. Moreover, it may contribute to peaceful resolution of difficult problems in building new civic nations in countries with significant Russian populations, such as Ukraine or Kazakhstan.

Hierarchies of national interests are different in Russia and in the United States. Diaspora issues rank very high among Russian priorities because they are linked to the fundamentals of Russian identity and self-perception. The United States should appreciate the concern of Russia for its sister communities in other states of the former Soviet Union. It is impossible for Russia to be indifferent to the plight of Russian-speaking minorities; the defense of their rights is an integral part of the Russian interest. To ensure that Russia's defense of its compatriots' interests is peaceful, the United States would be wise to give active support to positive aspects of regional integration in Eurasia. American understanding and constructive cooperation with Russia in this area could have a tremendous positive effect on bilateral relations and may secure cooperation in other areas, including those that are vital to the national security of the United States and the West in general.

. . . .

Notes

INTRODUCTION

1. The term "Russian idea" was coined by Fyodor Dostoevsky in 1860; see his *Polnoe sobranie sochineniy v tridtsati tomakh* (Collected Works in Thirty Volumes), vol. 18 (Leningrad: Nauka, 1972–1990), 35–40. For an analysis of the genesis and development of the "Russian idea," see an important book by Nikolai Berdyaev, *Russkaya ideya: Osnovnye problemy russkoi mysli XIX veka i nachala XX veka* (The Russian Idea: Main Problems of Russian Thought in the Nineteenth and Early Twentieth Centuries) (Moscow: Svarog, 1997). For a modern sympathetic study of the Russian idea, see Arsenii Gulyga, *Russkaya ideya i eyo tvortsy* (The Russian Idea and Its Creators) (Moscow: Soratnik, 1995). For a critical study of the concept, see Vladimir Khoros, "Russkaya ideya na istoricheskom perekryostke" (The Russian Idea at a Historic Crossroad), *Svobodnaya mysl'*, no. 6 (1992): 36–47. For the current political implications, see James Scanlan, "The Russian Idea from Dostoevskii to Ziuganov," *Problems of Post-Communism* (July/August 1996): 35–42. For a broad historic interpretation of the Russian idea as a set of perceptions about the distinctiveness of Russian culture and an ideal model of society, see Tim McDaniel, *The Agony of the Russian Idea* (Princeton, N.J.: Princeton University Press, 1996).

2. Aleksandr Solzhenitsyn argues: "The 'Russian question' at the end of the twentieth century stands unequivocal: Shall our people *be* or *not be*? The vulgar and insipid wave which seeks to level distinctions between cultures, traditions, nationalities, and characters has engulfed the whole planet. And yet how many withstand this onslaught, unwavering and even with their head held high! Not we, however. . . . If we persist in this way, who knows if in another century the time may come to cross the word 'Russian' out of the dictionary?" Aleksandr Solzhenitsyn, *The Russian Question at the End of the Twentieth Century* (New York: Farrar, Straus, and Giroux, 1995), 106–107.

3. It will be argued in chapter 4 that because of significant differences among the Russian communities in the near abroad, it is probably more appropriate to refer to them as different Russian diasporas, rather than a single Russian diaspora.

4. Aleksandr Solzhenitsyn, *Rossiya v obvale* (Russia in the abyss) (Moscow: Russkiy put', 1998), 3, 187, 156, 185, 203.

5. Ibid., 131.

6. Ibid., 69.

7. Ibid., 71.

8. See Margaret Canovan, *Nationhood and Political Theory* (Brookfield, Vt.: Edward Elgar, 1996), 20–21, 64.

9. See Liah Greenfeld, *Nationalism: Five Roads to Modernity* (Cambridge, Mass.: Harvard University Press, 1992), 261.

10. Anthony Smith, *The Ethnic Origins of Nations* (Oxford: Basil Blackwell, 1986), 150. Pierre van den Berghe was perhaps the first to introduce term *ethnie* into the English-language literature in the first edition of his *The Ethnic Phenomenon* (New York: Elsevier, 1981). He used it as a substitute for "ethnic group," which he found clumsy. Smith widely uses the term as synonymous with "ethnicity" and "ethnic group."

11. David Laitin, *Identity in Formation: The Russian-Speaking Populations in the Near Abroad* (Ithaca, N.Y.: Cornell University Press, 1998), 340.

12. For an excellent discussion of the term "diaspora," see Robin Cohen, "Diasporas and the Nation-State: From Victims to Challengers," *International Affairs* 72, no. 3 (1996): 507–20. For a discussion of the concept of the Russian diaspora, see Paul Kolstoe, *Russians in the Former Soviet Republics* (Indianapolis: Indiana University Press, 1995), 1–5. The term is widely used in Russian theoretical discourse by, for example, Solzhenitsyn in *The Russian Question*. It is also contained in the programs of both liberal and communist parties and organizations. See the programs of the liberal Yabloko party and Our Home Is Russia, and in the communist Spiritual Heritage, in V. A. Oleshchuk, V. V. Pribylovsky, and M. N. Reitblat, *Parlamentskie partii, dvizheniya, ob'edineniya: Istoriya, ideologiya, sostav rukovodyashchikh organov, deputaty parlamenta, programmnye dokumenty* (Parliamentary Parties, Movements, Associations: History, Ideology, Governing Bodies, Parliamentary Deputies, Program Documents) (Moscow: Panorama, 1996), 101, 200, 213. The term "diaspora" is also used in key governmental documents, for example, in the draft of the Concept of the State Policy of the Russian Federation toward Compatriots Abroad.

13. For an emotional discussion of these terms, see Semyon Agaev and Yuliy Oganisyan, "O kontseptsii gosudarsvennoy politiky RF v otnoshenii rossiiskoy diaspory: Po materialam obsuzhdeniya v ISPRAN" (On the Concept of the Russian Federation's State Policy toward the Russian Diaspora: Review of the Discussion in ISPRAN), *Polis*, no. 1 (1998): 181. The term "Russian-speaking" was especially attacked for its anti-Semitic flavor. David Laitin correctly noted that this term is often derogatory in Russia and quite neutral and acceptable in the newly independent states; see Laitin, *Identity in Formation*, 315.

14. See Ilya Prizel, *National Identity and Foreign Policy* (New York: Cambridge University Press, 1998).

15. Laitin, *Identity in Formation,* 335. See also Ronald Suny, *The Revenge of the Past: Nationalism, Revolution, and the Collapse of the Soviet Union* (Stanford, Calif.: Stanford University Press, 1993).

16. Prizel, *National Identity and Foreign Policy,* 8.

17. See Anatol Lieven, *Chechnya: Tombstone of Russian Power* (New Haven, Conn.: Yale University Press, 1998).

18. A rare exception is the pioneering work of the already-mentioned Ilya Prizel in his *National Identity and Foreign Policy.*

19. See Canovan, *Nationhood and Political Theory;* Smith, *The Ethnic Origins of Nations;* Walker Connor, *Ethnonationalism: The Quest for Understanding* (Princeton, N.J.: Princeton University Press, 1994); Rogers Brubaker, *Nationalism Reframed: Nationhood and the National Question in the New Europe* (New York: Cambridge University Press, 1996); Greenfeld, *Nationalism;* Robin Cohen, *Global Diasporas: An Introduction* (Seattle: University of Washington Press, 1997); Roman Szporluk, "The Fall of the Tsarist Empire and the USSR: The Russian Question and Imperial Overextension," in *The End of Empire? The Transformation of the USSR in Comparative Perspective,* ed. Karen Dawisha and Bruce Parrott (Armonk, N.Y.: M. E. Sharpe, 1997).

20. See Chauncy Harris, "The New Russian Minorities: A Statistical Overview," *Post Soviet Geography* 34, no. 1 (January 1993): 1–28; Vladimir Shlapentokh, Munir Sendich, and Emil Payin, eds., *The New Russian Diaspora: Russian Minorities in the Former Soviet Republics* (Armonk, N.Y.: M. E. Sharpe, 1994); Kolstoe, *Russians in the Former Soviet Republics;* Neil Melvin, *Russians Beyond Russia: The Politics of National Identity* (London: Royal Institute of International Affairs, 1995); Jeff Chinn and Robert Kaiser, *Russians as the New Minority* (Boulder, Colo.: Westview, 1996); Laitin, *Identity in Formation;* A. I. Ginzburg et al., eds., *Russkie v novom zarubezh'e: Programma etnosotsiologicheskikh issledovanii* (Russians in the New Abroad: A Program of Ethnic and Sociological Studies) (Moscow: Institute of Ethnology and Anthropology, 1993); V. I. Kozlov and E. A. Shervud, eds., *Russkie v blizhnem zarubezh'e* (Russians in the Near Abroad) (Moscow: Institute of Ethnology and Anthropology, 1994); Valery Tishkov, ed., *Migratsii i novye diaspory v postsovetskikh gosudarstvakh* (Migrations and New Diasporas in Post-Soviet States) (Moscow: Institute of Ethnology and Anthropology, 1996); V. A. Mikhailov et al., eds., *Natsional'naya Politika Rossii: istoriya i sovremennost'* (Nationality Policy of Russia: History and Contemporary) (Moscow: Russkii mir, 1997); T. Poloskova, *Diaspory v sisteme mezhdunarodnykh svyazey* (Diasporas in the System of International Relations) (Moscow: Nauchnaya kniga, 1998); G. Vitkovskaya, ed., *Problemy stanovleniya institutov grazhdanskogo obshchestva v postsovetskikh gosudarstvakh* (Problems of Civil Society Institutions' Formation in Post-Soviet States) (Moscow: Carnegie Moscow Center, 1998).

21. See Nikolai Rudensky, "Russian Minorities in the Newly Independent States: An International Problem in the Domestic Context of Russia Today," in *National Identity and Ethnicity in Russia and the New States of Eurasia,* ed. Roman Szporluk (Armonk, N.Y.: M. E. Sharpe, 1994); Elizabeth Teague, "Russians Outside Russia and

Russian Security Policy," in *The Emergence of Russian Foreign Policy,* ed. Leon Aron
and Kenneth Jensen (Washington, D.C.: United States Institute of Peace Press, 1994);
Neil Melvin, "The Russians: Diaspora and the End of Empire," in *Nations Abroad:
Diaspora Politics and International Relations in the Former Soviet Union,* ed. Charles
King and Neil Melvin (Boulder, Colo.: Westview, 1998); Aurel Braun, "All Quiet on the
Russian Front? Russia, Its Neighbors, and the Russian Diaspora," in *The New Euro-
pean Diasporas: National Minorities and Conflict in Eastern Europe,* ed. Michael Man-
delbaum (Washington, D.C.: Council on Foreign Relations, 2000).

CHAPTER 1: RUSSIAN NATION-STATE BUILDING AND
DIASPORAS IN THE SECURITY CONTEXT

1. See Yuri Afanasiev, "A New Russian Imperialism," *Perspective* 3 (February/
March 1994); Yuri Afanasiev, "Seems Like the Old Times? Russia's Place in the World,"
Current History 93 (October 1994); Yuri Afanasiev, "Russian Reform Is Dead," *Foreign
Affairs,* March/April 1994, 21–26.

2. See Stephen Sestanovich, "Geotherapy: Russia's Neuroses, and Ours," *The
National Interest* 45 (Fall 1996).

3. *Nezavisimaya gazeta,* December 19, 1996.

4. Geoffrey Hosking, *Russia: People and Empire* (Cambridge, Mass.: Harvard
University Press, 1997), 478–81.

5. See Richard Pipes, "Introduction: The Nationality Problem," in *Handbook of
Major Soviet Nationalities,* ed. Zev Katz et al. (New York: Free Press, 1975), 1.

6. Richard Pipes, "Birth of an Empire," *New York Times Book Review,* May 25,
1997: 13.

7. Martin Malia, "The Dead Weight of Empire," *Times Literary Supplement,*
June 20, 1997; as quoted in Lieven, *Chechnya,* 375.

8. Zbigniew Brzezinski, "The Premature Partnership," *Foreign Affairs,* March/
April 1994, 79. For a critical review of Brzezinski's views on a Russia that must "define
itself purely as Russia," see Valery Tishkov, *Ethnicity, Nationalism, and Conflict in and
after the Soviet Union* (London: SAGE Publications, 1997), 247.

9. Khachig Tololyan, "The Nation-State and Its Others: In Lieu of a Preface," in
Becoming National, ed. Geoff Eley and Ronald Grigor Suny (New York: Oxford University Press, 1996), 429.

10. Michael Howard, *The Lessons of History* (New York: Oxford University Press,
1991), 39.

11. See Hosking, *Russia: People and Empire,* 486.

12. Ibid.

13. Concrete border disputes in the post-Soviet space were analyzed in Tuomas
Forsberg, ed., *Contested Territory: Border Disputes at the Edge of the Former Soviet
Empire* (Brookfield, Vt.: Edward Elgar, 1995). Broader questions of the links between
geography and ideology in Russia were examined in Mark Basin, "Russia Between

Europe and Asia: The Ideological Construction of Geographical Space," *Slavic Review* 50, vol. 1 (Spring 1991): 1–17. Various cognitive maps of Russians in their relation to national identity were studied in Katheline Parthe, *Russia's "Unreal Estate": Cognitive Mapping and National Identity.* Occasional Paper 265 (Washington, D.C.: Kennan Institute for Advanced Russian Studies, July 1997).

14. Geoffrey Hosking, "The Freudian Frontier," *Times Literary Supplement,* March 10, 1995, 27, as quoted by Roman Szporluk in "The Fall of the Tsarist Empire and the USSR: The Russian Question and the Imperial Overextension," in *The End of Empire? The Transformation of the USSR in Comparative Perspective,* ed. Karen Dawisha and Bruce Parrott (Armonk, N.Y.: M. E. Sharpe, 1997), 70.

15. George Breslauer and Catherine Dale were the first to point out this striking contradiction. See George Breslauer and Catherine Dale, "Boris Yeltsin and the Invention of a Russian Nation-State," *Post-Soviet Affairs* 13, no. 4 (October–December 1997): 330.

16. Richard Pipes, "Is Russia Still an Enemy?" *Foreign Affairs,* September/October 1997, 73.

17. Smith, *The Ethnic Origins of Nations,* 135; emphasis added.

18. Ibid., 137.

19. See ibid., 147–49.

20. See Hans Kohn, *The Idea of Nationalism* (New York: Macmillan, 1946); Smith, *The Ethnic Origins of Nations,* 140–44; Johann Arnason, "Nationalism, Globalization, and Modernity," in *Global Culture: Nationalism, Globalization, and Modernity,* ed. Mike Featherstone (London: SAGE Publications, 1990), 231–32; Greenfeld, *Nationalism.*

21. See, for example, Featherstone, ed., *Global Culture;* Benjamin Barber, *Jihad vs. McWorld; How the Planet Is Falling Apart and Coming Together* (New York: Random House, 1995); Mathew Horsman and Andrew Marshall, *After the Nation-State: Citizens, Tribalism, and the New Global Disorder* (London: Harper Collins, 1995); John Agnew and Stuart Corbridge, *Mastering Space* (London: Routledge, 1995).

22. Ronald Robertson, "Globalization and Societal Modernization: A Note on Japan and Japanese Religion," *Sociological Analysis* 47 (Spring 1987): 38.

23. See Peter Rutland, "Globalization and the Transition in Eastern Europe," *Macalester International* 2 (Fall 1995): 3–7.

24. See John Spence, "Ethnicity and International Relations: Introduction and Overview," *International Affairs* 72, no. 3 (1996): 439; Seyla Benhabib, "Strange Multiplicities: The Politics of Identity and Difference in a Global Context," *Macalester International* 4 (Spring 1997), 28.

25. James Rosenau, "The Complexities and Contradictions of Globalization," *Current History* (November 1997), 361.

26. See Robin Cohen, "Diasporas and the Nation-State: From Victims to Challengers," *International Affairs* 72, no. 3 (1996): 517–20.

27. Benedict Anderson, "The Grammars of Modern Identity," *Macalester International* 4 (Spring 1997): 23.

28. On Chinatowns, see Cohen, "Diasporas and the Nation-State," 518–19.

29. Agnew and Corbridge, *Mastering Space*, 185.

30. Edward Said, *Orientalism* (New York: Vintage, 1979), 18.

31. See Salman Rushdie, *Imaginary Homelands* (London: Granta, 1990).

32. Cohen, "Diasporas and the Nation-State," 520.

33. Tololyan, "The Nation-State and Its Others," 428.

34. See, for example, Horsman and Marshall, *After the Nation-State*, x–xi.

35. Barber, *Jihad vs. McWorld*, 5–7.

36. Anderson, "The Grammars of Modern Identity," 24.

37. Eley and Suny, eds., *Becoming National*, 425.

38. Nationalist Chinese leader and founding father of the Republic of China Sun Yat Sen originally built his movement among the Chinese diaspora on Hawaii and in Hong Kong, Japan, and Europe.

39. Russians themselves usually address the issues of identity in a different way, and there are strong historical, not "structural," overtones in the discourse. The major themes are the relationship of modern Russia to the historical legacies of the Russian Empire and the Soviet Union. See more in Stephen Shenfield, "Post-Soviet Russia in Search of Identity," in *Russia's Future: Consolidation or Disintegration?* ed. Douglas Blum (Boulder, Colo.: Westview, 1994), 6.

40. Smith, *The Ethnic Origins of Nations*, 222.

41. The perils of the Turkish example for Russia were highlighted by Anatol Lieven in his "Restraining NATO: Ukraine, Russia, and the West," *The Washington Quarterly* (Autumn 1997): 73–74.

42. See more on the Romantic views of nationhood in Canovan, *Nationhood and Political Theory*, 6–9.

43. Hosking, *Russia: People and Empire*, 485.

44. See Connor, *Ethnonationalism*, 90.

45. Karen Barkey and Mark von Hagen, "Conclusion," in *After Empire: Multiethnic Societies and Nation-Building: The Soviet Union and the Russian, Ottoman, and Habsburg Empires*, ed. Karen Barkey and Mark von Hagen (Boulder, Colo.: Westview, 1997), 187.

46. Connor, *Ethnonationalism*, 29.

47. Breslauer and Dale, "Boris Yeltsin and the Invention of a Russian Nation-State," 330.

48. Ibid., 332.

CHAPTER 2: TRANSFORMATIONS OF RUSSIAN IDENTITY

1. See Connor, *Ethnonationalism*, 39–42, 91–100.

2. See Greenfeld, *Nationalism*, 490; Canovan, *Nationhood and Political Theory*, 62–64.

3. Berdyaev, *Russkaya ideya*, 307.

4. On the various concepts of the nation: As a "politically conscious ethnie," see van den Berghe, *The Ethnic Phenomenon*, 61; and Donald Horowitz, *Ethnic Groups in Conflict* (Berkeley: University of California Press, 1985). As a "cultural community," the perspective is based mainly on the views of German thinkers Johann von Herder (1744–1803) and Johann Gottlib Fichte (1762–1814), who stipulated that each linguistic group formed a separate nation. As "an act of willful consent and subjective identity," see Ernest Renan, "What Is a Nation?" in Eley and Suny, eds., *Becoming National*, 42–55; and Benedict Anderson, *Imagined Communities. Reflections on the Origins and Spread of Nationalism* (London: Verso, 1983). As a product of state modernization and nation-building, see Ernest Gellner, *Nations and Nationalism* (Ithaca, N.Y.: Cornell University Press, 1983).

5. For analysis of different perspectives on this issue, see Canovan, *Nationhood and Political Theory*, 8–9, 54–56.

6. Viktoriya Tokareva, a famous Russian writer and scriptwriter, recalled the key scene from the Soviet-era blockbuster play "Mimino," featuring a Georgian and an Armenian character who shared an elevator with two Japanese. One of the Japanese whispered to the other: "Look, those Russians are all alike." The scene was cut by the Soviet censors. See Viktoriya Tokareva, "Schast'e i blagopoluchie—ne material dlya tvorchestva" (Happiness and prosperity are not good themes for creative work), *Vzglyad* (December 19–25, 1997), 21.

7. Canovan, *Nationhood and Political Theory*, 51.

8. See Connor, *Ethnonationalism*, 90.

9. See a brief historiographical overview in Ronald Grigor Suny, "Russia, the Soviet Union and Theories of Empires" (talk given at the Center for International Security and Arms Control, Stanford University, March 14, 1996), 1–2.

10. See Afanasiev, "Seems Like the Old Times?"

11. See Dawisha and Parrott, eds., *The End of Empire?*; and Barkey and von Hagen, eds., *After Empire*.

12. See Suny, "Russia, the Soviet Union, and Theories of Empires."

13. See Yuri Slezkine, "The USSR as a Communal Apartment, or How a Socialist State Promoted Ethnic Particularism," *Slavic Review* 2 (Autumn 1994).

14. Mark Beissinger, "The Persisting Ambiguity of Empire," *Post-Soviet Affairs* 11, no. 2 (April–June 1995): 154.

15. Chinn and Kaiser, *Russians as the New Minority*, 19–22, 26–28, 65.

16. Solzhenitsyn, *Rossiya v obvale*, 113–14. Of course, such views are not shared by many scholars and ideologues in the newly independent states. Contemporary thinkers fight for usable past, and history is reinterpreted in many different ways.

17. See Sergei Savoskul, "Russkiye novogo zarubezhya" (Russians of the new abroad), *Obshchestvennye nauki i sovremennost'* 5 (1994): 93.

18. For comparative analysis of the Soviet Union and the Russian, Ottoman, and Habsburg empires, see Barkey and von Hagen, eds., *After Empire*.

19. Richard Pipes, "Introduction: The Nationality Problem," in *Handbook of Major Soviet Nationalities*, ed. Zev Katz (New York: Free Press, 1975), 1; Roman Szporluk, *Communism and Nationalism: Karl Marx versus Friedrich List* (New York: Oxford University Press, 1988), 206; Richard Sakwa, *Russian Politics and Society* (New York: Routledge, 1993), 101; Pipes, "Is Russia Still an Enemy?" 68.

20. See Hosking, *Russia: People and Empire.*

21. Nikholai Tsymbayev, "Rossiua i russkiye. Natsional'ny vopros v Rossiiskoi Imperii," in *Russkii narod: istoricheskaya sud'ba v XX veke*, ed. Yurii Kukushkkin (Moscow: ANKO, 1993), 39–50.

22. Sakwa, *Russian Politics and Society*, 101.

23. Pavel Milyukov, *Natsional'nyi vopros: proiskhozhdeniye natsional'nosty i natsional'nye voprosy v Rossii* (The nationality question: Genesis of nationalities and national questions in Russia) (Prague: Svobodnaja Rossija, 1925), 158–59.

24. See Andrei Zubov, "Sovetsky Soyuz: iz imperii v nichto?" *Polis*, no. 1(1992): 56–75; Aleksandr Vdovin, *Rossiiskaya natsiya* (Moscow: Libris, 1995): 136–38; Chinn and Kaiser, *Russians as the New Minority*, 65.

25. For the analysis of different trends in historiography on this issue, see Hugh Seton-Watson, "Russian Nationalism in Historical Perspective," in *The Last Empire: Nationality and the Soviet Future*, ed. Robert Conquest (Stanford, Calif.: Hoover Institution Press, 1986), 15–17. See also Szporluk, "The Fall of the Tsarist Empire and the USSR," 70–71; while struggling with historical myths in this article, Szporluk effectively creates a new "negative" myth concerning the nonexistence of links between Muscovy and medieval Kiev.

26. See Vdovin, *Rossiiskaya natsiya*, 105.

27. See Teresa Rakowska-Harmstone, "Chickens Coming Home to Roost: A Perspective on Soviet Ethnic Relations," *Journal of International Affairs* 42, no. 2 (1992): 519–48; and Szporluk, "The Fall of the Tsarist Empire and the USSR," 82–83.

28. See Ronald Grigor Suny, "Ambiguous Categories," *Post-Soviet Affairs* 11, no. 2 (April–June 1995): 190; and Brubaker, *Nationalism Reframed*, 28.

29. See Robert Kaiser, *The Geography of Nationalism in Russia and the USSR* (Princeton, N.J., Princeton University Press, 1994), 252–53 and 351. In contrast to his critique of the concept of a "Soviet people," Kaiser acknowledged "sovietization" of Russians in a separate set of arguments (p. 391).

30. See Slezkine, "The USSR as a Communal Apartment," 425.

31. Valery Solovey, "Russkiy natsionalism i vlast' v epokhu Gorbacheva," in *Mezhnatsional'nye otnosheniya v Rossii i SNG*, ed. Paul Goble and Gennady Bordyugov (Moscow: ITs "Airo-XX," 1994), 47–48.

32. *Literaturnaya gazeta*, November 15, 1972.

33. See Vdovin, *Rossiiskaya natsiya*, 184. See also Solovey, "Russkiy natsionalism," 58, 71.

34. Anatoly Chrenyaev, *Shest' let s Gorbachevym* (Six Years with Gorbachev) (Moscow: Progress-Kultura, 1993), 149.

35. Suny, "Russia, the Soviet Union, and Theories of Empire," 19.

36. Seton-Watson, "Russian Nationalism," 28.

37. There were several attempts to create a Russian republic as an entity exclusively for ethnic Russians in 1923, 1925, 1927, and 1949, but all of them failed. See Aleksandr Vdovin, "Russkaya natsiya i rossiiskaya nadnatsional'naya obshchnost'" (Russian nation and Russian supernational community), in *Russkaya natsiya: istoricheskoe proshloe i problemy vozrozhdeniya* (Russian Nation: Historic Past and Problems of Resurrection), ed. Evgenii Troitskii (Moscow: AKIRN, 1995), 45.

38. For a comprehensive analysis of the collapse of the Soviet Union, Czechoslovakia, and Yugoslavia from an institutional perspective, see Valerie Bunce, *Subversive Institutions: The Design and the Destruction of Socialism and the State* (New York: Cambridge University Press, 1999.)

39. Brubaker, *Nationalism Reframed,* 49.

40. See, for example, Bondarenko's account of a trip to the United States in *Zavtra* (December 1996).

41. See, for example, Greenfeld, *Nationalism,* 261–74.

42. Pavel Milyukov harshly criticized Nikolai Danilevsky for his "reactionary" and "retrograde" views; see Milyukov, *Natsional'nyi vopros,* 140.

43. Nikolai Danilevsky, *Rossiya i Evropa* (St. Petersburg: Glagol, 1995).

44. Fyodor Dostoevsky, "Pushkin: A Sketch," in *Russian Intellectual History,* ed. Marc Raeff (New York: Harcourt, Brace & World, 1966), 299.

45. Ibid.

46. Ibid., 300.

47. Though it seems that Dostoevsky and Danilevsky represented two opposite attitudes, Dostoevsky himself did not see it this way; he claimed that he was entirely in agreement with Danilevsky. See Dostoevsky's "Letter to Strakhov," in *Pisma,* vol. 2 (Dusseldorf: Brücker-Verlag, 1968), 181.

48. Vladimir Solovyov, "Natsional'nyi vopros v Rossii" (The national question in Russia), *Sochineniya,* vol. 1 (Moscow: Pravda Press, 1989), 333–49.

49. Vladimir Solovyov, "Mir Vostoka i Zapada" (The World of East and West)," *Sochineniya,* vol. 2, 604.

50. Ibid.

51. See Berdyaev, *Russkaya ideya,* 62.

52. KPRF leader Gennadi Zyuganov effectively endorsed the formula of orthodoxy, autocracy, and "national spirit," arguing that these principles, while being a conservative alternative to any attempts at reforms in Russia in the 1830s and 1840s, nevertheless adequately reflected the historical and cultural pillars of the Russian state. Moreover, he perceived the CPSU slogans of a "Soviet people as a new historical entity," "moral and political unity of the Soviet society," and even a "union multinational state" with a "single leading and guiding force" as a continuation of Uvarov's formula. See Gennadi Zyuganov, *Rossiya—Rodina moya: Ideologiya gosydarsvennogo* *patriotizma* (Russia Is My Motherland: The Ideology of State Patriotism) (Moscow: Informpechat', 1996), 224–25.

53. See E. G. Aleksandrov, "'Etnicheskoe samosoznnie' ili 'etnicheskaya identichnost'?" ("Ethnic self-consciousness" or "ethnic identity"?) *Etnographichescoe obozrenie* 3 (1996): 15.

54. For theoretical foundations of the outlined approach, see Gellner, *Nations and Nationalism;* Miroslav Hroch, *The Social Preconditions of National Revival in Europe* (New York: Cambridge University Press, 1985); and Eugene Weber, *Peasants into Frenchmen: The Modernization of Rural France* (Stanford, Calif.: Stanford University Press, 1976). For an application of this perspective to Russia, see Chinn and Kaiser, *Russians as the New Minority.*

55. Chinn and Kaiser, *Russians as the New Minority,* 61.

56. Pyotr Struve, "Patrioticheskaya trevoga 'renegata,'" (Patriotic concern of a 'renegade'), *Nezavisimaya gazeta,* February 7, 1995.

57. Milyukov, *Natsional'nyi vopros,* 173.

58. For an analysis of the Bolsheviks' approach to the nationalities question, see Aleksandr Vdovin, "Natsional'naya politika bol'shevikov i eyo al'ternativy," in Kukushkin, ed., *Russkii narod,* 119–78; and Kaiser, *The Geography of Nationalism,* 96–150.

59. One of the first Russian thinkers who pointed to this continuity was Nikolai Ustrialov.

60. For more on the impact of globalization on the strengthening of various types of "national ideas," see Al'gimantas Prazauskas, "Etnonatsionalism, mnogonatsional'noe gosudarstvo i protsessy globalizatsii," *Polis,* no. 2 (1997): 104–5.

61. To name but a few: Galina Starovoitova, adviser to President Yeltsin on nationalities issues in 1991–92; Valery Tishkov, minister of nationalities in 1992; Emil Payin, member of the Presidential Council; and Ramazan Abdulatipov, vice chairman of the Russian Federation's Federal Council and deputy prime minister in 1997–98.

62. Zviad Gamsakhurdia of Georgia, Levon Ter-Petrosyan of Armenia, Abulfazl Elcibey of Azerbaijan, and Vladislav Ardzinba of the self-proclaimed republic of Abkhazia in Georgia.

63. See, for example, Yulian Bromley et al., eds., *Sovremennye etnicheskie protsessy v SSSR* (Moscow: Nauka, 1975), 5. See also his *Ocherki teorii etnosa* (Moscow: Nauka, 1983) and *Etnosotsial'nye protsessy: teoriya, istoriya, sovremennost* (Moscow: Nauka, 1987).

64. Yulian Bromley, *Theoretical Ethnography* (Moscow: Nauka, 1984), 20.

65. Bromley et al., eds., *Sovremennye etnicheskie protsessy,* 10.

66. Valery Tishkov, *Ethnicity, Nationalism, and Conflict in and after the Soviet Union* (London: SAGE Publications, 1997), 3. Tishkov noted that Bromley's theory relied on the ideas of the Soviet scholar Sergei Shirokogorov, who developed his theory of ethnos in the 1920s; see ibid.

67. For a critical overview of Gumilev's perspectives, see Tishkov, *Ethnicity, Nationalism, and Conflict,* 2–9.

68. "O podgotovke k 50-letiyu obrazovaniya Soyuza Sovetskikh Sotsialistich-eskikh Respublik. Postanovlenie TsK KPSS," *Kommunist* 3 (1972).

69. Ramazan Abdulatipov, *O federal'noi i natsional'noi politike Rossiiskogo gosu-darstva* (Moscow: Slavyanskii Dialog, 1995), 19–20.

70. Ramazan Abdulatipov, "Russian Minorities: The Political Dimension," in *The New Russian Diaspora: The Russian Minorities in the Former Soviet Republics,* ed. Vladimir Shlapentokh et al. (Armonk, N.Y.: M. E. Sharpe, 1994), 40–41.

71. Leokadia Drobizheva, "Russian Ethnonationalism," in *Ethnic Conflict in the Post-Soviet World: Case Studies and Analysis,* ed. Leokadia Drobizheva et al. (Armonk, N.Y.: M. E. Sharpe, 1996), 129.

72. Tishkov, *Ethnicity, Nationalism, and Conflict,* 230, 275–76.

73. Ibid., 250.

74. Valery Tishkov, "O natsii i natsionalizme," *Svobodnaya mysl'* 3 (1996): 33–35.

75. Tishkov, *Ethnicity, Nationalism, and Conflict,* 260–61.

76. See *Rossiiskaya gazeta,* February 25, 1994; and Tishkov, *Ethnicity, National-ism, and Conflict,* 65–67.

77. *Nezavisimaya gazeta,* March 15, 1994; see also Tishkov's response in Tishkov, *Ethnicity, Nationalism, and Conflict,* 264–65.

78. *Nezavisimaya gazeta,* March 12, 1996.

79. See Aleksandr Vdovin, *Rossiiskaya natsiya: Natsional'no-politicheskie problemy XX veka i obshchenatsional'naya Rossiiskaya ideya* (Moscow: Libris, 1995), 201–202.

80. Tishkov, *Ethnicity, Nationalism, and Conflict,* 265.

81. Ibid., 276–77.

82. *Pravda,* February 4, 1995.

83. See *Sovetskaya Rossiya,* June 7, 1989.

84. Viktor Kozlov, "O sushchnosti russkogo voprosa i ego osnovnykh aspectakh," in Kukushkkin, ed., *Russkii narod,* 62.

85. V. Kabuzan, *Russkie v mire: Dinamika chislennosti i rasseleniya (1719–1989): Formirovanie etnicheskikh i politicheskikh granits russkogo naroda* (St. Petersburg: BLITs, 1996), 213–14.

86. Solzhenitsyn, *The Russian Question,* 108.

87. Berdyaev, *Russkaya ideya,* 322.

88. Ibid., 232.

89. Ibid., 93.

90. Solzhenitsyn, *The Russian Question,* 89–90.

91. Ibid., 94.

92. Solzhenitsyn, *Rossiya v obvale,* 43.

93. Ibid., 104–5.

94. Nikolai Pavlov, "Russkie: vremya vybora," *Nash sovremennik,* no. 1 (1995): 149.

95. Ibid., 165.

96. Ibid., 164.

97. Kseniya Myalo and Nataliya Narochnitskaya, " Eshche raz o 'evraziiskom soblazne,'" *Nash sovremennik,* no. 4 (1995): 132–34.

98. Kseniya Myalo and Nataliya Narochnitskaya, "Vosstanovlenie Rossii i evraziiskiy soblazn," *Nash sovremennik,* nos. 11–12 (1994): 218–19.

99. Nataliya Narochnitskaya, "Rossiya i russkie v mirovoy istorii," *Mezhdunarodnaya zhisn',* no. 3 (1996): 76.

100. Myalo and Narochnitskaya, "Vosstanovlenie Rossii," 218.

101. Narochnitskaya, "Rossiya i russkie," 86.

102. *Nezavisimaya gazeta,* February 27, 1997; see also the interview with Aksiuchits in *Etnograficheskoe obozrenie,* no. 4 (1996): 127.

103. See the minutes of the conference "Problemy razdelennosti i utverzhdeniya mezhdunarodno-pravovoy sub'ektnosti russkogo naroda v intersakh zashchity sootechestvennikov za rubezhom," State Duma Committee on CIS Affairs and Relations with Compatriots, Moscow, April 21, 1998.

104. *Zavtra,* no. 44 (November 1998).

105. T. I. Kutkovets and I. M. Klyamkin, "Russkie idei" (Russian Ideas), *Polis,* no. 2 (1997): 120.

106. Andrei Zdravomyslov, *Mezhnatsinal'nye konflikty v postsovetskom prostrnstve* (Interethnic conflicts in the post-Soviet space) (Moscow: Aspekt Press, 1997), 145.

107. Andrei Zdravomyslov, "Natsional'noe Samosoznanie i politicheskaya dinamika Rossii" (National self-consciousness and political dynamics in Russia), in *Istoriya natsional'nykh politicheskikh partii Rossii* (History of national political parties of Russia), ed. Aleksandr Zevelev and Vladimir Shelokhaev (Moscow: Rosspen, 1997), 61.

108. Zdravomyslov, "Natsional'noe samosoznanie," 53.

109. Kutkovets and Klyamkin, "Russkie idei," 120.

110. "Novyi russkii natsionalism: ambitsii, fobii, kompleksy," in *Economicheskie i sotsial'nye peremeny: monitoring obshchestvennogo mneniya,* no. 1 (1994): 16.

111. I. M. Klyamkin and V. V. Lapkin, "Russkii vopros v Rossii," *Polis,* no. 5 (1995): 82.

112. *Rossiiskie vesti,* April 15, 1997.

113. See results of the survey in Tishkov, *Ethinicity, Nationalism, and Conflict,* 252.

114. *Economicheskie i sotsial'nye peremeny: monitoring obshchestvennogo mneniya,* no. 1 (1995): 72.

115. Interfax, March 12, 1998.

116. Ibid.

117. Interfax, January 28, 1999.

118. Interfax, December 25, 1997.

119. Aleksandr Lebed, *Za derzhavu obidno—* (Moscow: Redaktsiya gazety "Moskovskaya Pravda," 1995), 409–10.

120. Calculations were made on the basis of data contained in Kutkovets and Klyamkin, "Russkie Idei," 120.

121. Klyamkin and Lapkin, "Russkii vopros v Rossii," 94.

122. Ibid., 87.

123. Ibid.

124. Ibid., 94.

125. Ibid., 96.

126. Canovan, *Nationhood and Political Theory*, 73.

CHAPTER 3: THE POLITICS OF NATION BUILDING IN MODERN RUSSIA

1. See the text of the program in V. V. Shelokhaev et al., eds., *Programmy Politicheskikh Partii Rossii: Konets XIX–Nachalo XX vv.* (Programs of Russia's political parties. Late nineteenth–early twentieth centuries) (Moscow: Rosspen, 1995), 326–36.

2. See ibid., 26–40 (especially 33–35).

3. See ibid., 341–49 (especially 342–43).

4. For instance, the 1905 program of the Russian Monarchist Party deplored the fact that "Traitors of Russia, united with various *inorodtsy* (non-Russians) living in the Russian Empire, have plans to split the borderlands of Russia and make Russia a primitive small state that would include only the Great Russians' *guberiyas* (regions)." Ibid., 427.

5. Ibid., 458.

6. See Pavel Milyukov, *Natsional'nyi vopros* (The nationality question) (Prague: Swobodnaja Rossija, 1925), 185–86.

7. See V. V. Zhuravlev, "Natsional'nyi vopros v programmakh obshcherossiiskikh politicheskikh partii nachala XX veka" (The nationality question in all-Russia's political parties' programs in the early twentieth century), in *Istoriya natsional'nykh politicheskikh partii Rossii* (History of nationalities' political parties in Russia), ed. A. I. Zevelev et al. (Moscow: Rosspen, 1997), 94.

8. Vladimir Kalina and Republican Party leader Vladimir Lysenko tried to apply the standard grouping of political forces (democratic, communist, and nationalist) to analyzing the politics of relations among nationalities. However, the approach fails to be sufficiently illustrative. See Vladimir Kalina and Vladimir Lysenko, "Mezhnatsional'nye otnosheniya v iter'ere politicheskikh partyi" (Interethnic relations in the context of political parties), *Rossiiskaya federatsiya*, no. 22–24 (November–December 1994): 22–25.

9. Alexander Pikayev described these two perspectives as "isolationist" and "revanchist." See Alexander Pikayev, "The Russian Domestic Debate on Policy toward the 'Near Abroad,'" in *Peacekeeping and the Role of Russia in Eurasia*, ed. Lena Johnson and Clive Archer (Boulder, Colo.: Westview, 1996), 51–66.

10. *Izvestiya*, June 10, 1995.

11. See Sakwa, *Russian Politics and Society*, 106–111.

12. See Connor, *Ethnonationalism*.

13. Thomas Hylland Eriksen, *Ethnicity and Nationalism: Anthropological Perspectives* (London: Pluto Press, 1993), 116–18.

14. Ibid., 116.

15. See Sakwa, *Russian Politics and Society*, 96, 104.

16. *Trud,* January 1, 1995.

17. Ibid.

18. See Robert Keohane, *After Hegemony: Cooperation and Discord in the World Political Economy* (Princeton, N.J.: Princeton University Press, 1984).

19. David Forsythe, *The Internationalization of Human Rights* (Lexington, Ky.: Lexington Books, 1991), 90.

20. Ibid., 91.

21. *Nezavisimaya gazeta,* January 12 and 15, 1994.

22. *Izvestiya,* January 2, 1992 ; *Mezhdunarodnaya zhizn,* March–April 1992.

23. *SNG: Nachalo ili Konets Istorii* (CIS: The beginning or the end of history) (Moscow: Institut Diaspory i Integratsii, 1997).

24. Author's interview with Konstantin Zatulin, Moscow, Summer 1997.

25. Nursultan Nazarbaev, *Evraziiskii Soyuz: Idei, Praktika, Perspectivy: 1994–1997* (Moscow: Foundation for the Assistance of Social and Political Sciences' Development, 1997), 45.

26. *Pravda,* September 12, 1996.

27. Similarities between some of the ideas advocated by Zyuganov and Solzhenitsyn were emphasized by Stephen Hanson in "Ideology and the Rise of Anti-System Parties in Postcommunist Russia" (paper prepared for the conference on "Party Politics in Postcommunist Russia," University of Glasgow, May 23–25, 1997), 14.

28. Zyuganov, *Rossiya—Rodina Moya,* 213–39.

29. Ibid., 215.

30. See ibid., 215–19.

31. Aleksei Podberezkin, *Russkii put'* (The Russian Path) (Moscow: RAU-Universitet, 1997), 11–13.

32. Mark Yoffe, "Vladimir Zhirinovsky, the Unholy Fool," *Current History* (October 1994), 324.

33. *Parlamentskie Slushaniya v Gosudarstvennoi Dume (Khronika, Annotatsii, Obzor)* (Parliamentary hearings in the State Duma: Chronology, annotations, review), vol. 6 (Moscow: Gosudarsvennaya Duma, 1997), 10.

34. Aleksei Mitrofanov, *Shagi novoi geopolitiki* (Steps of new geopolitics) (Moscow: Russkii Vestnik, 1997).

35. Sergei Baburin, *Territoriya gosudarstva: Pravovye i geopoliticheskie poblemy* (The state territory: legal and geopolitical problems) (Moscow: Moscow University Press, 1997), 476.

36. Oleshchuk, Pribylovsky, and Reitblat, *Parlamentskie partii, dvizheniya, ob'edineniya,* 388.

37. Vladimir Pribylovsky, *Russkie natsionalisticheskie i pravo-radikal'nye organi- zatsii, 1989–1995: Dokumenty i Teksty* (Russian nationalist and right-radical organi- zations, 1989–1995: Documents and texts), vol. 1 (Moscow: Panorama, 1995), 30.

38. Viktor Trushkov, "'Russkaya ideya' v Rossiiskom politichescom prostranstve," (The 'Russian idea' in Russia's political context), *Dialog*, no. 5 (1997): 12–15.

39. Nikolay Bindyukov, "O kontseptsii natsional'noy politiki KPRF v sovremen- nykh usloviyakh" (On the concept of the CPRF nationality policy under present con- ditions), *Dialog*, no. 6 (1997): 46–47.

40. See Pribylovsky, *Russkie natsionalisticheskie,* 32.

41. *Johnson's Russia List,* April 25, 1997.

42. Ibid.

43. See section 7.3 of the 1995 program of Our Home Is Russia and the sec- tion of Yabloko's 1995 political platform on "Relations with CIS Countries" in Oleshchuk, Pribylovsky, and Reitblat, *Parlamentskie partii, dvizheniya, ob'edineniya,* 81–82 and 100–101.

44. See the KRO's program in ibid., 248–49.

45. From Yuri Skokov's April 1995 report to the KRO congress in *Nezavisimaya gazeta,* April 22, 1995.

46. See Oleshchuk, Pribylovsky, and Reitblat, *Parlamentskie partii, dvizheniya, ob'edineniya,* 229–51 and 249.

47. See *Kongress russkikh obshchin. Manifest* (The Congress of Russian Commu- nities. Manifesto) (Moscow: Fenix, 1994); and Dmitriy Rogozin, *Formula raspada* (Formula of disintegration) (Moscow: Forum, 1998).

48. Rogozin, *Formula raspada,* 7–9, 44–47.

49. Hanson made this argument in his "Ideology and the Rise of Anti-system Parties," 1.

50. Dankwart Rustow, "Transition to Democracy," *Comparative Politics* 2, no. 3 (1970): 337–65; and Georg Sorensen, *Democracy and Democratization.* (Boulder, Colo.: Westview, 1993): 40–41.

CHAPTER 4: RUSSIANS OUTSIDE RUSSIA BEFORE AND AFTER THE BREAKUP OF THE SOVIET UNION

1. Eric Hobsbawm, *Nations and Nationalism since 1780: Programme, Myth, Reality* (New York: Cambridge University Press, 1992), 58, 62.

2. "Titular" is used here to mean an ethnic group whose name was used for giv- ing a title to a corresponding republic.

3. Dominique Arel and Valeri Khmelko convincingly argued that a self-reported "mother tongue" sometimes might mean the language one first learned as a child, or the language one speaks best at the present time, but not the language most used in daily intercourse, or "home language," or the language one feels more at ease with. See Dominique Arel and Valeri Khmelko, "The Russian Factor and Territorial Polarization in Ukraine," *Harriman Review* 9 (Spring 1996): 82. Therefore, it must be kept in mind that the figures in this section might seriously underestimate the actual use of Russian as a first language in many former Soviet republics. However, for the purposes of the analysis undertaken in this chapter, in the absence of other comparable data for all former Soviet republics, the indicator of a "native language" is demonstrative.

4. See ibid.

5. Seventy-five percent of urban ethnic Kazakhs and 66 percent of urban ethnic Kyrgyz indicated fluency in Russian as a second language in 1989. Calculated on the basis of data contained in *Itogi vsesoyuznoi perepisi naseleniya 1989 goda, tom VII: Natsional'nyi sostav naseleniya SSSR* (The results of the All-Union population census of 1989, vol. VII: National composition of the USSR population) (Minneapolis: East View Publications, 1993), 300–301, 552–53.

6. Chauncy Harris, "The New Russian Minorities: A Statistical Overview," *Post-Soviet Geography* 34, no. 1 (January 1993): 4–6.

7. See ibid., 22, 24; Kaiser, *The Geography of Nationalism*, 294; and I. Subbotina, "Migratsii russkikh v inoetnichnykh sredakh" (Migration of the Russians in other ethnic groups' environments), *Rasy i narody: Sovremennye etnicheskie i rasovye problemy* 22 (1992): 94.

8. Calculated on the basis of data contained in *Itogi vsesoyuznoi perepisi naseleniya 1989 goda, tom VII*, 154–55, 192–93.

9. Kaiser, *The Geography of Nationalism*, 302.

10. See A. A. Susokolov, "Natsional'no-smeshannye braki sredi russkogo naseleniya v raznykh regionakh strany" (Ethnically mixed marriages among Russians in different regions of the country), in *Russkie: etnosotsiologicheskie ocherki* (Russians: ethnological and sociological essays), ed. Yu. Arutiunian (Moscow: Nauka, 1995), 191–222; David Laitin, "Identity in Formation: The Russian-Speaking Nationality in the Post-Soviet Diaspora" (paper presented at the Annual Meeting of the American Political Science Association, New York, September 1994), as quoted in Pal Kolsto, "The New Russian Diaspora—An Identity of Its Own? Possible Identity Trajectories for Russians in the Former Soviet Republics," *Ethnic and Racial Studies* 19, no. 3 (July 1996): 634.

11. Ibid., 634–35.

12. See *Country Reports on Human Rights Practices for 1997: Report Submitted to the Committee on International Relations, U. S. House of Representatives, and the Committee on Foreign Relations, U. S. Senate, by the Department of State* (Washington, D.C.: U. S. Government Printing Office, 1998), 1070, 1073, 1164–1165, 1167; *Estonia and Latvia: Citizenship, Language and Conflict Prevention: A Special Report by the Forced Migration Projects* (New York: Open Society Institute, 1997), 22; *RFE/RL Newsline*, December 29, 1998.

13. See V. N. Belousov and E. A. Grigoryan, *Russkii yazyk v mezhnatsional'nom obshchenii v Rossiiskoi Federatsii i stranakh SNG* (The Russian language in inter-

national communication in the Russian Federation and the CIS countries) (Moscow: Institut Russkogo Yazyka, 1996).

14. See Sergei Savoskul, "Russkie novogo zarubezhya" (The Russians of the new abroad), *Obshchestvennye nauki i sovremennost'* 5 (1994): 96.

15. See Dominique Arel, "Language Politics in Independent Ukraine: Towards One or Two State Languages?" *Nationalities Papers* 23, no. 3 (September 1995): 613–14.

16. *Izvestiya*, July 22, 1997.

17. *Nezavisimaya gazeta*, April 4, 1997.

18. Canovan, *Nationhood and Political Theory*, 105.

19. Hugh Seton-Watson, "Russian Nationalism in Historical Perspective," in Conquest, ed., *The Last Empire*, 27.

20. Harris, "The New Russian Minorities," 221, table 5.6, 209, 223.

21. See table 1 of Pal Kolsto's "Integration or Alienation? Russians in the Former Soviet Republics." (Kolsto kindly shared the manuscript with the author.) See also Harris, "The New Russian Minorities," 17–19.

22. Calculated on the basis of data contained in Harris, "The New Russian Minorities," 18–19.

23. See table 4 in ibid. See also Subbotina, "Migratsii russkikh," 89.

24. Soviet equivalents of university and junior college education.

25. Regarding the Baltic states, these data challenge the myth that the Baltic Russians are backward, "uncultured" masses, performing menial jobs or working as industrial blue-collar workers at best. One interview with former Latvian president Guntis Ulmanis is revealing. When talking about Russians in Latvia, he mentioned only two real Russians—his kitchen help. Trying to show his tolerance, President Ulmanis said: "The other day, my wife asked me if I knew that there were two Russian women working in our kitchen. I knew that, so what?"; *Izvestiya*, October 20, 1993. These assumptions, uncorroborated by any statistics, are widespread in the literature and, in many cases, serve particular political goals. For example, Roman Levita and Mikhail Loiberg asserted that "as a rule, they [Russian migrants] were far below the local population in their educational and general cultural level"; Roman Levita and Mikhail Loiberg, "The Empire and the Russians: Historical Aspects," in *The New Russian Diaspora: Russian Minorities in the Former Soviet Republics*, ed. Vladimir Shlapentokh, Munir Sendich, and Emil Payin (Armonk, N.Y.: M. E. Sharpe. 1994), 16. See also Marika Kirch and Aksel Kirch, "Ethnic Relations: Estonians and Non-Estonians," *Nationalities Papers* 23, no. 1 (1995): 43. For a critical perspective on such assumptions, see Brian Boeck, "Legacy of a Shattered System: The Russian-Speaking Population in Latvia," *Democratizatsiya* 1, no. 2 (1992): 76–77. On the trend in Kyrgyzstan, it could be attributed to the low level of urbanization among the Kyrgyz. Those relatively few Kyrgyz who do live in the cities are predominantly a well-educated elite, while the majority living in the countryside are much less educated. Additionally, there are many less-educated blue-collar workers among Kyrgyzstan's Russians.

26. See Kaiser, *The Geography of Nationalism*, 394, 317–24.

27. See Suny, "Russia, the Soviet Union and Theories of Empires," 19; Chinn and Kaiser, *Russians as the New Minority*, 87; and Brubaker, *Nationalism Reframed*, 23, 29, 38.

28. Kaiser, *The Geography of Nationalism*, 396.

29. For an analysis of the phenomena, see Slezkine, "The USSR as a Communal Apartment," 434; Chinn and Kaiser, *Russians as the New Minority*, 4; Brubaker, *Nationalism Reframed*, 39; and Kaiser, *The Geography of Nationalism*, chapters 5 and 6.

30. Kaiser, *The Geography of Nationalism*, 231–33.

31. Ibid., 238–40, 242.

32. Ibid., 243.

33. Ibid., 248; Chinn and Kaiser, *Russians as the New Minority*, 74; Brubaker, *Nationalism Reframed*, 29.

34. Pal Kolsto, "Nation-Building in the Former USSR," *Journal of Democracy*, no. 1 (January 1996): 120.

35. The term is used by Walker Connor in his "The Impact of Homelands Upon Diasporas," in *Modern Diasporas in International Politics*, ed. Gabriel Sheffer (New York: St. Martin's Press, 1986).

36. Ibid., 18.

37. Kolsto, "Nation-Building in the Former USSR," 131.

38. See more on Romantic views of nationhood in Canovan, *Nationhood and Political Theory*, 6–9.

39. *Novye konstitutsii stran SNG i Baltii: Sbornik dokumentov*, 2e izdanie (New constitutions of the CIS and Baltic countries: Collected documents, 2d edition) (Moscow: Manuscript Press, 1997), 105.

40. Ibid., 508.

41. Ibid., 510.

42. Ibid., 227, 268, 309, 435.

43. Ibid., 623.

44. See Articles 29, 30, 31, 34, 36, 42, 44, 48, 54, and 56.

45. *Novye konstitutsii*, 582.

46. Michael Walzer, "Notes on the New Tribalism," in *Political Restructuring in Europe—Ethical Perspectives*, ed. C. Brown (London: Routledge, 1994), 188, as quoted in Conovan, *Nationhood and Political Theory*, 17.

47. See the constitution of Armenia in *Novye konstitutsii*, 107. See also the laws on citizenship in Kazakhstan, Kyrgyzstan, and Turkmenistan in *Kommentarii zakonodatel'stva gosudarstv—uchastnikov SNG o grazhdanstve* (Comments on the CIS countries legislation on citizenship) (Moscow: Yuridicheskaya Literatura, 1996), 127, 143, 219.

48. For example, the research conducted in five Kazakh cities by the international foundation Arkor showed that 93 percent of Russians condemned ethnically segregated education, while the corresponding figure for Kazakhs was only 33 percent. See *Monitor* 7, no. 3 (Summer 1996), 6. Such attitudes are very characteristic of Russians, who in many cases did not notice that their "internationalism" was perceived as Russification.

49. A vivid example of this phenomenon was municipal elections in Estonia in 1996, when Russian noncitizens were given an opportunity to vote. Partial success occurred only in Tallinn, while in northeastern Estonia, Russian voters chose not to participate or voted for the Estonian center-left parties See T. V. Poloskova, "Russkaya diapora stran Baltii" (Russian diaspora of the Baltic states), *Diplomatichesky vestnik*, no. 3 (1997): 41. For an analysis of the limited abilities of the Russian communities to struggle for their course in the Crimea and the strong element of Soviet loyalism, as opposed to Russian nationalism, in Pridnestrovye, see Anatol Lieven, *Chechnya: Tombstone of Russian Power* (New Haven, Conn.: Yale University Press, 1998), 243–59.

50. *CIS Migration Report 1996* (Geneva: IOM, 1997), 5.

51. Hilary Pilkington, *Migration, Displacement, and Identity in Post-Soviet Russia* (New York: Routledge, 1988), 139.

52. Ibid., 139; see also pp. 12–13, 200–204.

53. Subbotina, "Migratsii russkikh," 80–81.

54. See for example, Mikk Titma and Nancy Tuma, *Migration in the Former Soviet Union* (Koln: Bundesinstitut fur Ostwissenschaftliche und Internationale Studien, 1992).

55. See Robert Lewis and Richard Rowland, *Population Redistribution in the USSR: Its Impact on Society, 1897–1917* (New York: Praeger, 1979), 16–19. See also Pilkington, *Migration, Displacement, and Identity,* 14–18.

56. See Subbotina, "Migratsii russkikh," 82 (table 2); Anatolii Starkov, "Migratsionnye protsessy na postsovetskom prostranstve" (Migration processes on the post-Soviet space), *Otkrytaya politika*, no. 1–2 (1996): 15.

57. See Barbara Anderson and Brian Silver, "Demographic Sources of the Changing Ethnic Composition of the Soviet Union," *Population and Development Review* 15 (1989): 609–56.

58. See O. Komarova, "Migratsiya russkikh: novye tendentsii" (Migration of the Russians: new trends), *Etnopolis* 5 (1995): 125.

59. A. Michugina and M. Rakhmaninova, "Natsional'nyi sostav migrantov v obmene naseleniem mezhdu Rossiei i zarubezhnymi stranami" (Nationalities of migrants in population exchanges between Russia and foreign countries),*Voprosy statistiki* 12 (1996): 45.

60. *CIS Migration Report 1996*, 96.

61. Ibid.

62. Tim Heleniak, "Migration and Population Change in the Soviet Successor States" (paper presented at the 28th National Convention of the American Association for the Advancement of Slavic Studies, Boston, Mass., November 14–17, 1996), table 2.

63. Calculated on the basis of data contained in *Demograficheskii ezhegodnik Rossiiskoi Federatsii 1993* (Demographic yearbook of the Russian Federation 1993) (Moscow: Goskomstat Rossii, 1994), 380–83; and Heleniak, "Migration and Population Change," table 4.

64. Calculated on the basis of data contained in Michugina and Rakhmaninova, "Natsinal'nyi sostav," 44.

65. See Heleniak, "Migration and Population Change," table 7.

66. Michugina and Rakhmaninova, "Natsional'nyi sostav," 45.

67. *Oxford Analytica/East Europe Daily Brief,* March 20, 1997.

68. Agence France-Presse, December 29, 1998; *Johnson's Russia List,* December 30, 1998.

69. *CIS Migration Report 1996,* 9.

70. Natalya Kosmarskaya, "Otstavshie ot potoka" (Those who lag behind the stream), *Novoe vremya* 21 (1998): 27.

71. The data of the USSR State Committee on Statistics as presented in Valery Tishkov, ed., *Migratsii i novye diaspory v postsovetskikh gosudarstvakh* (Migrations and new diasporas in post-Soviet states) (Moscow: Institut Etnologii i Antropologii, 1996), 82.

72. See Starkov, "Migratsioonnye protsessy," 20–21.

73. See Viktor Iontsev, "Inostrannye rabochie v Rossii" (Foreign workers in Russia), *Economika i zhisn'* 7 (1997).

74. Ibid.

75. See statistics in Tishkov, ed., *Migratsii i novye diaspory,* 29, 72–73.

76. Unlike all other successor states of the former Soviet Union, Russia attracts significant numbers of non-Russians, including titular nationalities of other states. This trend is true primarily for Ukrainians, Armenians, Azerbaijanis, Georgians, and Belarusians; see ibid., 30–31. This suggests a more cosmopolitan nature of the Russian Federation in comparison with its neighbors. Nevertheless, ethnic Russians dominate immigration.

77. See the data provided by Tatyana Regent, head of the Russian Federal Migration Service, in *Russian Executive and Legislation Newsletter* 13, no. 65 (April 1997).

78. See Tishkov, ed., *Migratsii i novye diaspory,* 37.

79. *CIS Migration Report 1996,* 99.

80. Ibid., 100.

81. *Izvestiya,* August 3, 1995.

82. Pilkington, *Migration, Displacement, and Identity,* 177 (figure 8.2).

83. *Rossiiskaya gazeta,* June 8, 1996.

84. *Izvestiya,* August 3, 1995.

85. Ibid.

86. Rogers Brubaker, "Aftermaths of Empire and the Unmixing of Peoples: Historical and Comparative Perspectives," *Ethnic and Racial Studies* 18, no. 2 (April 1995): 189–218.

87. *CIS Migration Report 1996,* 88.

88. Results of a 1994 microcensus in a random poll of 5 percent of the Russian Federation's population; see *Rossiiskie vesti,* October 30, 1997.

89. See, for example, *CIS Migration Report 1996*, 5.

90. For the critique of this approach, see Pilkington, *Migration, Displacement, and Identity*, 185.

91. See ibid., 184–98.

92. The term "intermingling" was first used by Anatol Lieven for describing the situation in eastern Ukraine; see Lieven, "Restraining NATO," 65.

93. For overviews of the condition of Russians in Belarus and Ukraine, see R. A. Grigorieva and M. Yu. Martynova, "Russkoye naselenie Belarusi: etnokulturnaya situatsiya" (Russian population of Belarus: ethnocultural situation), 10–37; V. I. Kozlov and M. V. Kozlov, "Russkie i russkoyazychnye v Belarusi i na Ukraine" (Russians and Russian-speakers in Belarus and Ukraine," 38–52; and N. M. Lebedeva, "Russkaya diaspora ili chast' russkogo naroda? K probleme samoopredeleniya russkikh na Ukraine (Russian diaspora or a part of the Russian people? On the problem of self-determination of the Russians in Ukraine)," 53–59 in *Russkie v blizhnem zarubezhye* (Russians in the near abroad), ed. V. I. Kozlov and Ye. A. Shervud (Moscow: Institute of Ethnology and Anthropology, 1994).

94. For the analysis of the situation in the Crimea, see V. V. Stepanov, "Sovremennoye russkoe naselenie Kryma" (The modern Russian population of the Crimea)," in Kozlov and Shervud, eds., *Russkie v blizhnem zarubezhye*, 60–76. Russians do constitute a separate community in western Ukraine. The attitudes of local authorities and especially politically active Ukrainian nationalists toward Russians there are often hostile, leading to further differentiation between Ukrainians and Russians. For numerous reports of harassment toward Russians in Galicia see, for example, *Nezavisimaya gazeta*, April 4, 1997; and *Rossiiskaya gazeta*, April 29, 1997.

95. See, for example, Vladimir Malinkovich, "Russkii vopros v Ukraine" (The Russian question in Ukraine), *Otkrytaya politika*, no. 9–10 (1996): 77.

96. Returns of public opinion polls carried out by the Center for the Study of Public Opinion; see *Interfax*, October 27, 1997.

97. See Arel and Khmelko, "The Russian Factor," 81, 83, 85, 86.

98. See Lieven, "Restraining NATO," 65.

99. For an analysis of nation building in Belarus from a similar perspective, see Dmitri Furman and Oleg Bukhovets, "Belorusskoye samosoznanie i belorusskaya politika" (Belarusian identity and Belarusian politics), *Svobodnaya mysl'*, no. 1 (1996): 57–75. For a different interpretation of Belarusian history and recent developments, emphasizing the Belarusian "national idea," forced Russification, and the national-liberation movement, see Jan Zaprudnik, *Belarus: At a Crossroads in History* (Boulder, Colo.: Westview, 1993).

100. See the analysis of the roots of the conflict in Moldova in Pal Kolstoe, Andrei Edemsky, and Natalya Kalashnikova, "The Dniester Conflict: Between Irredentism and Separatism," *Europe-Asia Studies* 45, no. 6 (1993): 973–1000.

101. David Laitin, "Language and Nationalism in the Post-Soviet Republics," *Post-Soviet Affairs* 12, no. 1 (January–March 1996): 7.

102. See *Pravda-5*, May 16, 1997.

103. See *Segodnya*, September 5, 1995.

104. Most Russians are excluded from the privatization process in the Baltic states and are thus pushed into the finance and trade sectors; see, for example, Erik Andre Andersen, "The Legal Status of Russians in Estonian Privatization Legislation 1989–1995," *Europa-Asia Studies* 49, no. 2 (1997). The same could be said about Moldova, where about 80 percent of all businessmen are individuals of Russian descent; see T. V. Trapeznikova, "Russkie v Moldavii" (Russians in Moldova), *Diplomaticheskii vestnik*, no. 4 (1995): 42.

105. Kaiser, *The Geography of Nationalism*, 399.

106. See Sergei Savoskul, "Rossiya i russkie v blizhnem zarubezhye" (Russia and the Russians in the near abroad), *Ethnopolis*, no. 3 (1995): 132.

107. See the theoretical approach to this problem in Smith, *The Ethnic Origins of Nations*, 151–52.

108. See Lieven, *Chechnya*, 260.

109. See Kolsto, "The New Russian Diaspora," 610–11.

CHAPTER 5: POLICY OF THE RUSSIAN FEDERATION TOWARD THE RUSSIAN DIASPORAS

1. This wave of non-Russian immigration to the Russian Federation often contains individuals with "indefinite citizenship status, profession, and . . . place of residence"; T. V. Poloskova, "'Diaspory stran blizhnego zarubezhya' v Rossii" ('The near abroad diasporas' in Russia), *Diplomaticheskiy vestnik*, no. 10 (October 1997): 29.

2. See "Conflict Prevention, the Rights of Non-Citizens, and the Institution of the OSCE Human Rights Ombudsman" (paper prepared by Open Society Institute Forced Migration Project, June 1996), 4–5.

3. Andrei Kozyrev, *Preobrazhenie* (Transfiguration) (Moscow: Mezhdunarodnyye Otnosheniya, 1995), 98.

4. *Rossiyskaya federatsiya*, no. 22–24 (November–December, 1994): 55.

5. See details in chapter 3 and Igor Zevelev, "Building the State and Building the Nation in Contemporary Russia," in George Breslauer et al., *Russia: Political and Economic Development* (Claremont, Calif.: Keck Center for International and Strategic Studies, 1995).

6. The term was used frequently since then by Boris Yeltsin and Andrei Kozyrev.

7 *Nezavisimaya gazeta*, January 1, 1994.

8. Ibid.

9. *Voyennaya mysl'*, no. 5 (November 1993): 5.

10. Such a "change of landmarks" in Russian diplomacy was hailed by the official Russian press (see, for example, *Rossiyskaya gazeta*, January 21, 1994) but received sharp criticism both from the Baltic states and members of the CIS, including friendly Kazakhstan. See the articles by Umirserik Kasenov, director of Kazakhstan's Presidential Institute for Strategic Studies, in *Nezavisimaya gazeta*, March 12, 1994, and *Aziya,* March 1994.

11. See Article 2.2 in "Federal'naya migratsionnaya programma" (The federal migration program), in *Pereselentsy: Federal'naya migratsionnaya programma* (Migrants: Federal migration program) (Moscow: Izdatel'stvo "Rossiskaya gazeta," 1994), 37.

12. According to the law signed by President Boris Yeltsin on February 19, 1993, a "forced migrant" is an individual who moves to another country because of serious abuses or threats of abuses to his or her human rights. The individual might be a Russian citizen or a former Soviet citizen who lived in any successor state and acquired Russian citizenship after moving onto Russian territory. See "Zakon Rossiyskoy Federatsii o vynuzhdennykh pereselentsakh" (Law of the Russian Federation on forced migrants), in *Pereselentsy*, 9–10. For an analysis of the current legal status of refugees and forced migrants in Russia, see L. Andrichenko and Ye. Belousova, "Bezhentsy i vynuzhdennye pereselentsy" (Refugees and forced migrants), *Gosudarstvo i pravo*, no. 5 (1995).

13. Sergei Savoskul, "Russkie novogo zarubezhya" (Russians of the new abroad), *Obshcestvennye nauki i sovremennost'*, no. 5 (1994): 100.

14. "Tri Voprosa Strane" (Three questions to the country), *Tsentral'no-Aziatskoe obozrenie*, no. 1 (1993): 51.

15. See texts of agreements in *Diplomaticheskiy vestnik*, no. 1 2 (January 1994): 27–29; and *Diplomaticheskiy vestnik*, no. 10 (October 1995): 24–26.

16. For a unique comprehensive legal analysis of the treaty between Russia and Turkmenistan, see George Ginsburg, "The Question of Dual Citizenship in Russia with the Successor States in Central Asia," *Central Asian Monitor*, no. 4 (1994): 25–26.

17. See ibid., 26–28.

18. *Kommersant-Daily*, February 2, 1995.

19. See *Diplomaticheskiy vestnik*, no. 12 (December 1995): 34.

20. See the text of the treaty in *Diplomaticheskiy vestnik*, no. 7 (July 1997): 35–41.

21. "Dogovor o druzhbe, dobrososedstve, i sotrudnichestve mezhdu Rossiyskoy Federatsiey i Respublikoy Belarus" (Treaty on friendship, good-neighborliness, and cooperation between the Russian Federation and the Republic of Belarus), *Rossiyskaya gazeta* (departmental supplement), May 5,1995.

22. "Dogovor mezhdu Respublikoy Kazakhstan i Rossiyskoy Federatsiey o pravovom statuse grazhdan Respubliki Kazakhstan, postoyanno prozhivayushchikh na territorii Rossiyskoy Federatsii, i grazhdan Rossiyskoy Federatsii, postoyanno prozhivayushchikh na territorii Respubliki Kazakhstan" (Treaty between the Republic of Kazakhstan and the Russian Federation on the legal status of citizens of the Republic of Kazakhstan who are permanently residing on the territory of the Russian Federation, and citizens of the Russian Federation who are permanently residing on the territory

of the Republic of Kazakhstan), *Rossiyskaya gazeta* (departmental supplement), February 25,1995; "Soglashenie mezhdu Respublikoy Kazakhstan i Rossiiskoy Federatsiey ob uproshchennom poryadke priobreteniya grazhdanstva grazhdanami Respubliki Kazakhstan, pribyvayushchimi dlya postoyannogo prozhivaniya v Rossiyskuyu Federatsiyu, i grazhdanami Rossiyskoy Federatsii, pribyvayushchimi dlya postoyannogo prozhivaniya v Respubliku Kazakhstan" (Agreement between the Republic of Kazakhstan and the Russian Federation on simplified acquisition of citizenship by citizens of Kazakhstan coming to Russia for permanent residency and by citizens of Russia coming to Kazakhstan for permanent residency), *Rossiyskaya gazeta* (departmental supplement), February 25, 1995. See also *Diplomaticheskiy vestnik*, no. 2 (1995).

23. Russia and Kyrgyzstan signed a similar agreement in 1996.

24. "Strategicheskiy kurs Rossii s gosudarstvami–uchastnikami Sodruzhestva Nezavisimykh Gosudarstv" (The strategic course of Russia in its relations with the states that are parties to the Commonwealth of Independent States), *Rossiyskaya gazeta*, September 23, 1995.

25. *Nezavisimaya gazeta*, February 23, 1995.

26. "Deklaratsiya Uchreditel'nogo S'yezda upolnomochennykh predstaviteley zaru-bezhnykh rossiyskikh obshchin, organizatsiy i ob'yedineniy" (Declaration of the Constituent Assembly of the empowered representatives of Russian communities, organizations, and associations living abroad), *Delovoy mir*, July 11, 1995.

27. T. V. Poloskova, "Nekotorye voprosy grazhdanstva v stranakh SNG i Baltii" (Some issues of citizenship in the CIS countries and the Baltics), *Diplomaticheskiy vestnik*, no. 5 (May 1996): 50.

28. Article 62 of the Russian Constitution. See *Konstitutsiya Rossiiskoy Federatsii* (Moscow: INFRAM-NORMA, 1996), 21.

29. "Zakon o grazhdanstve Rossiyskoy Federatsii" (The law on citizenship of the Russian Federation), *Vedomosti S'yezda narodnykh deputatov Rossiiskoy Federatsii i Verkhovnogo Soveta Rossiyskoy Federatsii*, item 1112, no. 29 (1993).

30. For subsequent changes and amendments to the law, see *Sobraniye aktov Prezidenta i Praviiel'stva Rossiyskoy Federatsii* 4 (1994); *Rossiyskaya gazeta*, October 26, 1994; *Sobraniye zakonodalel'stva Rossiyskoy Federatsii*, item 496, no. 7 (1995).

31. See Article 18 of the law's 1995 version in *Sobraniye zakonodalel'stva Rossiyskoy Federatsii*, item 496, no. 7 (1995).

32. Author's interview with Abdulakh Mikitaev, former chief of the Presidential Administration's Citizenship Directorate, Moscow, Summer 1996.

33. See Abdulakh Mikitaev, "Gosudarstvennaya politika Rossii v oblasti grazhdanstva: Praktika realizatsii zakona 'O grazhdanstve Rossiiskoy Federatsii'" (Russian state policy in the field of citizenship: Implementation of the law 'On citizenship of the Russian Federation'), in *Aktual'nye problemy grazhdanstva: Materialy mezhdunarodnoy nauchno-prakticheskoy konferentsii po problemam grazhdanstva, 23–24 fevralya 1995 g.g. Moskva* (Current problems of citizenship: Proceedings of the international academic-practical conference on the problems of citizenship, February, 23–24, 1995,

Moscow), ed. S. A. Avakyan (Moscow, February 23-24, 1995), 11. See also the statement of Mikitaev's successor O. Kutafin, "Perspektivy razvitiya instituta rossiiskoga grazhdanstva i realizatsii deysvuyushchego v etoy oblasti zakonodatel'stva" (Prospects for the development of the Russian citizenship institution and implementation of the current legislation in this field), *Diplomaticheskiy vestnik,* no. 2 (February 1997): 42.

34. *Diplomaticheskiy vestnik,* no. 2 (February 1997): 44.

35. See the briefing of A. F. Molochkov, head of the Russian consular group, in *Diplomaticheskiy vestnik,* no. 5 (May 1995): 39–41.

36. *Diplomaticheskiy vestnik,* no. 2 (February 1997): 44.

37. "Konventsiya ob uproshchennom poryadke priobreteniya grazhdanstva grazhdanami Gosudarstv—uchastnikov Sodruzhestva Nezavisimykh Gosudarstv" (Convention on simplified acquisition of citizenship by the citizens of the states that are parties to the Commonwealth of Independent States), *Rossiiskaya gazeta,* March 16, 1996.

38. *Diplomaticheskiy vestnik,* no. 2 (February 1997): 45.

39. According to Articles 19a and 19d of the law, one could obtain Russian citizenship by application without having to reside in the Russian Federation for a total of five years (or three consecutive years), if one had formerly held Soviet citizenship, or if one had at least one direct ancestor who was a Russian citizen. See "Zakon o grazhdanstve Rossiiskoy Federatsii." An overwhelming majority of the people in the near abroad are former Soviet citizens who could easily become Russian citizens under this provision.

40. "Russian Election Survey," *OMRI Special Report,* December 22, 1995. Author's interview with Abdulakh Mikitaev, Moscow, Summer 1996.

41. ITAR-TASS, January 28, 1997, as quoted in *OMRI Daily Digest,* January 29, 1997.

42. "Perspektivy razvitiya instituta rossiiskogo grazhdanstva," 41.

43. Ginsburg, "The Question of Dual Citizenship," 24.

44. The author personally knows many individuals who are effectively dual citizens.

45. *Kazakhstanskaya pravda,* February 25, 1995.

46. *Nezavisimaya gazeta,* June 28, 1996.

47. See I. P. Blishchenko, A. Kh. Abashidze, and Ye. V. Martynenko, "Problemy gosudarstvennoy politiki Rossiiskoy Federatsii v otnoshenii sootechesvennikov" (Problems of the state policy toward the compatriots), *Gosudarstvo i pravo,* no. 2 (1994): 8.

48. See ibid., 9.

49. *Rossiyskaya federatsiya,* no. 22–24 (November–December, 1994): 56.

50. Kozyrev, *Preobrazheniye,* 105.

51. *Diplomaticheskiy vestnik,* no. 2 (1995): 52.

52. "Ukaz Prezidenta Rossiyskoy Federatsii 'Ob osnovnykh napravieniyakh gosudarstvennoy politiki Rossiyskoy Federatsii v otnoshenii sootechestvennikov prozhivayushchikh za rubyezhom" (Decree of the President of the Russian Federation "On the basic directions of the Russian Federation's state policy toward compatriots living abroad"), *Rossiyskaya gazeta*, August 18, 1994. "Osnovnyye napravieniya gosudarstvennoy politiki Rossiyskoy Federatsii v otnoshenii sootechestvennikov, prozhivayushchikh za rubezhom" (Basic directions of the Russian Federation's state policy toward compatriots living abroad), *Rossiyskaya gazeta*, September 22, 1994. See also *Rossiyskaya federatsiya*, no. 22–24 (November–December, 1994).

53. "Programma mer po podderzhke sootechestvennikov za rubezhom" (Program of actions to support compatriots abroad), *Rossiiskaya gazeta*, May 30, 1996.

54. See ibid.

55. Draft of "Kontseptsiya gosudarstvennoy politiky Rossiiskoy Federatsii v otnoshenii zarubezhnykh sootechestvennikov" (Concept of the Russian Federation's state policy toward compatriots abroad).

56. Ibid., 1. This definition is much broader than ethnocentric ones, which were suggested, for example, by V. M. Chubarov, the Council member of the Rodina Association, an important group advocating support of the compatriots. According to Chubarov, individuals belonging to titular nationalities in the former Soviet republics could by no means be regarded as compatriots. See V. M. Chubarov, "Eshche raz o sootechestvennikakh za rubezhom" (On the compatriots abroad, once again) *Diplomaticheskiy vestnik*, no. 6 (June 1997): 41.

57. "Kontseptsiya gosudarsvennoy politiki," 2–4.

58. Ibid., 5.

59. Author's interview with Vladimir Chernous, consultant to the Russian Federation Government's Department for the CIS Affairs, Moscow, April 3, 1998.

60. *Nezavisimaya gazeta*, December 17, 1998. See also the resolution of the Council of Compatriots in the State Duma, "On the Recommendation of the Parliamentary Hearings 'On the International Legal State of the Russian Compatriots in the States of the CIS and the Baltics: Analysis and Perspectives.'" June 1–2, 1998.

61. Author's interviews with Vladimir Chernous in summer 1997 and spring 1998.

62. See Blishchenko, Abashidze, and Martynenko, "Problemy gosudarstvennoy," 3–14.

63. "O gosudarsvennoy politike Rossiiskoy Federatsii"; see specifically Articles 20 and 33.

64. Author's interview with Vyacheslav Igrunov, Moscow, April 2, 1998.

65. See the text of the decree in *Rossiiskaya gazeta*, April 18, 1996.

66. See *Moskovskiy komsomolets*, June 11, 1998.

67. Kozyrev, *Preobrazhenie*, 99.

68. "Parlamentskie slusnaniya v Komitete Gosudarstvennoy Dumy po delam SNG i svyazyam s sootechestvennikami za rubezhom" (Parliamentary hearings in the State Duma's Committee on CIS Affairs and Compatriots Abroad), *Diplomaticheskiy vestnik*, no. 5 (May 1997): 42.

69. "Deklaratsiya o soblyudenii suvereniteta, territorial'noy tselostnosti i neprikosnovennosti granits gosudarstv—uchastnikov Sodruzhestva Nezavisimykh Gosudarstv" (Declaration on observing the sovereignty, territorial integrity and inviolability of the borders of states that are parties to the Commonwealth of Independent States), *Diplomaticheskiy vestnik,* no. 9–10 (1994).

70. "Memorandum o podderzhanii mira i stabil'nosti v Sodruzhestve Nezavisimykh Gosudarstv" (Memorandum on the maintenance of peace and stability in the Commonwealth of Independent States), *Diplomaticheskiy vestnik,* no. 3 (1995).

71. For the text of the convention, see *Diplomaticheskiy vestnik,* no. 21–22 (November 1994): 43–46.

72. "Konventsiya Sodruzhestva Nezavisimykh Gosudarstv o pravakh i osnovnykh svobodakh cheloveka" (Convention of the Commonwealth of Independent States on human rights and fundamental freedoms), *Rossiyskaya gazeta* (departmental supplement), June 23, 1995.

73. *UN International Covenant on Civil and Political Rights* (New York: United Nations, 1985), 31.

74. After the May 1995 referendum on the issue, Belarus upgraded the status of Russian to that of a state language. The action was not the result of Russian pressure; rather, it was a reaction against attempts by the Belarusian elite to construct a new state, despite the low level of ethnic consciousness within the country and the lack of popular support for independence. More than 80 percent of voters who participated in the May 1995 referendum approved the change of the Russian language's status.

75. Gennadi Zyuganov, ed., *Sovremennaya Russkaya ideya i gosudarstvo* (The modern Russian idea and the state) (Moscow: RAU-Korporatsiya, 1995), 87–93.

76. Kolstoe, *Russians in the Former Soviet Republics,* 271.

77. See the description of these events in ibid., 284–85. Many politicians in Moscow, including the liberal Vladimir Lukin, argued postfactum that it would have been bad to promise the withdrawal of troops and not do so, but even worse to threaten not to withdraw and actually withdraw.

78. "Sud'by russkoyazychnogo naseleniya v stranakh SNG i Baltii" (Destiny of the Russian-speaking population in the CIS and Baltic countries), *Mezhdunarodnaya zhizn',* no. 6 (1995): 116–17.

79. In this respect, a parallel can be drawn with the policy of the People's Republic of China (PRC) toward Chinese diasporas in Southeast Asia. Between 1909 and 1955, authorities in Beijing followed an assertive policy of treating any person of Chinese ethnic origin as a Chinese subject, irrespective of his or her place of birth or residence. However, in 1955, PRC leaders decided to compromise the defense of overseas Chinese to Beijing's foreign policy interests. At the Bandung Conference that year, Beijing endorsed a policy of "peaceful coexistence" and expressed a willingness to conclude agreements regulating the nationality and citizenship status of overseas Chinese. Subsequently, the PRC went even further and abandoned the idea of dual nationality, advising overseas Chinese to choose local citizenship. Despite these changes, some tensions remained between Beijing and the governments of Southeast

Asian countries. Sentimental ties and ethnocentric obligations force China to maintain special links with coethnics, a circumstance that concerns other governments, regardless of the formal citizenship status of their Chinese minorities. See Milton Esman, "The Chinese Diaspora in Southeast Asia," in Sheffer, ed., *Modern Diasporas in International Politics.*

80. Stephen Sestanovich, "Vozdat' Rossii dolzhnoye" (Give Russia credit), *Polis,* no. 1 (1995): 78.

81. Gail Lapidus, "A Comment on 'Russia and the Russian Diasporas,'" *Post-Soviet Affairs* 12, no. 3 (July–September 1996): 287.

82. Teague, "Russians outside Russia and Russian Security Policy."

83. Gellner, *Nations and Nationalism,* 105.

84. James Mayall, "Irredentist and Secession Challenges," in *Nationalism,* ed. John Hutchinson and Anthony Smith (New York: Oxford University Press, 1994), 272.

85. George Breslauer, "Yeltsin's Political Leadership: Why Invade Chechnya?" in Breslauer et al., *Russia: Political and Economic Development,* 9.

CONCLUSIONS AND IMPLICATIONS

1. Alexander Motyl, *Sovietology, Rationality, Nationality: Coming to Grips with Nationalism in the USSR* (New York: Columbia University Press, 1990), x.

2. Ian Bremmer and Ray Taras, eds., *Nations and Politics in the Soviet Successor States* (New York: Cambridge University Press, 1993), xix.

3. *New York Times,* October 10, 1999.

4. I would like to mention the important writings of George Breslauer, who has analyzed Yeltsin's attempts to build a new Russian nation-state; in this context, see Breslauer and Dale, "Boris Yeltsin and the Invention of a Russian Nation-State," 303–332. See also the works of John Dunlop, one of the few authors who have attempted to address the problems confronted by Russians as a "people" after the collapse of the Soviet Union; see John Dunlop, "Russia: In Search of Identity?" in Bremmer and Taras, eds., *New States, New Politics,* 29–95. Wayne Allensworth has analyzed the issue of Russian post-Soviet identity as an attempt to grapple with modernity; see Wayne Allensworth, *The Russian Question: Nationalism, Modernization, and Post-Communist Russia* (Lanham, Md.: Rowman & Littlefield, 1998).

5. The term "Soviet civilization" was used by Andrei Sinyavsky, a prominent writer and Soviet-era dissident, to describe the cultural context of the Soviet Union; see Andrei Sinyavsky, *Soviet Civilization: A Cultural History* (New York: Arcade Publishing, 1990).

6. Laitin, *Identity in Formation,* 363.

7. Pilkington, *Migration, Displacement, and Identity,* 206.

8. See, for example, proposals of the mainly nongovernmental Brno Programme in *Charta Gentium et Regionum: Brno Programme.* (Munchen: Intereg, s. a.)

9. Igor Ivanov, "Rossiya v menyayuschemsya mire" (Russia in a changing world), *Nezavisimaya gazeta*, June 6, 1999, 6.

10. "'Vybory—eto bor'ba za vlast', no ne protiv gosudarstva.' Vystuplenie Vladimira Putina pered deputatami Gosudarstvennoy Dumy 16 avgusta 1999 goda" ("Elections are a struggle for power, not against the state." Vladimir Putin's address to the deputies of the State Duma on August 16, 1999), *Nezavisimaya gazeta*, August 19, 1999, 3.

11. *Nezanisimoe voennoe obozrenie*, January 14, 2000.

12. *Nezavisimaya gazeta*, April 22, 2000.

13. Zbigniew Brzezinski called this policy a strategy of supporting "geopolitical pluralism" in the region; see Brzezinski, "The Premature Partnership," 79.

14. Ibid., 77.

15. Zbigniew Brzezinski, "A Geostrategy for Eurasia," *Foreign Policy* 76, no. 5 (September/October 1997): 56.

16. Ibid., 87, 197.

17. Zbigniew Brzezinski, *The Grand Chessboard: American Primacy and Its Geostrategic Imperatives* (New York: Basic Books, 1997), 120; emphasis added. Brzezinski also wrote that "Russia . . . will have no choice other than eventually to emulate the course chosen by post-Ottoman Turkey, when it decided to shed its imperial ambitions and embarked very deliberately on the road of modernization, Europeanization, and democratization" (p. 119).

18. See the discussion of Russia's place in a new world order in Alexei Salmin, "Rossiya, Evropa, i novyi mirovoy poryadok" (Russia, Europe, and the new world order), *Polis*, no. 2 (1999): 10–31.

19. Remarks by James A. Baker III given at the Kennan Institute's Twenty-Fifth Anniversary Dinner, October 4, 1999, Washington, D.C.

20. Lieven, "Restraining NATO," 74–75.

21. Hopmann, Shenfield, and Arel, *Integration and Disintegration in the Former Soviet Union*, 52.

22. *Izvestiya*, October 28, 1994.

23. Yevgeny Primakov, "Fragmenty iz glavy 'Poshel v razvedku'" (Fragments from the chapter "Went to Intelligence"), *Sovershenno sekretno* 9 (1999): 9–10. Louis Sell, a well-informed retired U. S. foreign service officer who served as minister-counselor for political affairs at the U. S. embassy in Moscow during 1991–1994 and as director of the Office of Russian and Eurasian Analysis at the State Department during 1996–1998, contends: "The U. S. approach toward the CIS has been a key element in convincing most Russians that the real aim of U. S. policy has been to keep their country weak. . . . The U. S. has almost always taken the side of the former Soviet republics in their abundant quarrels with Moscow." His advice is to conduct a very different policy: "We should encourage integration among the independent states of the former Soviet Union. . . . This does not mean re-creating the Soviet Empire but rather encouraging the states of the former Soviet Union to re-establish the economic, cultural, and human links that are essential to rebuilding prosperity in the region"; Louis Sell, "Who Lost Russia?" (remarks to the Maine Foreign Policy Forum, October 21, 1999), as reprinted in *Johnson Russia List,* October 21, 1999.

24. Sherman Garnett, "Russia's Illusory Ambitions," *Foreign Affairs,* March/April 1997, 67.

Index

Abdulatipov, Ramazan, 49
Abkhazia, 85, 86
Afanasiev, Yuri, 11
Akaev, Askar, 136–137
Aksiuchits, Viktor, 56, 69
Alexander III, 44
Alexievich, Svetlana, 121
All-Russian Center for the Study of
    Public Opinion (VTsIOM), 57,
    58, 59
All-Russia's Union "Renewal," 74
All-Union Communist Party of Bolshe-
    viks (VKPB), 83
Ambartsumov, Yevgeny, 72
Anderson, Benedict, 19, 20–21
Andropov, Yuri, 38
Arel, Dominique, 173
Armenia
    armed conflict, 104, 117
    citizenship policies, 114
    constitution of, 113
    and Convention on the Rights of
        Persons Belonging to National
        Minorities, 150–151
    ethnic Russian community, 96–97,
        100, 102
    nationalism, 34, 104
    Russian emigration to Russia, 117,
        118
    Russian-language speakers, 95–100

Armenian diaspora, 4, 128, 156
Astafiev, Mikhail, 69, 81
Austria, 24
Azerbaijan
    armed conflict, 104, 117
    constitution of, 113
    and Convention on Human Rights
        and Fundamental Freedoms,
        151
    and Convention on the Rights of
        Persons Belonging to National
        Minorities, 150–151
    ethnic Russian community, 96–97,
        100
    Russian emigration to Russia, 117,
        118, 121
    Russian-language speakers, 95–100

Baburin, Sergei, 56, 83, 84–85, 86
Bagramov, Eduard, 50
Baker, James A. III, 170
Baltic states. See also Estonia, Latvia,
    and Lithuania
    citizenship policies, 104–106, 114,
        126, 136, 139, 141
    constitutions of, 113, 114
    and Convention on the Rights of
        Persons Belonging to National
        Minorities, 150
    economic conditions, 103–104

Baltic states *(cont.)*
   education of Russians compared
      with indigenous groups, 109, 110
   ethnic Russian communities, 96–97,
      100, 102, 104, 125, 126–127, 168
   key to "Russian question," 127
   language policies, 106, 153
   nationalism, 34, 36, 104
   role of Baltic-Americans in, 21
   Russian assimilation, 122
   Russian emigration to Russia, 126
   Russian-language speakers, 95–100,
      153
   Russification, 95, 96–97, 101
   stability of, 168
Barber, Benjamin, 20
Barkey, Karen, 25
Beissinger, Mark, 33
Belarus
   constitution, 113
   and Convention on Human Rights
      and Fundamental Freedoms, 152
   and Convention on the Rights of
      Persons Belonging to National
      Minorities, 150–151
   and dual citizenship, 137
   economic condition, 103
   education of Russians compared
      with indigenous groups, 109, 110
   ethnic Russian community, 61, 96–
      97, 100, 122, 124–125
   language policies, 106–107
   reunification with Russia, 24, 53,
      54, 55, 56, 61
   Russian emigration to Russia, 120
   Russian-language speakers, 95–100,
      102, 106, 153
   and Russian nationalism, 36, 43,
      53, 54, 55, 56
   Russification of titular population,
      95, 101
   U.S. policy toward, 174, 175
Belov, Vasily, 52, 69
Berdyaev, Nikolai, 1, 30, 42, 53

Black Hundred, 69, 70
Bolsheviks, 45–46, 50, 66–67
Bondarenko, Vladimir, 39
Borders
   confusion over Russian boundaries,
      15–16, 33–39
   defining, 15
   intellectual history perspective,
      40–46
   public opinion on, 57–62
   redrawing along ethnic lines as
      security threat, 166
   Russian goal of building state within
      current borders, 16–17, 29
   states versus nations, 3, 32
   territorial versus ethnic nations,
      17–18
   theoretical perspectives, 3, 16, 30–33,
      46–56
Braun, Aurel, 7
Breslauer, George, 26, 157
Bromley, Yulian, 47
Brotherhood of Saints Cyril and
      Methodius, 41
Brubaker, Rogers, 7, 39, 111
Brzezinski, Zbigniew, 11, 13, 169–170
Bukharin, Nikolai, 36, 37
Bund, 65
Burbulis, Gennadi, 68

Canovan, Margaret, 7, 32, 62, 107
Catherine the Great, 42
Center for Sociological Analysis of
      Interethnic Conflicts, 57–58
Center of Social Prognosis and
      Marketing, 58
Central Intelligence Agency, 174
Chechnya, 4, 6, 16, 17, 25, 72, 157, 168
Chernomyrdin, Viktor, 75, 144
Chernous, Vladimir, 146
Chernyaev, Anatoly, 38
China, 6
Chinese diaspora, 4
Chinn, Jeff, 7, 33, 44

Christian Democratic Party, 69
CIS Migration Report, 118, 121
Citizenship
    agreements on, 120, 138, 140, 142
    dual citizenship, 54, 89, 106, 132–
        142, 147, 155
    identification cards, 147–149
    protection of Russian citizens
        abroad, 134, 142, 155, 165, 176
    and status of Russians in former
        Soviet republics, 104–106, 114,
        138
    Universal Declaration of Human
        Rights and, 133
Citizenship Directorate of the Russian
    Presidential Administration, 133
Civic Union, 74
Clinton, Bill, 161
Clinton administration, 169
Cohen, Robin, 7, 20
Colton, Timothy, 59
Commission on the Affairs of Com-
    patriots Abroad, 144, 146, 168
Committee for International Affairs
    and Foreign Economic Rela-
    tions of the Russian Supreme
    Soviet, 72
Committee for State Security (KGB), 38
Committee on CIS Affairs and Rela-
    tions with Compatriots, 56, 138,
    147, 168
Committee on Geopolitics, 82
Common Course, 77, 86–87
Communism, fall of, 2, 67
Communist Party of the Russian
    Federation (KPRF), 8, 71, 77,
    83–86
Communist Party of the Soviet Union
    (CPSU), 37, 38, 46
"Compatriots living abroad" concept,
    1–2, 142–149, 165, 176
"Concept of the Russian Federation's
    State Policy Toward the Com-
    patriots Abroad," 144

Congress of Russian Communities
    (KRO), 87–88
Connor, Walker, 7, 25–26, 70, 112
Constitutional Democratic Party, 44,
    65, 69
Constitutions of Soviet successor states,
    113–114
"Constructivist" school, 50
Convention on Human Rights and
    Fundamental Freedoms, 151–152
Convention on the Rights of Persons
    Belonging to National Minori-
    ties, 144, 150–151
Council of Compatriots, 138
Council of Europe, 150, 166
Crimea, 85, 86, 115, 124, 125, 153, 154
Croatia, 24
Cultural identity, 31, 33, 92, 101,
    128–129

Danilevsky, Nikolai, 40, 41, 42, 43,
    81, 163
De Gaulle, Charles, 154–155
De-Russification, 82
"Declaration of the Constituent
    Congress," 138
"Declaration on Observing the Sover-
    eignty, Territorial Integrity, and
    Inviolability of Borders," 150
"Declaration on the Russian Federation
    Support of Russia's Diaspora
    and on Protection of Russia's
    Compatriots," 146
Democratic Choice, 86–87
Democratic Party of Russia, 74, 86–87
Democratization, 14, 88–89
Derzhava, 69, 73, 83, 84
Diasporas
    concept of Russian diaspora, 3–4
    and nation-state building, 14,
        26–27
    as potential security threat, 18–22
    Russian diaspora compared with
        other diasporas, 21–22, 156

Diasporas *(cont.)*
  Russian Federation policy toward
    Russian diasporas, 131–158,
    164–168
  typology and future prospects,
    123–129, 155–158
Dostoevsky, Fyodor, 1, 40, 41–42, 43,
  45, 55, 162, 163
Drobizheva, Leokadia, 49–50
Dual citizenship, 54, 89, 106, 132–142,
  147, 155
Duma Committee on CIS Affairs and
  Relations with Compatriots, 56,
  138, 147, 168

E-mail, 19, 21
Economic conditions
  and migration to Russia, 120
  of post-Soviet states, 103–104
Economic reintegration, 74–75, 158,
  161, 172–176
Economic Union, 74
Education
  factor in consolidation of ethnic
    Russians, 108, 109
  of Russians compared with indige-
    nous groups, 109
Emigration. *See* Migration
Energy resources
  dependency of new states on Russia,
    154
  oil pipeline routes, 174, 175
Eriksen, Thomas Hylland, 70
Estonia
  citizenship policies, 104–106, 114,
    126, 136, 139, 141
  constitution of, 113, 114
  economic conditions, 103–104
  education of Russians compared
    with indigenous groups, 109,
    110
  ethnic Russian community,
    96–97, 100, 102, 104, 125,
    126–127, 168

  as key state for "Russian question,"
    127
  language policies, 106, 153
  Russian-language speakers, 95–100,
    153
  stability of, 168
Estonian diaspora, 21
Ethnic versus territorial nations, 17–18
Ethnonationalism
  factors precluding rise of, 5
  factors strengthening, 46–47
  historical tradition of, 66
  integration as alternative to, 158,
    172–176
  and integrationalists, 87
  and new Russian diasporas, 5–6,
    91–92
  perspective on nation building,
    69–71
  public opinion on, 58–59, 60–61
  representation in the Russian State
    Duma, 76–77, 78
  and restorationalists, 80–86
  as security threat, 23–24, 164,
    165–166, 171–172
  theoretical ethnonationalism, 51–56
Ethnos
  Bromley's theory of, 47–48
  Gumilev's theory of, 48
Eurasian Union, 74–75
"The Eurasians," 44–45, 163
External Intelligence Service, 173–174

Fatherland–All Russia, 77
Federal Migration Program, 135
Federal Migration Service (FMS), 135
Fichte, Johann Gottlib, 93
First Congress of People's Deputies, 52
Forward Russia!, 77
Fourth Congress of Russian National-
  ists, 85
Framework Convention for the Protec-
  tion of National Minorities, 150
France, 134, 154–155, 166

"Free union of flourishing nations,"
36
Frolovsky, Georgi, 44

Gellner, Ernest, 50, 156
Genocide, 24
"Geomourners," 11–12
Georgia
    armed conflict, 104, 117
    Baburin's ethnonationalism and,
        84, 86
    citizenship policies, 138
    constitution of, 113
    and Convention on the Rights of
        Persons Belonging to National
        Minorities, 150
    education of Russians compared
        with indigenous groups, 109,
        110
    ethnic Russian community, 96–97,
        100
    language policies, 106
    nationalism, 34, 104
    Russian emigration to Russia, 117,
        118, 121
    Russian-language speakers, 95–100,
        153
    U.S. financial aid, 174
"Geotherapists," 11–12, 13
"German question," 18
Germany, 6, 18, 56, 166
Ginzburg, A. I., 7
Glazunov, Ilya, 71–72
Glazyev, Sergei, 87
Globalization
    features of, 19
    and nation building, 14–15, 18–19,
        161
    and nationalism, 39
    as potential security threat, 18–22
    Russian backlash against, 39, 46–47
    and theoretical framework for
        Russia, 161, 172
Gorbachev, Mikhail, 37, 46, 74

Goryacheva, Svetlana, 84
Governmental Commission on the
        Affairs of Compatriots Abroad,
        144, 146, 168
Grachev, Pavel, 134–135
Gramsci, Antonio, 72
"Great Russian" chauvinism, 37
Grebennikov, Valery, 149
Greek diaspora, 4, 21, 128, 156
Greenfeld, Liah, 7
Guboglo, Mikhail, 59
"Guest" workers, 116, 120
Gumilev, Lev, 48

Hague Convention, 142
Harris, Chauncy, 7
Hegemony
    areas of Russian success, 154
    defense of rights of Russian
        minorities as instrument of,
        1–2, 153–154, 167
    dual citizenship as instrument of,
        134, 136
    multilateral agreements as barrier
        to, 152
    perspective on nation building,
        72–73, 81
    representation in the Duma, 76, 77,
        78–79
    Russian goal of, 1–2
    Russia's weakness and, 5, 167
    U.S. policy against Russian hege-
        mony, 169–176
Hobsbawm, Eric, 50, 93
Hopmann, Terrence, 173
Hosking, Geoffrey, 13, 15, 35
Hough, Jerry, 59, 125
Howard, Michael, 15
Human rights
    as instrument of Russian hegemony
        and dominance, 1–2, 153–154,
        167
    and integration, 172
    and multilateralism, 149–152, 166

Human rights *(cont.)*
  protection of rights of "compatriots
    abroad," 87, 142–152, 165, 166
  U.S. policy, 165, 166–167
Huntington, Samuel, 162

Identification cards, 147–149
Immigration. *See* Migration
Imperialism
  compared to ethnonationalism, 171
  hegemony and dominance as step
    toward, 72–73, 165–166
  Imperial Russia, 13, 65–66
  integration as barrier to, 158,
    172–176
  neo-imperialism, 22–23, 55, 71
  perspectives on Russian imperialism,
    11–12, 13, 23, 33–34, 169–170,
    171–172
  representation in the Duma, 76
  rethinking Russian imperialism,
    171–172
  and Russian national identity, 35–36
  Solzhenitsyn's condemnation of,
    53–54
  U.S. policy against Russian imperi-
    alism, 169–176
  verbal, 152–155
Inorodtsy, 43
Institute for Ethnic and Anthropolog-
    ical Studies, 127
Institute of Diaspora and Integration,
    73
Institute of Ethnology and Anthro-
    pology, 68
Institute of Sociological Analysis, 57, 60
Integrationalism
  as alternative to ethnonationalism,
    158, 171, 172–176
  perspective on nation building,
    74–75
  representation in the Duma, 76, 77,
    78–79, 86–87
  U.S. policy, 75, 161, 169–176

Intellectuals
  problems of identity in Russian
    intellectual history, 40–46
  as source of Russian ethnonation-
    alist doctrine, 52
  Soviet and post-Soviet theoretical
    discourse on Russian nation-
    hood, 46–56
Interfronts, 101
International institutions
  distrust of, 39
  Russian integration into, 170
International Organization for
    Migration, 115
Irish diaspora, 21, 128
Israel, 21, 32
Ivanov, Igor, 85, 166

Japan, 6
Jewish diaspora, 4, 21, 32, 128, 156

Kabuzan, V. M., 52–53
Kaiser, Robert, 7, 33, 37, 44, 111, 127
Karlsruhe Agreement, 166
Kazakhstan
  citizenship policies, 114, 120, 137,
    138, 141
  constitution of, 113, 114
  and Convention on Human Rights
    and Fundamental Freedoms, 151
  and Convention on the Rights of
    Persons Belonging to National
    Minorities, 150–151
  education of Russians compared
    with indigenous groups, 109, 110
  ethnic Russian community, 16, 61,
    96–97, 100, 102, 104, 108, 109,
    125–126, 127, 168
  and integrationalism, 74
  as key state for "Russian question,"
    127
  language policies, 107–108
  reunification with Russia, 24, 53,
    54, 55, 56, 61

Kazakhstan *(cont.)*
  Russian emigration to Russia, 117, 118, 120, 121
  Russian-language speakers, 95–100, 153
  Russification of titular population, 95, 101
  stability of, 168
Kazakov, Aleksandr, 148–149
Keohane, Robert, 72
KGB. *See* Committee for State Security
Khrushchev, Nikita, 36
Kiev International Institute of Sociology, 124
Kissinger, Henry, 11, 154–155
Klyamkin, Igor, 57, 58
Kolstoe, Paul, 7, 103, 112, 113
Kostomarov, Nicholas, 41
Kozlov, Viktor, 52
Kozlov, Vladimir, 7
Kozyrev, Andrei, 73, 133, 134, 135, 136, 142–143, 149–150, 153, 173
Kuchma, Leonid, 137
Kuleshov, Sergei, 7
Kutafin, O. E., 140–141
Kyrgyzstan
  citizenship policies, 114, 120, 135, 136–137
  constitution of, 113, 114
  and Convention on the Rights of Persons Belonging to National Minorities, 150–151
  education of Russians compared with indigenous groups, 109, 110
  ethnic Russian community, 96–97, 100, 102, 109
  language policies, 106, 107
  Russian emigration to Russia, 118, 120, 121
  Russian-language speakers, 95–100, 153
  Russification of titular population, 101

Laitin, David, 3, 5, 7, 103, 125, 163
Language and language policies
  mass media, 107, 143, 166
  protection of bilingualism, 166
  Russian-language speakers outside Russia, 93–101, 102, 106, 124, 153, 175
  "Russian-speakingness" as national form, 36, 93, 100, 163
  in Soviet successor states, 106–108, 124, 153
  Stalin's promotion of Russian language in non-Russian republics, 38
Latvia
  citizenship policies, 104–106, 114, 126, 136, 141
  education of Russians compared with indigenous groups, 109, 110
  ethnic Russian community, 96–97, 100, 125, 126–127, 168
  as key state for "Russian question," 127
  language policies, 106, 107, 153
  Russian emigration to Russia, 126
  Russian-language speakers, 95–100, 153
  stability of, 168
Latvian diaspora, 21
"Law of colonial ingratitude," 108–115
Lebed, Aleksandr, 60, 85
Leman, Susan, 59
Lenin, Vladimir, 37, 45, 47, 111
Leontiev, Konstantin, 81, 163
Lewis, Robert, 117
Liberal Democratic Party of Russia, 8, 12, 82, 84
Liberals, 36, 49–51
Lieven, Anatol, 6, 171
Lithuania
  constitution of, 113, 114
  ethnic Russian community, 96–97, 100, 102

Lithuania *(cont.)*
  Russian emigration to Russia, 118
  Russian-language speakers, 95–100
Lithuanian diaspora, 21
Locke, John, 2
Lukin, Vladimir, 12
Luxembourg, 166
Luzhkov, Yuri, 73, 77, 85, 86
Lysenko, Nikolai, 69

Malia, Martin, 13
Marriages between Russians and
    non-Russians, 33, 36, 48, 102,
    109–110, 117, 124
Marx, Karl, 2–3, 45
Mass media
  and "compatriots abroad," 107,
    143, 166
  and globalization, 19
  and "virtual" nationality, 19
Mayall, James, 157
"Melting pot" paradigm, 19–20, 36, 101
Melvin, Neil, 7
"Memorandum on the Maintenance
    of Peace and Stability in the
    CIS," 150
Migrant workers, 116, 120
Migranyan, Andranik, 72
Migration
  attitudes toward migrants, 2,
    121–122
  categories of migrants, 116
  dual citizenship as preventative
    measure for mass migration,
    133
  forms of, 116
  "repatriation," 123
  Russian emigration from non-
    Russian republics, 109, 117,
    118, 120, 121, 126, 132
  in territory of former Soviet
    Union, 2, 107, 115–123
Mikhail Archangel Russian People's
    Union, 66

Mikitaev, Abdulakh, 133, 136, 140,
    142, 143
Military
  condition of Russian military, 11
  conditions for military intervention,
    157
  as constituency for restorationalism,
    71
  intervention to protect compatriots
    in the near abroad, 134, 168
  joint U.S.-Central Asian military
    exercises, 174
  and Russian hegemony, 154
Military Doctrine of the Russian
    Federation, 168
Mill, John, 2–3
Milyukov, Pavel, 35, 40, 44, 45, 50, 65,
    66–67, 88
Ministry for Nationalities Policy, 168
Ministry of CIS Affairs, 145
Ministry of Foreign Affairs, 139–140,
    148, 151, 168
Ministry of Nationalities and Federa-
    tive Relations, 145
Minorities
  self-determination, 66–67
  self-victimization of Russian mi-
    norities, 114–115
Mitrofanov, Aleksey, 82
Moldova
  armed conflict, 104
  Baburin's ethnonationalism and,
    84, 86
  citizenship policies, 135
  constitution of, 113, 114
  and Convention on the Rights of
    Persons Belonging to National
    · Minorities, 150–151
  education of Russians compared
    with indigenous groups, 109,
    110
  ethnic Russian community, 96–97,
    100, 104
  language policies, 106, 107

Moldova *(cont.)*
regionalism, 125
Russian emigration to Russia, 117
Russian-language speakers, 95–100,
153
Russification of titular population,
101
Motyl, Alexander, 160
Multilateralism, 149–152
Multinational institutions
distrust of, 39
Russian integration into, 170

Narochnitskaya, Nataliya, 55–56
Narodnost', 42
Nash sovremennik, 52
Nation building
destructiveness of, 15
and diasporas, 19–22, 156
distinction between nation and
state, 3, 32
and ethnonationalism, 23–24,
69–71
and fostering of indigenous non-
Russian nationalism, 110–111
and globalization, 14–15, 18–19, 161
noncongruence of states and nations
in former Soviet Union, 162
perspectives on, 65–75
politics of, 63–89
Russia's double challenge of, 4
scenarios of, 22–27
as a security threat, 13–18
state institutions and, 39
National-Republican Party of Russia,
69, 85
Nationalism. *See also* Ethnonationalism;
Russian identity
and diasporas, 19–22
and globalization, 18–19
nationalist rhetoric and the imperatives of state building, 152–155
in Russia today, 64, 167–168
and Russian identity, 29–62

Russian nationalists compared to
white militants in U.S., 39
states versus nations, 3, 32
and war, 15
Western versus Eastern, 18
Nazarbaev, Nursultan, 74–75, 141
"Near abroad," 2
New state building. *See also* State
building
and integration, 86–87
policy of, 68–69, 134
Putin as a new state builder, 167–168
representation in the Duma, 76,
78–79
Nicholas I, 81
Nomenklatura, 69, 71, 73
North Atlantic Treaty Organization
(NATO), 127
Northern Ireland, 21, 36
Nuclear weapons, 15, 170

"Official nationalism," 42
Oktyabrists, 65
"On Creation of 'Rossiyane,' the Fund
for the Support of the Compa-
triots Abroad," 148
Organization for Security and Coop-
eration in Europe (OSCE), 151,
166
Otechestvo movement, 73
Our Home Is Russia, 86, 149

Pamyat', 69
Party for Russian Unity and Accord, 74
Pavlov, Nikolai, 55
Payin, Emil, 7
Peasants, 43
People's Patriotic Union, 84
Peter the Great, 42
Pilkington, Hilary, 116, 121
Pipes, Richard, 13, 35
Plekhanov, Georgi, 45
Podberezkin, Aleksei, 82
Poland, 43

Political parties
 alliances and rivalries, 80–89
 framework for analyzing politics of
  nation building, 63–64, 67–75
 historical traditions, 65–67
 and nation building, 75–79
Poloskova, T., 7
Presidential Commission on Citizen-
  ship, 133, 134, 139–140, 141
Pridnestrovye, 85, 86, 104, 115, 125, 153
Primakov, Yevgeny, 73, 77, 85, 140, 174
Primordialists, 47–49
Prizel, Ilya, 5
"Program of Actions to Support the
  Compatriots Abroad," 144
Public opinion, 57–62
Public Opinion Fund, 57, 59, 60, 61
Pushkin, Aleksandr, 42
Putin, Vladimir, 3, 16, 64, 167–168

Rasputin, Valentin, 52, 69
Refugees. *See* Migration
"Relative deprivation theory," 33
"Repatriation," 123
Restorationalism, 71–72, 78, 81–86
Robertson, Ronald, 19
Rogozin, Dmitri, 87–88
Rosenau, James, 19
Rossiiskie, 65–66
Rossiyane fund, 148–149
Rowland, Richard, 117
Rudensky, Nikolai, 7
Rushdie, Salman, 20
Russia and Europe (Danilevsky), 41
*Russia Is My Motherland: The Ideology
  of State Patriotism* (Zyuganov),
  81–82
Russian Academy of Sciences, 127
Russian All-People's Union (RAPU),
  83, 84–86
Russian Assembly, 66
Russian Communist Labor Party
  (RKPB), 83
"Russian idea," 1, 162, 163

Russian identity
 civic, 22, 24–26, 33
 civilizational identity, 161–164
 collapse of Soviet Union and loss
  of, 12, 15–16
 collective identity, 5, 14, 17–18, 31,
  128–129
 cultural identity, 31, 33, 92, 101,
  128–129
 defining boundaries of Russian
  people, 30–33
 and democratization, 14, 88–89
 ethnic identity, 5, 17–19, 24, 101,
  128–129
 intellectual history and problems
  of, 40–46
 mythology of common descent,
  17, 31
 options for, 22–27
 public opinion on, 57–62
 redefinition of, 6–7
 "Russian-speakingness" as, 36, 93,
  100, 163
 security implications, 17, 22–27
 theoretical perspectives, 30–33,
  46–56
 weakness of post-Soviet Russian
  identity, 5, 33–39
Russian Independent Institute for
  International Law, 146
Russian language. *See* Language and
  language policies
Russian Monarchist Party, 66
Russian National Unity, 85
Russian Party of Communists (RPK),
  83
"Russian question," 1–9, 25, 26, 127,
  164–168, 174–176
*The Russian Question at the End of
  the Twentieth Century* (Solzhenitsyn), 54
Russian Soviet Federated Socialist
  Republic (RSFSR), 39, 106, 111
Russianness. *See* Russian identity

Russians outside Russia
    characteristics of, 92
    "compatriots living abroad" con-
        cept, 1–2, 142–149, 165, 176
    concept of Russian diaspora, 3–4
    diversity of Russians and Russified
        groups, 102–108
    and ethnonationalism, 91–92
    "law of colonial ingratitude,"
        108–115
    migrants and refugees, 115–123
    Russians and Russian speakers,
        93–101, 102, 106, 124, 153, 175
    typology of Russian diasporas and
        future prospects, 123–129, 155–
        158, 164–168
Russia's Democratic Choice (DC), 77
Russkie, 61, 65–66, 82
Rutskoi, Aleksandr, 69, 71, 73, 153
Ryakhovsky, Boris, 121

Sakwa, Richard, 35
Savitsky, Pyotr, 44
Savoskul, Sergei, 7, 34
Second World Russian Council, 52
Seleznev, Gennadi, 85
Sendich, Munir, 7
Serbia, 5, 24, 26
Serfdom, abolition of, 43
Sestanovich, Stephen, 11, 154–155
Seton-Watson, Hugh, 38, 108
Sevastopol, 86, 137
Shafarevich, Igor, 69
Shakhrai, Sergei, 74
Shenfield, Stephen, 173
Shevchenko, Taras, 41
Shlapentokh, Vladimir, 7
Sidorov, V. S., 150
Simferopol, 139
Sixth Congress of People's Deputies,
    134
Skokov, Yuri, 87
Slezkine, Yuri, 33
Smith, Anthony, 3, 7, 17, 23, 50

Solovey, Valery, 38
Solovyov, Vladimir, 1, 40, 42, 55, 163
Solzhenitsyn, Aleksandr, 2, 6, 34, 35,
    53–54, 69, 81, 82
Soviet Union as homeland, 121–122,
    123, 127
Special Provision 2103, 148
Spiritual Heritage, 82
Stalin, Joseph, 37–38, 47
Stankevich, Sergei, 153
State building. *See also* Nation build-
    ing; New state building
    future prospects, 155–158, 167–168
    nationalist rhetoric and the imper-
        atives of state building, 152–155
    noncongruence of states and nations
        in former Soviet Union, 162
    states versus nations, 3
State Statistics Committee, 140
Steps of New Geopolitics (Mitrofanov),
    82
Struve, Pyotr, 40, 44
Suny, Ronald Grigor, 5, 50
Susokolov, A., 103
Suvchinsky, Pyotr, 44
Switzerland, 166
Szporluk, Roman, 7, 35

Tajikistan
    armed conflict, 104, 117, 121
    citizenship policies, 136
    and Convention on Human Rights
        and Fundamental Freedoms, 152
    and Convention on the Rights of
        Persons Belonging to National
        Minorities, 150–151
    education of Russians compared
        with indigenous groups, 109, 110
    ethnic Russian community, 96–97,
        100, 102
    Russian emigration to Russia, 117,
        118, 121
    Russian-language speakers, 95–100
Teague, Elizabeth, 7

Territoriality
  territorial versus ethnic nations,
    17–18
  waning importance under global-
    ization, 19
Tikhonov, Georgi, 56
Tishkov, Valery, 7, 49, 50–51, 68
Tkachev, Pyotr, 45
Tololyan, Khachig, 14, 20
Toynbee, Arnold, 162
Tribalism, 20
Trubetskoy, Nikolai, 44
Tsymbayev, Nikolai, 35
Tuleev, Aman, 81
Turkey, 24, 175
Turkmenistan
  citizenship policies, 114, 136, 138
  constitution of, 114
  and Convention on Human Rights
    and Fundamental Freedoms, 151
  education of Russians compared
    with indigenous groups, 109, 110
  ethnic Russian community, 96–97,
    100
  migration rate, 118
  Russian emigration to Russia, 117
  Russian-language speakers, 95–100

Ukraine
  Baburin's ethnonationalism and,
    84, 86
  citizenship policies, 137, 139
  constitution of, 113–114
  and Convention on Human Rights
    and Fundamental Freedoms, 151
  and Convention on the Rights of
    Persons Belonging to National
    Minorities, 150–151
  economic conditions, 103
  ethnic Russian community, 61,
    96–97, 100, 102, 104, 122,
    124–125, 127
  as key state for "Russian question,"
    127

  language policies, 107–108, 124
  mixed marriages, 124
  reunification with Russia, 24, 53,
    54, 55, 56, 61, 80
  Russian emigration to Russia, 120
  Russian-language speakers, 95–100,
    124, 153
  and Russian nationalism, 36, 43,
    53, 54, 55, 56
  Russification of titular population,
    95, 101
  stability of, 168
  Treaty on Friendship, Cooperation,
    and Partnership, 85, 137
  U.S. policy toward, 171, 174
UN Declaration on the Rights of
    Persons Belonging to National
    or Ethnic, Religious, and Lin-
    guistic Minorities, 150
UN International Covenant on Civil
    and Political Rights, 151
Union of Communists, 83
Union of October 17, 65
Union of Right Forces, 77, 86–87
Union of Russian People, 66
United Kingdom, 36
United States
  Central Intelligence Agency, 174
  ethnic Americans, 19–20
  forging a new U.S. approach to Eur-
    asia, 13, 165, 166–167, 169–176
  "melting pot" paradigm, 19–20, 36
  policy implications of Russian dias-
    poras, 159–176
  policy supporting Eurasian "geopo-
    litical pluralism," 75
  policy toward Soviet successor
    states, 16–17, 131, 171, 174
  protection of citizens abroad, 134
  tolerance of Chechen war, 16
  U.S. history and approach to
    nation-state building, 14
  white militants compared with
    Russian nationalists, 39

Universal Declaration of Human Rights, 133

"Universalism," 22–23

Uvarov, Count Sergei, 42 43

Uzbekistan
    citizenship policies, 135
    constitution of, 113
    and Convention on Human Rights and Fundamental Freedoms, 151
    economic conditions, 104
    education of Russians compared with indigenous groups, 109, 110
    ethnic Russian community, 96–97, 100
    Russian emigration to Russia, 118, 121
    Russian-language speakers, 95–100, 102

Vdovin, Aleksandr, 51

"Virtual" nationality, 19

Vitkovskaya, G., 7

Von Hagen, Mark, 25

Von Herder, Johann, 93

Voskhozhdenie fund, 149

Walzer, Michael, 114

Working Russia, 83

Yabloko, 12, 77, 86, 147

Yakovlev, Aleksandr, 38

Yavlinsky, Grigori, 74

Yeltsin, Boris
    and Chechen war, 16
    and "compatriots living abroad" concept, 134, 136, 137, 138, 142, 143, 148, 153
    and de-ethnicized nation building, 26–27, 50
    and "de-Russification," 82
    downplaying of national themes, 3, 16, 53, 64
    and ethnonationalism, 70, 158
    and presidential power, 75
    and Russian hegemony, 73
    on Soviet Union, 68

Yoffe, Mark, 82

Yugoslavia, 24, 26, 48

Zatulin, Konstantin, 73, 85, 138

Zdravomyslov, Andrei, 58

Zhirinovsky, Vladimir, 12, 56, 71–72, 82, 84, 85

Zhirinovsky Bloc, 78–79. *See also* Liberal Democratic Party of Russia

Zhuravlev, V. V., 67

Zubakov, Yuri, 140

Zyuganov, Gennadi, 35, 38, 56, 64, 81–82, 83–84, 85, 86

Igor Zevelev is professor of Russian studies at the George C. Marshall European Center for Security Studies in Garmisch, Germany, following his position as head research associate at the Institute of World Economy and International Relations (IMEMO) of the Russian Academy of Sciences, which he also served as deputy director of its Center for Developing Countries. Professor Zevelev has also been a distinguished visiting professor at the University of California, Berkeley; the Jackson School of International Studies at the University of Washington; and Macalester College in St. Paul, Minnesota. He was a fellow at the Woodrow Wilson International Center for Scholars in Washington, D.C. in 1996–97. During 1997–98, he was a senior fellow at the United States Institute of Peace, where he completed the research for this study. Among Professor Zevelev's other published works are *Global Security Beyond the Millennium: American and Russian Perspectives* (co-edited with Sharyl Cross), *Urbanization and Development in Asia,* and *Southeast Asia: Urbanization and Problems of Social Development* (1985). He holds doctorates in history from Moscow State University and in political science from IMEMO.

Jennings Randolph Program
for International Peace

This book is a fine example of the work produced by senior fellows in the Jennings Randolph fellowship program of the United States Institute of Peace. As part of the statute establishing the Institute, Congress envisioned a program that would appoint "scholars and leaders of peace from the United States and abroad to pursue scholarly inquiry and other appropriate forms of communication on international peace and conflict resolution." The program was named after Senator Jennings Randolph of West Virginia, whose efforts over four decades helped to establish the Institute.

Since 1987, the Jennings Randolph Program has played a key role in the Institute's effort to build a national center of research, dialogue, and education on critical problems of conflict and peace. Nearly two hundred senior fellows from some thirty nations have carried out projects on the sources and nature of violent international conflict and the ways such conflict can be peacefully managed or resolved. Fellows come from a wide variety of academic and other professional backgrounds. They conduct research at the Institute and participate in the Institute's outreach activities to policymakers, the academic community, and the American public.

Each year approximately fifteen senior fellows are in residence at the Institute. Fellowship recipients are selected by the Institute's board of directors in a competitive process. For further information on the program, or to receive an application form, please contact the program staff at (202) 457-1700, or visit our web site at www.usip.org.

Joseph Klaits
Director

Russia and Its New Diasporas

This book was set in the typeface Minion; the display type is Giovanni. Cover design by The Creative Shop in Rockville, Md. Interior design by Mike Chase. Page makeup by Helene Redmond of HYR Graphics in Gaithersburg, Md. Copyediting and proofreading by EEI Communications, Inc., in Alexandria, Va. Production supervised by Marie Marr. Peter Pavilionis was the book's editor.